Audacious Democracy

Audacious Democracy

Labor, Intellectuals, and the
Social Reconstruction of America

Edited by
Steven Fraser and Joshua B. Freeman

A MARINER ORIGINAL
HOUGHTON MIFFLIN COMPANY
Boston · New York 1997

Library of Congress Cataloging-in-Publication Data
Audacious democracy : labor, intellectuals, and the social
    reconstruction of America / edited by Steven Fraser
    and Joshua B. Freeman.
        p. cm.
    "A Mariner original."
    ISBN 0-395-86682-0
    1. Labor movement — United States. 2. Working class —
United States. 3. Intellectuals — United States. I. Fraser,
Steve, 1945– . II. Freeman, Joshua Benjamin.
HD8066.A93 1997
331.88'0973 — dc21 97-25125 CIP

Printed in the United States of America

Book design by Robert Lowe

QUM 10 9 8 7 6 5 4 3 2 1

Contents

Audacious Democracy

Introduction

Steven Fraser and Joshua B. Freeman

BETTY FRIEDAN tells us, in her essay in this book, about her "historic Geiger counter," a remarkably reliable internal device that has in the past alerted her to the eruption of big social upheavals, most spectacularly the feminist revolution she helped inaugurate. Her historic Geiger counter is ticking again. She, and all the contributors to this volume, sense that something is shifting in the social metabolism of the country. The labor movement, reviled, held in contempt, or ignored entirely for a generation, is making sounds like a giant waking from a long slumber. Class conflict, a concept that Americans instinctively shy away from, even vehemently deny any legitimate place in our national narrative, is nonetheless forcing itself into public consciousness. At one time — two political generations ago at least — organized labor fired the engines of democratic advance. As a social movement its doings produced tremors from the top to the bottom of American society. How might a newly aroused and combative labor movement similarly reconfigure the face of *fin de siècle*, "postindustrial," "postmodern" America? That is the question animating this book.

Social prophecy is a hazardous occupation. At the close of a century that has become justly notorious for its disastrously misguided apocalyptic visions of "the end of days," it would be reckless in the extreme to enter the crystal ball–gazing business. Neither the editors nor the contributors think of themselves as prophets. All of us, however, sense a sea-change occurring in the nation's social chemistry. All of us sense that it may be possible to rebuild a vigorous alliance between the intellectual community and a labor movement undergoing its own revitalizing sea-change. And all of us, for these reasons, joined in a great "teach-in" last fall at Columbia University. It was called "The Fight for America's Future: A Teach-in with the Labor Movement," and sparked nearly twenty similar events at college campuses around the country. The teach-in movement is the immediate ancestor of this book. Whether the book, in turn, will produce its own offspring no one can know.

Looking back at all the excitement and energy generated by the teach-ins, two equally baffling questions arise: Given the labor movement's reputation as our society's sclerotic dinosaur, why did anyone attend — much less the thousands who did so? And looking back a bit further prompts the query. What ever happened to the alliance between the intellectual community and the labor movement, which for generations had been a potent part of our public life, extending the boundaries of democracy, challenging the presumptuous power of corporate America, fighting for social justice?

Who but veterans of the labor movement and their historians remembers? Still, some of the most illustrious intellectuals in the country's history have found a home in the house of labor and married their work to its cause. (It is indubitably the case that others of equal fame have lined up on the other side.) From Tom Paine to John Dewey, from Walt Whitman to Jack London, American writers, artists, and scholars have discovered a deep moral affinity between their visions and aspirations and those of what used to be called "the laboring classes." Moreover, beginning with the "workingmen's" parties in the age of Jackson and continuing through the era of the New Deal, this otherwise cerebral and spiritual relationship took on institutional body. The worlds of letters, journalism, and social science periodically joined labor's crusades against the domineering presence of industrial and financial leviathans. Whether busting the trusts in the Gilded Age and allying with the Populist Party, or confronting the "malefactors of great wealth" in the age of Roosevelt, a segment, at least, of the cultural community mobilized its special resources to champion the struggles of labor in both the political and industrial arenas. Nor was this strictly a matter of defending the downtrodden.

For nearly a century, the labor question was universally regarded as the primordial social question. All of America's vexing worries regarding equality and the concentration of wealth, war and peace, the fate of working women and children, racial and ethnic hatred — all of these and a dozen other seemingly intractable dilemmas — were absorbed and reinterpreted within the capacious embrace of the labor question. Its solution promised not only to emancipate a group tormented by the drudgery, indignities, and privations of industrial labor, but to transform and democratize the social and political order of which the working classes were only a part. For that reason, a world of writers and artists and intellectuals took up the labor question as its own and made common cause with the moral ambitions of the labor movement. And that is why an event like last year's Columbia University teach-in would have seemed wholly unexceptionable at more or less any time up to about 1948.

But then that alliance withered away and for nearly a half-century vanished from the public stage. The reasons are legion, but the first may be that the labor question, which for so long had given that alliance life, seemed to have found its answer in postwar American prosperity. Incendiary issues of class inequalities lost their urgency, subsided, and even fell off the public agenda. Then the Cold War chilled the climate for considering a broad spectrum of democratic and egalitarian initiatives once jointly cherished by progressive intellectuals and labor activists. And then, of course, the sixties happened. The divergent reactions of the labor movement and the intellectual community to Vietnam, race relations, and the counterculture explain much of the estrangement. Trade union leadership feared a break with national administrations that still seemed friendly to its interests; unions reaped the benefits of the lower unemployment and growing enrollments that were secondary effects of an economy super-heated by the war in Vietnam. And because it shared the ideological fixations of the national security state, much of the labor leadership reacted to the students' uncompromising denunciations of the war as if they were the ravings of traitors. The academic world, where even earlier noted social scientists had pronounced the exhaustion of the labor metaphysic, now retaliated by dismissing the trade unions as hopeless captives of the corporate liberal state. Meanwhile, a labor movement that, since the 1930s, had laid legitimate claim to a pioneering role in the fight against discrimination, now found itself condemned by liberal intellectuals for betraying the cause of the black poor, and accused by more radical elements of the student movement of seeking to skim the cream from an imperial world order that exploited people of color at home and abroad. In a final irony, the counterculture, which in the early sixties drew explicitly on the tradition of labor protest and focused its anger on America's exploitation of the working poor, was by the end of the decade preoccupied with its own alienation from the conformity of consumer culture and intent on displaying its contempt for all those values still cherished across broad stretches of working-class America.

Since then, a wall of mutual suspicion and recrimination has virtually terminated any communication between these two worlds. The alliance, which for nearly a century acted as a potent counterweight to the single-minded commercial calculus of the corporate order, seemed beyond repair; its absence has been bitterly felt. Rushing in to fill the vacuum has been a culture of greed and meanness whose features are painfully familiar: gross and growing disparities of wealth and income not seen since the Gilded Age; a political system neck-deep in banality and cynicism; a new reign of sweating, overwork, and intimidation at the workplace; a veritable epidemic of economic insecurity; a chilling indifference to the well-being of poorer women and children; a frightening escalation of racial, ethnic, and homophobic scapegoating and paranoia; and a purging from our national vocabulary of such clear and potent terms as *class* and *economic democracy* and *egalitarianism,* consigning to exile even that once-inspiring, now quaint-sounding cry of *solidarity.* We live now under the sign of the "Market Republic," a "republic" which celebrates such predatory CEOs as "Chain Saw Al" Dunlap of Sunbeam and "Neutron Jack" Welch of GE for their Darwinian ruthlessness, a "republic" with the hubris to announce itself as the "end of history." From this particular brave new world, the realm of the visionary and the sense of possibility have been officially banished.

But the worm turns. Words like *class* and phrases like *class structure* are resurfacing in public debate, signaling once again serious maldistributions of power and wealth, carrying with them at least a hint of the moral opprobrium once directed at landed, financial, and industrial elites. A modern specter, *downsizing,* appearing regularly on the evening news and in every major metropolitan daily, bears a family resemblance to the villainous plutocrats caricatured in an earlier age. It is the "great fear" that haunts America in the 1990s. The country is embarrassed and scandalized to discover that sweatshops, once thought to be extinct, flourish like poisonous weeds, tainting some of our favorite consumables and the media stars who promote them. The abrasions of social class remain an abiding reality, not only because of the obscene divisions of wealth and income, but because of the gross disparities in public education, the quality of housing, the mercenary rationing of health care, the erecting of walled and gated compounds to protect the privileged, even in the tragic divergence in life expectancies between poor and wealthier newborn babies.

Hierarchy produces its own political reactions. To overcome rampant political disaffection, politicians like Bill Clinton are finding it useful to assume a vaguely populist posture. Meanwhile, on the right, Patrick Buchanan clearly located a raw nerve of resentment about a party system that for too long had consigned the working classes to political oblivion. And outside the somnolent precincts of the two parties is an extraordinary volatility suggested by the rise of the Perotistas. It points to an underlying social instability that, at least in part, has to do with that nagging "labor question," which turns out not to have received its final answer after all.

However, the best sign that the labor question is indeed alive and well is the recent upheaval within the AFL-CIO. In the fall of 1995, in an unprecedented contest for the leadership, a new president, executive vice president, and secretary-treasurer were elected. John

Sweeney, Linda Chavez-Thompson, and Richard Trumka, on assuming office, pledged to increase dramatically the resources devoted by the union federation to organizing millions of unorganized workers. Their platform proclaimed as well a commitment to restoring the political muscularity and independence of the labor movement. John Sweeney talked about turning trade unionism once again into a "social movement" that would speak on behalf of all working and poor Americans, not merely that portion which pays dues to a trade union. An institution whose nearly moribund state had become practically axiomatic finally decided to do something about it . . . or risk a headlong descent into irrelevance. Signs of early success are visible, if not to be exaggerated. An upward revision of the minimum wage, a subject at first not even on the political agenda and then given less than no chance of passage, became law, almost entirely thanks to the energy of the new labor movement. During the presidential election season, conservative Republicans rediscovered an old nemesis, bitterly complaining that "big labor" (for some time dismissed as small and shrinking) was making their lives miserable back in their home districts.

Perhaps most astonishing, the new labor movement seems determined to overcome its own insularity. The defensive and sometimes complacent mentality that was in part responsible for isolating AFL-CIO headquarters in Washington is receding. Now the federation is actively seeking allies from within the feminist, environmentalist, religious, and university communities. It recognizes that, from the standpoint of women and racial minorities and immigrants, organized labor had for a long generation largely excluded the powerless rather than acting as their champion. Moreover, while not so long ago it might have dismissed "identity politics" as diversionary and divisive, the new view acknowledges its real accomplishments and seems prepared to bridge class and other forms of "identity." Whether the new movement can and will realize its good intentions, whether we live at the dawn of a new era of a transformed labor question, only time will tell. But there is no doubt that without the rise of the new leadership, the historic Columbia University teach-in would never have been conceived, much less taken place. So, too, this book, which carries that dialogue between the labor movement and the intellectual community one step further, exists only because of the rumblings in the house of labor.

If indeed America is once again about to grapple with the labor question, however, it won't be the same one our ancestors wrestled with. The globalization of at least parts of the economy, massive new waves of immigration, the revolution in gender relations, the central role of women workers, racial polarization, the dismembering of the welfare state, the explosion of the service sector, the disintegration of urban life, the birth of the "multiversity" — all of these are altering the very nature of the "labor question" as we enter the new millennium. So, too, will the relationship between the labor movement and the intellectual world assume new form. The essays that follow explore these new reinvigorating possibilities and put a period to those premature proclamations about the "end of history." Our country is threatening to become less, not more democratic. To reverse that dangerous slide, we propose here the creation of a new and more audacious democracy.

A revived alliance between labor and intellectuals would be unthinkable if not for the ascension of John Sweeney and his colleagues, who actively seek coalition with social sectors that their predecessors shunned. In the essay that opens this collection, Sweeney blames the current erosion of economic and moral standards largely on corporate leaders, who broke a social compact with labor that brought decades of prosperity following World War II. But he blames labor, too, for becoming parochial, defensive, and ineffective in the face of corporate challenge and cultural change. Sweeney sees our best hope for national renewal in a social movement that would include a revitalized labor movement but transcend it, bridging the fault lines of gender and race in the quest for social justice and economic security.

Betty Friedan's interest in labor goes way back; fresh out of college she worked as a union journalist. Here she recounts her growing sense that recent radical economic and social changes demand that the feminist movement — and, for that matter, other embattled social movements — break with their past political practice. Increasing income inequality, corporate downsizing, and unbridled greed are undermining the economic and psychological security of even privileged groups. So deep is the social crisis, she argues, that for anyone to advance toward justice and equality we need to create political formations that transcend separate interests, linking social activists with organized labor to fight corporate gluttony and extend our democratic rights.

Insecurity has taken up permanent residence in working-class homes. Lillian Rubin, author of *Worlds of Pain,* a classic account of the social psychology of working-class life, documents what the new economic order has meant for working families. Rubin dissects the linguistic sleight-of-hand by which neologisms like "downsizing" and "rightsizing" are used to rationalize the firing of workers, and cant about family values replaces discussion of the plight of the working class.

Intellectuals long have concerned themselves with workers and their families. Eric Foner, Richard Rorty, and David Montgomery explore the complex history of the relation of intellectuals to labor and social reform. Foner, past president of the Organization of American Historians, chronicles how from the earliest days of our history an impressive array of intellectual and cultural leaders joined forces with labor to seek social equity, while the labor movement produced its own long line of influential thinkers and writers. But Foner cautions that most intellectuals, in the past and present, have backed the established powers. The celebrated philosopher Richard Rorty decries the ignorance of Americans about labor's bloody battle to win for workers a degree of decency and democracy. Progressive intellectuals, he argues, must end their quarter-century disengagement from the class struggles taking place outside academic precincts (and recently within them as well). The Yale labor historian David Montgomery, enjoining us not to romanticize the post–World War II era of seeming labor triumph, delineates the limits as well as the benefits brought by Cold War liberalism. He calls for intellectuals and labor activists to imagine a new type of society that subordinates market values to human ones.

Many contributors to this volume share Montgomery's sense that, even as we grapple with immediate crises, we need to broaden our vision of the possible. But a quarter-century of defeats at the hands of business and the political right has yielded a hard-headed realism in devising strategies to revitalize labor. Robert W. Welsh, executive assistant to John Sweeney, describes the initiatives the AFL-CIO has taken under its new leadership and its plans for reversing the union movement's decline, such as broad, multiunion organizing campaigns, like one targeting the booming Las Vegas construction industry, greater rank-and-file involvement in organizing efforts, and a Union Cities program to give organized labor greater local prominence. The veteran unionist José La Luz — who is presently organizing public workers in Puerto Rico — discusses the role of worker education in union revival. He contrasts strategies that promote worker empowerment with more traditional, top-down efforts.

The AFL-CIO director of corporate affairs, Ronald Blackwell, discusses the challenges economic globalization presents to workers. Blackwell sharply dissents from the pundits who portray globalization as the inevitable product of technological innovations. It is the accumulation of unrestrained corporate power, according to Blackwell, not computers or telecommunication advances, that accounts for the growing international flow of goods, capital, and people. Three case studies — the Gap, Firestone Tire and Rubber, and California strawberry growers — illustrate how unions can fight the effects of globalization.

With workers carrying a union card now below 15 percent, organizing the unorganized stands as labor's foremost task. Frances Fox Piven — a noted scholar of poverty and poor people's movements — argues that the new federal mandate forcing welfare recipients into workfare threatens all workers with job insecurity and declining wages. Only by extending its arm to the lower strata of the work force, Piven contends, can organized labor hope to give America the raise that John Sweeney argues it needs. The AFL-CIO education director, Bill Fletcher, frames the issue of welfare reform in the context of the international movement toward limiting government regulation of the economy and ensuring minimal social standards. Citing W.E.B. Du Bois's account of divisions among unionists over the issue of slavery, he shows how, throughout its history, the labor movement has had competing tendencies toward including and excluding the poorest and most exploited workers. President Clinton's "end of welfare as we know it," Fletcher concludes, presents an opportunity for labor to reconceive itself as a *movement,* promoting the interests of all workers, whether or not they currently belong to a union.

When labor tries to organize low-paid workers, the obstacles are enormous, including a hostile legal climate in which the right of workers to organize without fear of reprisal, enshrined in the 1935 National Labor Relations Act, has all but disappeared. Lawyers working with labor, argues the legal historian William E. Forbath, must develop new organizing strategies that circumvent the limitations of the law, like industrywide drives toward union recognition without federal involvement, and boycotts led by community groups not subject to the same restrictions as unions. Simultaneously, labor and its allies must fight for labor-law reform that restores to workers the civil rights they once had.

Audacious democracy entails balancing the common good with a recognition that some groups of Americans suffer particular discrimination, face particular hardships, and have particular needs. Many of the essays in this volume indirectly address this issue, but the sociologist and political columnist Todd Gitlin takes it head-on in his plea to move beyond identity politics toward a common politics that can advance the interests of all. The revival of organized labor, writes Gitlin, represents the essential prerequisite for such a departure. Michael Eric Dyson — a broad-ranging scholar of African-American studies — cautions that in seeking common ground we must not take whiteness as normative, as some critics of identity politics do. While rejecting the notion of "special interests," he argues that, given the country's long history of racism, any movement for radical democracy must openly confront the many ways race shapes our situations and outlooks.

The AFL-CIO's new leadership recognizes the need to ameliorate past discrimination and provide vehicles for subgroups to pursue their particular concerns even as they pursue shared ones. But labor must go further. Karen Nussbaum, the head of the AFL-CIO's newly created Working Women's Department, argues that, with women forming an ever-greater proportion of the wage workforce, the success or failure of the labor movement will rest on its ability to represent and speak for them. While dissatisfaction with working conditions is endemic among women, Nussbaum cites polling data indicating that when women have a problem on the job, they more often turn to their mothers than to labor, women's, or civil rights groups. For this to change, Nussbaum argues, the AFL-CIO, already the largest working women's organization in the country, must start acting like it.

Mae Ngai, a historian and founder of the Asian Pacific American Labor Alliance, calls on organized labor to change its stance toward immigrants and immigration policy. In her look at the history of labor and Asian Americans, she shows that worker solidarity often failed to cross lines of race or nationality, while giving examples of how unionists can tap the energy and support of immigrant communities. Manning Marable, the director of the Columbia University Institute for Research in African-American Studies, chronicles sharp debates among black leaders that pitted strategies of self-help against efforts to build alliances along class lines, setting them in a context of economic hardship and discrimination. Marable believes that a class approach, in which unionism plays a leading role, makes the most sense.

In different ways, Paul Berman and Norman Birnbaum make the case for intellectuals joining force with labor. Berman, the author of the recent *A Tale of Two Utopias,* takes a personal and ideological approach, detailing what labor's victories have meant for him, and how, at critical junctures, labor had the political foresight that many intellectuals lacked. Though often accused of group selfishness, labor, Berman argues, has had an impressive record of standing for the interests of the society as a whole, from its support for the New Deal to its work on behalf of civil rights legislation. Birnbaum, University Professor at Georgetown University Law Center, takes a largely historical approach, charting how ties with trade unionism and social reform invigorated successive generations of intellectuals, especially during the Progressive era and the New Deal. The changing conditions of intellectual life, including the growth of the university, have given intellectuals both a certain remove from the daily mechanics of social life and a degree of autonomy that can be used to buttress labor revival.

Audacious democracy in the end is a matter of political action. Joel Rogers, University of Wisconsin Professor of Law, Political Science, and Sociology, proposes that labor's new organizing and political strategies be closely linked, with both aimed at blocking corporations from taking the "low road" to globalization — wage cutting, job shifting, and environmental despoilment. Rogers sets forth a set of practical steps for creating progressive electoral alliances that are independent of, if not totally divorced from, the Democratic Party. Finally, the Harvard theologian Cornel West places the fledgling effort by labor and intellectuals to join forces, of which this book is a part, in the tradition of struggle for radical democracy. Fully cognizant of the darkness of our times and the difficulty of the challenges we face, he calls for us to go forth, armed with hope and history, to battle for nothing less than the social reconstruction of America.

1

America Needs a Raise

John J. Sweeney

I AM A PRODUCT of the social compact that lifted America out of the Great Depression and lifted working Americans into the middle class. My parents were Irish immigrants. My father was a New York City bus driver, and a proud member of the Transport Workers Union. My mother was a domestic worker. They lived and worked and raised a family in tough times. But during those times most working people, business people, and public officials shared certain understandings.

Here's what working people knew. If you got up every morning and did your job, you could earn a better life for yourself and a better chance for your children — especially if you joined a union. Here's what business people knew. If you paid your workers fairly, tried to provide some job security, and plowed some of your profits back into their communities, you could count on loyal employees and loyal consumers. For employers back then, decent wages and benefits and high standards of corporate responsibility were seen as good business and good for business. And our leaders in government, business, and labor understood what President Kennedy said best: "A rising tide lifts all boats."

It's not that things were perfect — far from it. Business, government, and labor had confrontations; we were beset by age, race, and sex discrimination; poverty was a serious problem. But for almost thirty years after winning World War II, our nation prospered because we prospered together — in striking contrast to the exploding income inequality of the past decade. We were concerned with raising the standard of living for all Americans, not just accumulating wealth for a fortunate few.

As the postwar economy grew, along with increased productivity and rising union membership, a fair portion of the newly created wealth was distributed among the American workforce. The result, in the 1950s and 1960s, was the most dramatic increase in living standards in history. Together we built the most competitive economy and the largest middle class this world has ever known. Most workers had enough time off to pay attention to their families and enough money to enjoy basic pleasures like going to a movie or to the beach for a week. And our economy was so dynamic that we were able to create safety nets for those being left behind — Social Security, Medicare, and Aid to Families with Dependent Children chief among them.

Those days began to come to an end in the early 1970s, when corporate America made a fateful decision to compete in the new global economy, not through team work and know-how, but by driving down labor costs. Rather than compete on the basis of quality and expand the markets for their goods and services, corporations chose to widen their profit margins by moving plants, outsourcing into low-wage markets, and shipping jobs overseas. Even employers with proud histories of doing right by their workers joined the rush to speed up work, freeze wages, slash health benefits, and eliminate pensions.

As a result, the rich got richer while America's working families got left behind. Over the last twenty years, real earnings declined, average family income stagnated, and purchasing power eroded, leaving the United States with the most uneven distribution of wealth of any major industrialized nation. By 1992, the top 20 percent controlled 80 percent of the wealth.

A few simple statistics tell the story. From 1980 to 1995, a period when consumer prices increased 85 percent, factory wages rose only 70 percent and the minimum wage increased a measly 37 percent — while productivity rose 24 percent, corporate profits shot up 145 percent, and CEO pay skyrocketed a whopping 499 percent, with the average CEO receiving an unbelievable $4.5 million a year in salary alone!

American families tried all kinds of coping mechanisms. They sent husbands, wives, and teenage kids into the labor force. They took second and third jobs. Despite their efforts, median family income fell 5 percent between 1989 and 1994.

By mid-decade, American workers were forced to add job insecurity to their bag of economic woes. Giant corporations discovered they could enhance their short-term profit picture and jack up the price of their stock by downsizing. Mobil announced big layoffs, and its stock went up. Chase Manhattan and Chemical Bank announced a merger that put twelve thousand people out of work, and their stocks went up. AT&T said it planned to lay off forty thousand men and women, and its stock went up while its chairman, Robert Allen, took in his highest total compensation package ever, $15.9 million. Boeing CEO Frank Shrontz pocketed $5.9 million while laying off twenty-three thousand. American Home Products Corporation chairman John R. Stafford scored a package of $9.7 million, up 132 percent, when he announced four thousand layoffs.

And then there was Al "Chain Saw" Dunlap, who, in under two years at Scott Paper, handed out pink slips to 11,200 workers, sold off the remains of the company, and walked away with a personal fortune of $100 million. Then he took over Sunbeam, laid off 350 workers, and rolled out a grand scheme to eliminate half of Sunbeam's 12,000 jobs, shutter eighteen of its twenty-six factories, and close thirty-seven of its sixty-one warehouses.

According to the Institute for Policy Studies, the top twenty-two CEO job slashers of 1995 were rewarded with $37 million — the increased value of their stocks and stock options — in addition to their multimillion-dollar paychecks. *Business Week* reported that executive salaries and bonuses jumped 25 percent at the twenty companies with the largest announced layoffs.

Corporate irresponsibility became the strategy of choice in our new winner-take-all economy, and entire working-class towns were blindsided. In Decatur, Illinois, workers at Caterpillar helped their company achieve record profits, only to be forced out on strike over company demands for a two-tier wage structure and weekend work with no overtime.

After helping Bridgestone-Firestone overcome the effects of an overpriced leveraged buyout, employees in five cities found themselves on the street and permanently replaced when they resisted massive contract concessions. In Milwaukee, a greedy multinational grabbed up Pabst Brewing, milked dry a 152-year-old plant, then shut it down and put five hundred workers out of jobs without looking back. In Solway, New York, the citizens were delighted when Landis Plastics decided to open a new plant in their job-starved little community. Three years later, they came to know Landis as a company that gave demerits to workers who had to take their children to emergency rooms, discriminated in pay scales and job assignments between men and women, fired workers for trying to organize a union, canceled health insurance for disabled workers, and ran a plant that chewed off fingers in the name of extra profits from the chewing gum it manufactured.

For American workers and their families, these are snapshots from hell. They paint an ugly portrait of a country that has lost respect for workers and the jobs they do. American workers are running out of money, running out of options, and running out of hope. They've exhausted their savings, and they are loaded with debt. They have little time off from work to spend with their children or their friends, and they can't afford small things like eating out once a week, much less a real vacation. They see 20 percent of our society paying $3 for a cup of coffee and driving $40,000 automobiles and they wonder, "Who's getting my share?" They are frustrated and bitter, and their anger is exceeded only by anxiety over keeping their jobs.

The human toll has been staggering. And I'm convinced that at some point our nation will face even harsher consequences from the reckless pursuit of lower and lower wages by American business. People who don't have money can't spend money, and that can be disastrous for an economy historically driven by optimism and consumer purchases. People who make less money pay less in taxes, and twenty years of depressed wages are taking a toll on local, state, and federal tax coffers and undermining our Social Security system. Finally, people who have no money can't save money, and our savings rate is already flagging.

It doesn't take an economist or a sociologist to conclude that America desperately needs a raise, and not just in wages and benefits, but in hope for the future and in corporate responsibility.

So how do we push our nation back on the road to higher wages and more lofty standards and expectations? No one has all the answers, but we do know that it won't happen one corporation at a time, or without fundamental changes in the way our country works. One of the things we need most is a strong counterbalance to the power of corporations — in the workplace, in the marketplace, and in our policy-making arenas. And the only institution that can play that role is the American labor movement.

But in order to play that role, unions must change. Here's the truth. The weakness of labor encouraged employers to take the low road. It isn't just a coincidence that a disastrous decline in the power and influence and membership of unions accompanied this twenty-year decline in living standards of working families. We fell down on the job, some say, because we paid too much attention to preserving our contracts; others fault a rightward drift in our political advocacy.

My own view is that the labor movement, when faced with a changing culture as well as a changing economy, hunkered down. To paraphrase the Reverend Jesse Jackson, we spent too much time looking in the mirror and not enough time looking out the window. Relationships with natural allies torn apart in the 1960s and 1970s went unrepaired. The labor movement became isolated and introverted, concerned more with our own deepening crisis than with the crisis in the world around us. The fact is that we allowed our membership to decline from about 27 percent of the workforce in 1980 to less than 15 percent by the time I was elected to head the AFL-CIO in 1995, just a year after radical right-wingers swept the congressional elections and took control of the United States Congress.

Only by rebuilding our strength can we bring American business back to the high road of decent wages, job security, and corporate responsibility. And only if we substantially increase our membership can working families regain some control over our national agenda and our federal government. That is why I began my first term as president by challenging every union to put millions of dollars into organizing, from the Sunbelt to the Rustbelt and from health care to high tech. And that is why we began pouring money and people into rebuilding our grassroots political strength.

We also know we have to reach out energetically to our natural allies in the movements for civil rights and women's rights, as well as in the gay and lesbian and intellectual and student communities. For far too long, we told ourselves we were fighting a fight for all of America, while we cut ourselves off from — or formed hollow, patronizing alliances with — the organizations that advocate most forcefully for the soul of progressive America. For instance, without ever becoming serious partners with feminist leaders and women's groups we told ourselves that unions were the best vehicle by which women could achieve economic equality. We cannot even rebuild our movement, much less reclaim America, without these allies.

Academics and intellectuals have a special role to play. We need help in making basic economic education available and accessible to every American so that all people can understand what is happening to their family budget and who is doing it to them.

We need help in telling the world about the shameful exploitation of children and women workers in the awful sweatshops we thought were a thing of the past, both here and overseas. We need help in exposing the flaws in our movement and, more important, exposing the flaws in our society. We need help in arousing an older generation to the defense of their retirement security and in alerting a younger generation to the foolishness of turning their future over to the friendly folks who brought us the savings-and-loan debacle and, indeed, the Great Depression. And we need help in telling millions of unrepresented workers that, while it takes a village to raise a child, it takes a union to get a raise.

The 1996 election season brought a glimpse of a labor-led progressive revival. We decided that working families deserved a better voice, so we voted ourselves a $35 million special assessment and spent it on independent expenditures, rather than giving it to political parties. We decided to transform the AFL-CIO from a Washington-based policy-making operation into a grassroots political machine, so we put 138 highly skilled staffers out in the field to help us reconnect working families to the political system and build for the future. We decided to change our membership approach from an endorsement process to an educational process, so we provided our members with a lot more information and a lot less baloney.

On Election Day, the results validated our efforts. Twenty-one million voters from union households accounted for 23 percent of the overall vote, up from 14 percent in 1994 and 19 percent in 1992. We retired eighteen of the ugliest Americans ever to besmirch the United States Congress, men and women who had spent the previous two years bashing workers while attempting to radically downsize our federal government and destroy most of the programs and protections working families depend on for their very survival. Most analysts failed to note that we lost eleven other races — enough to change the leadership in the House — only by a total of twelve thousand votes.

It would of course take much more to elect a government that really stands for and fights for our values and beliefs. And none of this is to say that the efforts we put together were more than a thin, hasty start at taking on a still abysmal political situation.

But we were 23 percent of the vote, and we voted 68 percent Democratic. It doesn't take a rocket scientist to figure out that what we need to better influence our national agenda is more union members!

A bigger, stronger labor movement can be the core and catalyst for a new social movement extending well beyond our ranks, a movement that will push for public policies promoting economic security and social justice. And that movement itself will help bridge some of the racial and social gaps in our country and restore a sense of purpose to public life. As our unions become stronger and smarter, we will be in a position to offer business some challenges. Take some of your profits and invest them in growing the American economy, American workers, and American wages. Offer your workers the training they need for tomorrow's jobs — not just the big shots in the executive suites, but all your employees. Work with your employees and their unions. Stop sending jobs out of the country. Pay people better so that they can spend and save and support the thousands of small businesses that are struggling to survive.

Give us a voice in decision-making — give us half a chance to improve the quality of our goods and services.

A revitalized labor movement will also be able to issue some challenges to our government and our elected officials. Restore some sanity to a tax code that has reduced taxes on millionaires by one-third over the past fifteen years while raising taxes by a similar amount on middle-income Americans. Put some new limits on the Wall Street wizards who are operating dangerously beyond the fringe of current regulation. End expense deductions for obscene levels of corporate pay and bounties to corporations to send jobs overseas, as well as other forms of corporate welfare. Stop stealing from the poor, the young, and the elderly through back-door tax deals, side-door business subsidies, and front-door program cuts. Beef up Social Security and Medicare; don't destroy them. And by all means don't turn workers' hard-earned payroll tax dollars over to money managers who simply want to collect their commissions and run, regardless of whether individuals' investments pay off or workers are left destitute in their old age. Honor the wishes of 80 percent of the American people and spend more money, not less, on Headstart, education, and job training, Americorps, the National Endowments for the Arts and Humanities, and on helping care for those who are in need.

"More." That's what the first president of the American Federation of Labor, Samuel Gompers, said nearly a century ago when he was asked, "What does labor want?" "More schoolhouses and less jails," he replied, "More books and less arsenals, more learning and less vice, more constant work and less crime, more leisure and less greed, more justice and less revenge."

And what do working Americans want as we draw close to a new century? What we want is to work together to build an America that holds true to the values we honor in our homes and in our houses of worship.

We want to live in a country where you can raise a family without having to hold down three jobs. Where you don't have to spend so much time at work that you have no time left to go to a movie or to a ball game with your kids or grandchildren. Where your lot in life is determined by what you do, and not by the color of your skin, the accident of your birth, or the selection of your partner. Where our children and grandchildren can look forward to pay raises instead of layoff notices. To going to college instead of into dead-end jobs. To enjoying life more, not less, than we've been able to.

Our idea of a just society is one in which honest labor raises the standard of living for all, rather than creating enormous wealth for just a few. And our notion of a moral nation is one that cares for its young, its old, and its poor, and leaves the rich to fend for themselves.

2

History's Geiger Counter

Betty Friedan

I HAVE A PRETTY GOOD historic Geiger counter. It clicked thirty years ago, when the explosive reaction to *The Feminist Mystique* and the first law against sexual discrimination in employment led to what became the modern women's movement in 1966. And that counter is clicking again, because I think we are on the verge of something new: a movement for social justice, a movement to transcend the separate interests, the special interests, even the very good interests of identity politics that have been at the cutting edge of democratic progress. We are beginning a new period of history. The resurgence of a progressive spirit in the labor movement, an urge to break the status quo, has resulted in the election of John Sweeney as head of the AFL-CIO. That same progressive resurgence in the intellectual community is giving new life to the idea of an alliance between intellectuals and labor. It was just a few years ago that my historic Geiger counter started clicking again when I saw the need to transcend feminism's focus on women's needs alone.

I am having a fruit-and-cottage-cheese lunch with a new friend near her bank. She happens to be the top woman at that bank, with no other woman anywhere near her level, and she gets lonesome at lunchtime. The guys at her level all go out together; they don't have lunch with the women anymore. Some new kind of sex discrimination? Oh, no, she says, it's just that there's so much talk about sexual harassment suits these days. No one knows what is or isn't, so they figure, why risk it? But she isn't looking for feminist advice. What is really beginning to get her down is that her husband, who was downsized at one of our biggest corporations three years ago, hasn't been able to find a job and has almost stopped looking. "I'm carrying it all," she says. "It's okay; we'll make it. But it's not good, at home, the way he feels now. It's as if he's given up. I could get a divorce, I suppose. But he is the father of my children. And I still love him. So that's not an option. But, ambitious as I am, I never figured it would end up like this."

That same summer week, in 1994, I see an item in the *Times* that, during the last five years, there has been a significant drop in income — nearly 20 percent — of college-educated white American men. Not minority, high school-educated, blue-collar, but white management men, the masters of the universe. And it is hitting mainly men in their forties. But no such decline is taking place among women. Of course, women, on the whole, are not making as much money as men, but more women are coming out of professional programs into management jobs. And the service jobs, which most women hold, are the ones now on the increase in our economy; they are not being downsized, like the blue-collar jobs and layers of middle management. These service jobs, I later learn, are being contracted out, outsourced, put on a temporary or contingency basis, without benefits or job security. Nevertheless, it seems that women are now carrying some 50 percent of the income burden in some 50 percent of families.

Downsizing had not yet hit the headlines; "the angry white male" had not yet surfaced in the 1994 elections. But my inner Geiger counter clicked, the way it does in the presence of something contrary to definition, expectation, accepted truth. I trust that click now. Though my thinking the last thirty years — and that of many other women — has been conducted within the liberating frame of reference of the women's movement for equality, I again feel an urgent sense of the need for change. With all the reservations, mistakes, omissions, and downright objections that my feminism has surmounted these years, its liberating force, for women, for our whole society, has always prevailed. But my inner Geiger counter does not lie. What I sense here is something basic, something that cannot be evaded or handled at all in the usual feminist terms.

What I sense here is the need for a paradigm shift, beyond feminism, beyond sexual politics, beyond identity politics altogether. A new paradigm for women and men. And the more I think about this, the more I realize that a lot of other people, of very different political persuasions from mine, are moving to a similar realization. There's a mounting sense that the crises we are now facing, or denying, cannot be solved as we previously and variously conducted our personal or political or business or family lives. They can no longer be seen in terms of women alone or women versus men — gender. The old paradigm that still shapes our thinking may keep us from seeing these problems for what they are, much less solving them. We must create a new paradigm.

The Feminine Mystique represented such a paradigm shift; breaking through that age-old definition of woman only in sexual relation to man — wife, mother, sex object, housewife, never as a person, defining herself by her own actions in society — that was, in fact, a paradigm shift. The *personhood of woman* made the whole gestalt different. After that paradigm shift, the problem became defined as: What keeps American women from moving, participating, as full equals in every area of American society?

Before the modern women's movement, our maps in every field were defined by men, and women were defined in relation to men. It was a paradigm shift when we began to define our own terms and to challenge the rubrics of theory and practice which in every field had been developed only from male experience. It opened up every field, as women began to move, in great numbers, through the 1960s and 1970s and 1980s into law and medicine, all the sciences, business, art, politics, the humanities, and to preach the sermons, in church and synagogue. "It changed my life," I hear from women of three generations who still stop me in street, restaurant, airport. It opened life, personal and political, family and professional, in complex new directions.

But as I sense my Geiger counter pulsing again, I look back and admit anomalies that kept making me try to stretch the box of feminism long before this crisis, which requires breaking out of that box, no matter how comfortably, or uncomfortably, it has served us up until now.

For me, the unwritten, inviolable law against which any and all thinking about women must be tested is simply life itself: Does it open or close real life as women live it; does it permit more choice, autonomy, freedom, control over one's life; does it empower or restrict? In fact, that's where I came in, in the 1950s, after I was fired from a newspaper job for being pregnant with my second child, and retreated guiltily to the life of a suburban housewife in a beautiful old Victorian house in Rockland County, New York. In those days a wife and mother who worked outside the home was supposed to be losing her femininity, undermining her husband's masculinity, and neglecting her children, no matter how much her paycheck was needed to help pay the bills.

For those of us who started the modern women's movement — mothers, most of us, housewives, League of Women Voters and other volunteer leaders, midlife educators back to school, and formerly invisible women in corporate or government office or trade-union hall — the paradigm shifted overnight, it seemed. The new paradigm was simply the ethos of American democracy — equality of opportunity, our own voice in the decisions of our destiny — but applied to women in terms of daily life as it was being lived as the theory and practice of democracy may never have been applied before.

And how truly empowering it was, those first actions we took as an organized women's movement, getting Title VII of the Civil Rights Act enforced against sex discrimination, when its own commissioner, like the congressmen who passed it, was treating it as a joke. They stopped laughing when we began the class-action suits, when the telephone company had to pay millions of dollars in reparations to women who had never been allowed to apply for jobs beyond operator. How empowering when we demanded to be served in the Oak Room of the Plaza, where women had never been allowed to lunch, where men made their business deals. How world-enlarging when we used the law to make newspapers stop advertising all the good jobs under "Help Wanted Male," and saleswoman, clerk, waitress, cleaner under "Help Wanted Female." And women began enrolling in great numbers in law school (from less than 4 percent to more than 40 percent in two decades), medical school, M.B.A. and Ph.D. programs.

For younger women, coming into organizations from the student movement of the 1960s, without much experience of the life most women had led and were still leading, the paradigm shift came from a different place, though that wasn't clear at first. Sexual politics created a model of gender based on class warfare and racial oppression — and I had trouble with it from the beginning, because it didn't fit *life* — life as I'd known it personally, other women's lives, even scientific knowledge about life. It expressed a lot of rage, that was true, rage that had to be suppressed when women were completely dependent on men, or rage taken out on men and children covertly or on our own bodies. But did it really open life to new evolution to see women as oppressed victims, the whole sex, rising against man as a whole sex, the oppressors — down with men, down with marriage, down with motherhood, down with everything women ever had done to attract men, down with everything men had done in history, the patriarchs, the brutes?

When I left the presidency of NOW, in 1970, sexual politics was already dividing our strength. I began putting most of my energy into teaching, lecturing, and writing again — all of it geared to what I saw as the need for feminist thought to evolve. In *The Second Stage* I proposed coming to new terms with family, with motherhood, with men, with careers, going beyond the dilemmas of the old paradigm, the male model or its sexual obverse, the no-win supposed "choice" of family versus job.

In this period when feminist consciousness was supposedly at the cutting edge, women of childbearing years were dividing into bitterly antagonistic camps as they were forced into no-win, either-or choices, motherhood versus career. I myself saw no real equality unless women could "have it all," as men could. But they can't do it exactly as men do, can they, as long as women are the ones who give birth to children, and still take, or are supposed to take, most of the responsibility for raising them?

All through the 1980s, the women's movement for equality was clearly spreading throughout society, as women in great numbers were moving into and out of professional schools, community colleges, into jobs and professions. Women were using affirmative action to get skilled trade jobs, were seeking leadership positions in unions and professional organizations. Women's legal and policy advocacy groups grew, and African-American, Asian, and Latino women, women sociologists and scientists, Catholic nuns and Jewish rabbis formed their own caucuses. And following the "baby bust," in those years when women were liberating themselves from the feminine mystique, many of these new women were choosing to have babies when they were in their thirties and forties.

Yet polls began showing that younger women did not want to call themselves feminists, though they seemed to identify with every item of women's agenda of equality. During the Reagan years, a backlash was also forming, pushed by the religious right, and evident in the mass media, with cover stories of gray-suited career women setting down briefcases, picking up babies, and putting on aprons. A law providing unpaid parental leave couldn't even get through Congress.

"Identity politics," they started calling it inside the Beltway in Washington. "Special interests," the politicians and the pundits were calling the women, the blacks, the gays, labor, the handicapped, the Latinos, the people whom the government and laws of our democracy were supposed to protect from the overwhelming tyranny of corporate power — the real "special interests" of the oil industry and the lumber barons. Surely, women — who are 52 percent of the American people — should never have let themselves be defined by such a model, based originally on corporate power. Can we find the strength *to put the interests of the people first,* weakened as we increasingly organize over separate, single issues, and define our enemy in terms of race or gender or sexual orientation — black versus white, women versus men, gay versus straight?

Most of the energy of the leading feminist organizations has recently been focused on abortion or sexual politics — rape, date rape, pornography. The religious right and other far-right groups instigated the bombing of abortion clinics and a "gag rule" prohibiting hospitals or clinics that receive federal funds from giving women any information about abortion possibilities. (Clinton got rid of that.) There is no question in my mind that the major reason for the focus on abortion by demagogues of the far right is its symbolic message of woman's independence, autonomy, control over her own body, and destiny. But were we somehow letting those who opposed all our rights, our very personhood as women, box us in, define the terms of our unfinished battle too narrowly? After all, year after year we spent most of our organizational energy and funds fighting for the right to abortion, the battle we had already won, in Congress and the courts and public opinion.

Ought not at least as much energy go into breaking down the remaining barriers to women's earning and advancement in our economy until they achieve equality with men? Key to that, in the United States, would be to change the structures that make it difficult for American women to combine childbearing and advancement in business and professions. I discovered about this time that the countries where women's earnings were now virtually equal to men's — Australia, for instance — were those with strong national policies on child care, parental leave, flexible hours.

A poll that truly crosses lines of race, class, and generations, to find out the concerns of women in the 1990s, was conducted and released as "Women's Voices" by the Center for Policy Alternatives and the Ms. Foundation. It shows, to the amazement of the politically correct, that none of the sexual issues, including abortion, are among the main problems concerning women today, younger or older, black or white. They are for choice, overwhelmingly. But the percentage ranking any of the sexual issues — rape, date rape, sexual harassment, pornography, abortion — as of major concern is very low.

For the great majority of women today, according to the poll, the main problems are jobs — getting them, keeping them, getting ahead in them — and "work and family" — how to put it all together, how to meet the responsibilities of children and career, how to live the equality we've fought for. The economy itself is now based on the two-paycheck family. Women now constitute nearly 50 percent of the workforce. And in some 50 percent of families, women now earn 50 percent or more of the family income.

My sense of real crisis arrived in the summer of 1994, as I prepared to go to Washington as guest scholar at the Woodrow Wilson Center for International Scholars. As I packed up my papers, I did a double-take at a number of random items I'd been clipping from the business pages of newspapers.

1. ITEM: *Male, Educated and in a Pay Bind* (*New York Times*, February 11, 1994)
> For the first time since World War II, college-educated men in their late forties and early fifties — normally the prime earning years — are suffering a steep decline in wages, finally getting caught in the downward mobility that has hit most other groups of male workers.
>
> By comparison, the million or so college-educated women in this age group have seen their median incomes, adjusted for inflation, rise slightly since 1988. But at $25,818, the median is still well below that of their male peers, although in many households the women's earnings cushion the men's losses.

2. ITEM: *The War Between the Sexes* (*The Economist*, March 5, 1994)
> Women have been the job market's big success story during the past two decades. But as they have found jobs, men have lost them. Have women driven men from the workplace?

3. ITEM: *Good Jobs in Hard Times, $5.25 an Hour, $7 to $8 an Hour* (*New York Times*, October 3, 1993)
> Almost unnoticed, discount retailers like Wal-Mart, Kmart, Target, Venture, and Home Depot have become a huge source of new employment in America. The jobs they offer, mostly at $5 to $9 an hour, are turning out to be one of the best deals that corporate America offers. As the discounters expand, offering hundreds of barnlike stores to meet the demand for low-priced mer-

chandise of Americans pinched by stagnant incomes, many other industries shrink and lay off workers . . . That gives the discounters a huge pool of idle people from whom to choose. The stores report that five to ten people, many of them experienced and skilled, compete for each job.

My inner Geiger counter is clicking again, urgently. I see the paradox for women. They are doing better than ever before, benefiting from the changes in the economy, with more control over their lives than their mothers ever dreamed of. And the great majority now work at jobs that, though they may not be the greatest, give them a life in their forties and fifties after their kids are off, even though the juggling of children and job in their thirties is tough. Many women are doing as well or better than downsized men. Not at the very top still, *but the women are achieving what begins to look like equality because the men are doing worse.* Is their loss really our gain?

Studying the pattern in these news items, I sense a backlash much more serious than Robert Bly's drum-beating, loincloth-wearing masculine impersonators. I notice the new custody decisions, in Michigan and California, where a woman loses custody of a child because she has a demanding job, or is getting her law degree or Ph.D., and her child spends part of the day in day care, while the father's new wife or mother would stay home all day with the child. And the "family values" cry is being spread by the religious right even as it continues to bomb abortion clinics. Feminist groups mobilize to defend abortion clinics, but who is mobilizing to confront economic inequality, disequilibrium, and dislocation, which are far more threatening to family values and to the survival and stability of families than is abortion or pornography? They are also far more dangerous to women, endangering all our gains, all the rights we have won, the autonomy and independence, during this past quarter-century.

I see that there has to be a paradigm shift from our previous thinking about women, and not just the sexual politics, though it seems clear to me that the increased violence against women and abuse of children may be symptoms of the rage and anger of men dispossessed of their dominance. But the sole focus on women's status *vis à vis* men is a diversion. If women are winning and men are losing, how long can we really win? The fact is, most women still live in some kind of family with men, and will subtly suffer — economically, emotionally — if the downsizing and insecurity of the men continue. We must face the real economic threat to family values.

As for women alone, single parents, lesbian couples, the politics of hate that is rising from and stirring up the rage of the threatened men will surely turn on them. I hear that Rush Limbaugh calls me a feminazi. If "jobs" and "work and family" are what concern women most, we have to mobilize to protect our children, our families, ourselves in a new coalition with men. The women's attitude cannot be "Up with women; forget the men."

While we weren't looking, something really dangerous was going on in America: the accumulation of more and more and obscenely more of the wealth and resources of this nation by those who are already rich. It is a dangerous income inequality. And none of us — women, blacks, gays — none of the separate groups that our own movements comprise are going to advance much further unless we join with labor in confronting this crisis of income inequality. We have to take on the culture of greed with specific measures to restore the priorities of this nation. Should we not — women, black, all of us — join with labor as Americans did fifty years ago when they fought for the forty-hour week, and fight for a thirty-hour week, which would mean more jobs for everybody? That would meet the crying needs of women and men in the child-rearing years, who shouldn't be working fifty- and sixty-hour weeks to make ends meet. We must take on the corporate culture of greed to defend and extend democracy, to revitalize our vision of the common good, a humane vision that places the highest priority on people's lives and not on the stock market index and the corporate bottom line.

3

Family Values and the Invisible Working Class

Lillian B. Rubin

WE AMERICANS have a long history of using words to obscure unpleasant realities. We spin, we twist, we label. Sometimes a new label makes sense. The shift from *cripple,* with the ugly associations it has for so long evoked in both literature and life, to the more neutral *handicapped* has enabled us to look the disabled in the face with greater ease. But whether for good or ill, the words we choose, *downsizing,* for example — and those we *don't* choose to use, like *working class* — have social and political consequences that too often go unnoticed.

In the last several years hardly a week has gone by when some corporate giant hasn't announced the firing of more workers. Only we never use that word anymore. We talk instead about *layoffs,* a word that implies that these workers are caught in some temporary company downturn, something like what my mother used to experience during what's known as the "slack season" in the garment industry. But for today's worker, the "regular" season never comes around again.

Not only don't we fire people anymore, but we have a whole new corporate language, words designed to make the process seem harmless, as if we were doing nothing more than tinkering with the corporate structure. So we *downsize, restructure, re-engineer,* or, most bizarre of all, *rightsize.*

Rightsize! It's a word coined by IBM's CEO Louis Gerstner and designed to shield companies from criticism by obscuring the human consequences of these greedy moves to increase corporate profits — not to mention their CEOs' earnings. After all, if a company is right-sized — the implication being that something wrong is now being righted — how can anyone complain? For each company that right-sizes or restructures itself, however, thousands of women and men lose their jobs, and with them their hold on the American dream.

But why worry about this now? Government officials and the press keep citing various economic indicators to show that the recession of the early 1990s is over: unemployment is down; despite the recent gyrations on Wall Street, the economy is growing; we've added an impressive ten million new jobs since 1993.

So why are so many American families in such pain? Perhaps because the experts forgot to say that nearly 8.5 million people — one out of every fourteen workers, most of them women and men in working-class families — were fired in the two years between 1993 and 1995. That's on top of the nine million workers who were rendered jobless in the first three years of this decade. Nor do they explain that the official unemployment rate is different from the *real* one, since the Labor Department figures include only those who have been looking for work in the week of the count. Which leaves out the millions of workers who, after months of looking, have given up hope and abandoned the search.

The experts don't tell us either that, while the official unemployment rate may have declined, the number of workers who are down-sized out of their jobs continues to climb. Nor do they bother to add that most of the newly created jobs are low-level service jobs that pay a fraction of what these millions of men and women were earning before they got rightsized and downsized out of work. And they ignore the fact that a very large number of these same new jobs are temporary, which means that they offer no benefits and pay less than permanent full-time work.

Characteristically, we now have a new name for these "temps" as well. "Contingent workers," the Labor Department calls them, a name that allows us to look away from the fact that these are, in the words of some labor economists, "throwaway workers." Tens of millions of women and men live with that grim reality every day — with the knowledge that, for their employers, they're interchangeable and, like objects that are no longer useful, just as easily disposable. Emotionally, it corrodes their inner sense of themselves and their value; economically, they live with fear and uncertainty, worrying when they wake each day that by nightfall they'll be out of even the inadequate job they cling to so desperately.

In my recent study of working-class families, *Families on the Fault Line* — those whose voices are seldom heard in the cacophony of noise and demand that make up our public life — I interviewed 162 families who live in cities across the country.[1] The sample consisted of ninety-two white ethnic families, thirty African Americans, twenty Latinos, and twenty Asians. The median age of the women was thirty-two; of the men, thirty-seven. Sixteen percent of the families were headed by a woman — three-fourths because they were divorced; the rest, except for one who was widowed, because they had never married. Roughly a third were second marriages for at least one of the partners. The husband-wife families had been married at least five years; the range was five to thirty years. Whenever possible, I interviewed wives, husbands, and teenage children, for a total of 388 separate in-depth, face-to-face, focused interviews.

Over the course of the last decade about a quarter of the men and women I met learned firsthand about the pain and uncertainty of being disposable workers. And all spoke bitterly of the experience. "It's like they don't see you like a person," complained a thirty-two-year-old father of three children; "like you don't have bills and kids. They don't need you anymore, so they toss you out like you're not a real human being. I've been looking for steady work for eight or nine months, but there ain't none, least none I can get. So me and my wife, we live scared. I've got to depend on these temporary jobs, where the pay's lousy and you don't get any benefits. But at least with both of us working, we can pay the rent. What happens when I can't even get one of these rotten jobs? We'll be out on the street."

The *Wall Street Journal* and others like it keep telling us that the changes in corporate America are good for the country. I don't know whose country they're talking about, but it's certainly not the one in which most working-class families struggle to feed, clothe, and educate their children. In reality, whatever the gains of the lean corporate culture of the 1990s, they come at the expense of both the workers and the nation. For when a person cannot count on a permanent job, a critical element binding him or her to society is lost, and the consequence to both family and national life is devastating.

With millions of poor and working-class American families in just this situation, the current cant about family values, which displays no understanding of the social and economic bases necessary to sustain those values, becomes a shameful kind of political sophistry. Certainly some of the changes in family and social life in recent decades are cause for concern. Old rules have given way in every facet of family life, from the public world of work to the private arena of sex, while a new order is not yet fully in place. As we continue to move into uncertain social and emotional territory, anxieties rise and breed nostalgia for a past when, in retrospect, life seemed simpler, safer, and saner.

From this perspective, it's easy to understand the appeal of the family-values discourse. But it's a discussion in a vacuum. For as the values advocates frame it, the family itself *becomes* the context, as if families were atoms afloat in space, unconnected to the social and institutional life in which they are embedded.

If we're going to preach the politics of virtue, then we need to promote the social conditions that dispose people to be virtuous. The family-values champions, for example, complain endlessly that two working parents don't spend enough time with their children. But when the choice is between time and the money to pay the rent, time loses. If the values partisans care so much about time for family life, they would serve their cause better by, among other things, joining a movement to restructure the world of work and decrease the standard forty-hour work week to thirty-two hours.

Visionary? Yes. But that's what people said a century ago when the reformers of that era engaged the struggle for the forty-hour week that we now take as given in nature.

A job that pays a living wage and affords decent, safe housing — these are the fundamental needs, the twin girders on which family stability rests. Yet now, after two decades of rising rents and falling wages, millions of poor and working-class families have neither. Our national response to this reality? The President signs into law new housing legislation that puts an end to the decades-long promise to subsidize decent housing for low-income families. And the family-values band plays on.

In the real world, IBM rightsizes and families tremble as un-counted numbers of men who have supported their families for twenty years sit home and watch their wives go off to work. Or a single mother finds herself on welfare — that is, in the good old days when there was still a welfare program in place. Or a family that prided itself on its self-sufficiency suddenly finds itself buying grocer-ies with food stamps instead of dollars. Or a child's illness goes untreated because the medical benefits that went with the job are gone and her parents can't afford the care that could help. Or the family loses their home and with it whatever stability they had managed to achieve.

In such circumstances, rates of depression rise markedly and alco-hol abuse increases as people — usually men — seek some respite from the voices of shame and blame inside them. Among the families in my study, a fifth of the men were serious drinkers, a problem usually exacerbated by unemployment and underemployment. "My husband drinks a lot more now; I mean, he always drank some, but not like now," said a twenty-eight-year-old nurse's aide and mother of three children. "I guess he tries to drink away his troubles, but it only makes more trouble. I tell him, but he doesn't listen. He has a fiery temper, always has. But since he lost his job, it's real bad, and his drinking doesn't help it none."

As tensions heighten, so does family violence, leaving already fragile families even more at risk. "I worry a lot when he drinks, because he treats my little boy so terrible, punches him around," the same woman continued.

But it's not just the child who gets "punched around." When I asked if she, too, had felt the pain of her husband's violence, she looked away while her fingers plucked agitatedly at her jeans. Fi-nally, as if in an unconscious wish to deny the reality, she shook her head no, but the words she spoke said something else. "Yeah, but only when he has too many beers. He doesn't mean it. It's just that he's so upset about being out of work."

Some kind of violence — sometimes against children only, more often against both women and children — is the admitted reality in about 14 percent of the families in this study. I say "admitted reality," because this remains one of the most closely guarded secrets in family life, a hidden shame that both women and men deny, even when the evidence is clearly visible. It's reasonable to assume, therefore, that the proportion of families victimized by violence is considerably higher.

Alcoholism, family violence, depression — these are old news, problems of family living that always escalate in times of stress. But now there's a new one to add to family tensions — the fear of homelessness. Over and over, people in this study talked about their terror that they might soon find themselves "on the street" — a fear that clutches at the heart and gnaws at the soul as unemployment and underemployment become a way of life in so many families.

Nothing exemplifies the change in the twenty years since I last studied working-class families, in *Worlds of Pain,* than the fear of being on the street.[2] Then, not a single person worried about being homeless. For them, homelessness was something that happened somewhere else, in India or some other far-off and alien land. Then, we wept when we read about the poor people who lived on the streets in those other places. *What kind of society doesn't provide this most basic of life's needs?* we asked ourselves. Now, the steadily growing numbers of homeless in our own land have become an ever-present and frightening reminder of just how precarious life in this society can be. Now, they're in our face, on our streets, an accepted category of American social life — "the homeless."

Just how readily accepted they are was brought home to me recently when my husband, who volunteers some time in the San Francisco schools, reported his experience with a sixth-grade class. He had been invited to talk to the children about career opportunities and, in doing so, talked about his own past as a restaurateur. The students listened, engrossed. But instead of the questions he had expected when he finished, they were preoccupied with how he managed the problem of the homeless. Did he feed homeless people when they asked for food? He explained that at the time he had restaurants in the Bay Area, there were no homeless on the streets. Undaunted, they wanted to know what he did when he found a homeless person sleeping in the doorway of the restaurant. He reminded them that he had just told them that homelessness wasn't an issue when he was in business. They listened, he said, but they couldn't really grasp the idea of a world without the homeless. How could it be otherwise? At their age, homelessness is so much a part of their daily world that they take it for granted, a phenomenon not of their time but of all times.

Obviously, all these family problems aren't with us *only* because IBM and a host of other companies have downsized, rightsized, and restructured. But these structural changes in the corporate economy have human consequences, and the words we have devised to speak of these events, mask that reality and enable us to look away from the anguish they cause.

It's true, too, about the words we choose *not* to speak. Take the words *working class* — perfectly good words elsewhere in the world, but ones that have been written out of the American lexicon. It's another example of our American ingenuity, especially when it comes to using language to cloud reality. We call something by another name and behave as if we've made it so. Except that it doesn't work that way.

Everyone who has ever asked the question knows that most Americans, whether they're rich or poor, identify themselves as middle class. Occasionally, a working-class man in one of my studies will say, "I'm a working man" — a statement made sometimes with pride, sometimes with anger, but rarely with any consciousness of class and its meaning in his life.

Not a surprise in a country where the media and the experts join in defining the middle class by the car in the driveway, the TV and VCR in the living room, the brand-name sneakers, the designer jeans, and all the other symbols that are the marks of status in our consumer-driven society. Or where the Congressional Budget Office lumps together as middle class all families of four with annual incomes between $19,000 and $78,000 — a range so wide as to be nonsensical to anyone but a politician.

Some progressive writers also now argue that we must cast aside the distinctions between the working and middle classes. In a recent article in *The Nation* (October 7, 1996), for example, Richard Parker insists that we must redefine *"progressive politics — clearly, bluntly and without compromise — as being about the permanent enlargement of the middle class"* (emphasis in original). I have no quarrel with his goal of improving the lot of all Americans, only with his argument that the idea of a working class no longer has any real meaning; only with his insistence that it's "antiquated and out of touch" to talk about the differences between the working and middle classes; only with his belief that progressive politics is best served by an enlarged middle class.

I agree that the old Marxist notion of class no longer applies to the American experience — that is, if it ever did. But that doesn't mean the divisions in this society should be blurred into irrelevancy. Rather, it suggests that we must find new ways to conceive and speak of them. Until we do, the language of class is all we have, and, its problems notwithstanding, it explains more than it obscures.

Even a cursory look at the statistics of the 1996 election reveals that, excepting those with postgraduate training, Americans vote more conservatively as they move up the education and income ladder, which means also the class ladder. In the congressional races, 55 percent of high school graduates — almost certainly working-class men and women — cast their vote for Democrats, while 57 percent of college graduates voted Republican. Voters with annual family incomes under $50,000 fell heavily in the Democratic column — the lower the income, the wider the margin. As income increased, so did support for the Republicans, rising from 53 percent to 63 percent as earnings climbed from $50,000 to $100,000 a year. And a convincing 63 percent of union households threw their support to Democratic contenders.

Certainly, as Mr. Parker points out, the middle class is larger today than it has ever been. Certainly, too, the weekly earnings of some workers at the top tier of the blue-collar pyramid may match those of middle-level white-collar managers. But these are the rare working-class jobs, the dream jobs of a world in which most workers have to settle for very much less. Equally important, even those in the most desirable blue-collar jobs are paid by the hour, while the middle manager earns a weekly wage. Since hourly work isn't as steady, the *annual* income of blue-collar workers is likely to be substantially less than the earnings of their white-collar counterparts, even when the hourly wage is higher.

Still, it's reasonable to ask what difference it makes if we distinguish between working-class and middle-class families. The label we affix doesn't change their lives, does it? The answer is both yes and no. In the immediate sense, no matter what we call people, their daily lives remain the same. But in the larger scheme, it makes a difference.

For one thing, despite all the media attention to the middle-class professionals who have been downsized out of their jobs, it is the blue-collar workers who were hit first and hardest in the new corporate culture. For another, the idea of the middle class is not just a handy social category, a shorthand way to describe a segment of the population. It has broad political and policy implications as well. For the way we conceive of our people determines how we think of their needs and, therefore, how government policy is made.

Someone benefits, someone loses each time a policy is promulgated. If the popular political language denies the very existence of a sector of the population, its needs aren't likely to be taken into account. Take housing, for example. While the federal government says it can no longer afford to subsidize rents for working-class families who have been priced out of the market, the mortgage-interest and property-tax deductions it grants to homeowners — benefits that accrue most heavily to the middle and upper-middle classes — cost the public treasury billions every year.

At a more basic level, it makes a difference in how people define themselves, because they can't see their own self-interest if they don't have the language to affirm it. For words are more than just words; they embody ideas, *our* ideas. Words are the symbols that frame our thoughts and guide our actions. Without the words, ideas are hard to come by — if they come at all. And without an idea that binds people together in some common cause — the idea of a working class that transcends race, ethnicity, and religion, for example — it's virtually impossible for people to organize in their own behalf.

The language of "working families" that dominated the recent presidential campaign — and that was adopted by the unions and other progressives — may serve the political need to appear inclusive. But the very breadth of the idea makes it problematic, since it encompasses the families of the Fortune 500 CEOs along with the families of the janitors, the machine operators, the truck drivers, and the shipping clerks who work for them. Without the language of class — and the *idea* it embodies — these most elementary class realities are obscured, and ordinary working-class families become invisible, swallowed up in the large, amorphous category of "working families." In this setting, the "working" part of the "working families" rhetoric too easily falls away, and we're left with a discourse about families and family values that is disconnected from the social and economic realities that determine the quality of family life.

Psychologically, too, the blurring of class issues makes a difference. In the short run, given the stigma attached to being working class in this country, calling themselves middle class may make people feel better about their social situation and enhance their self-esteem. Over the long haul, however, the denial of their class position leads to a confused and contradictory social identity that leaves working-class people riven with status anxiety and impairs their ability to join together to act in their own behalf.

The fact is that class inequalities not only exist in our society, they're handed down from parents to children in the same way that wealth is passed along in the upper class. True, American society has always had a less rigid and clearly defined class structure than many other nations. Poor people climb up; wealthy ones fall. These often well-publicized figures help to support the myth about equality of opportunity. But they're not the norm. Nor is the perpetuation of our class structure accidental. The economy, the polity, and the educational system all play their part in ensuring the continuity and stability of our social classes.

Look at public education. Myth tells us that it's the great equalizer, the one institution in our society that promises every child the same education and, therefore, an equal chance at the good life. Yet educational researchers have known for years that a school's achievement record is closely correlated with its students' socioeconomic status. It's no secret either that schools in poor and working-class neighborhoods have fewer resources and worse physical plants than those in the wealthier ones. The best teachers, the cleanest books, the most supplies seem to find their way more often into the schools that serve white middle-class children than into those attended by the poor and working class.

The problem is not only that schools for middle-class children are more pleasant, better-equipped places, although surely the environment has something to do with how well children learn. These differences also count because they send a message about who and what this society values — a message that working-class children hear very clearly.

Despite their social and political invisibility and the disparity in the resources allocated to their schools and communities (just look at the difference in the maintenance of the streets in urban working-class and middle-class neighborhoods), working-class families are the single biggest group of families in the country. These are the men and women who provide our services and who make our goods in what's left of the manufacturing sector — workers whose education is limited, whose mobility options are restricted, and who work for an hourly rather than a weekly wage. They don't tap public resources; they reap no benefit from either the pitiful handouts to the poor or from huge subsidies to the rich.

But all too often they live on the edge. Any unexpected event threatens to throw them into the abyss. Credit, if they're able to get it at all, is stretched to the limit. The machine spits out the plastic card that helped them deal with the steady erosion of income in recent years; the clerk hands it back to them with an embarrassed

"Sorry, the machine won't take it. Do you have another card?" They probably do, but it won't make any difference; the machine will know that one, too, is "maxed out."

For large numbers of working-class families, then, their much vaunted middle-class lifestyle has turned out to be a house of cards built on debt. The American dream — a life filled with goods and comforts bought on credit; goods that in our consumption-driven society are the symbols of worth, the emblems of success — has become a nightmare of uncertainty, if not despair. But even the bankruptcy court — the last refuge of the middle class — is too often closed to the working class.

It takes a certain amount of knowledge, sophistication, and access to legal advice to plan for a bankruptcy — commodities in short supply among most working-class families. In my recent research into the lives of these families, I heard story after story about people who lost everything they had — including their children's beds — because they didn't understand that they could have declared bankruptcy. As a thirty-eight-year-old father of two teenage children remarked bitterly, "After the finance people came, I found out I could have gone bankrupt. Maybe if I'd known about it before, we could have saved some things from those damn vultures. But I never found out about it until it was too late. I mean, I heard of people going bankrupt, but I always thought it was only businesses did that, not plain people. How would I know? Nobody tells you stuff like that; then, when you find it out, it's too late, and you're stuck."

But even if he had known, he might have discovered that he couldn't afford the luxury of having himself declared officially broke. For bankruptcy isn't for the poor and the near-poor, since they rarely have the $1000 or more it takes in court costs and legal fees. Instead, they lose the possessions that a bankruptcy filing would have protected and remain buried under debts that the bankruptcy court would have canceled. One of the men who found himself in just this position explained angrily, "I read in the paper about people declaring bankruptcy, and I figured I had to do something or we'd drown in those goddamn bills. So I went to see this lawyer, and he said, yeah, sure, I could go bankrupt and all my bills would be wiped out. Only problem was, it would cost about a thousand dollars. Christ, if I had a thousand, I wouldn't be bankrupt, would I?"

These are not just the sad stories of an unlucky few. Every person in this study had either suffered the loss of a job or had friends, neighbors, or family members who suddenly found themselves on the unemployment line. Some found other jobs, but almost always they were earning substantially less than they had before they were fired.

It's true, of course, that many of the issues confronting families today know no class boundaries. Middle-class families also feel the credit crunch; they too have had to strain their resources nearly to the breaking point to maintain their lifestyle; they too know the anxiety of not being able to spend enough time with their children. Even families at the high end of middle-class incomes are feeling strapped by the cost of housing, feeding, clothing, and educating a family today. But what turns those issues into problems, as well as how families attend to them, is related to the resources at their disposal, which, of course, means their class position.

Middle-class families may be unable to afford the house of their dreams, may find it a strain to pay for their children's private school, may have to go into debt to buy a new car or take a vacation. But will anyone argue that these problems are as wrenching as those of the working-class family earning $35,000 and struggling to come up with the money for the rent, a doctor's bill, or a winter coat for a growing child? The subjective experience of deprivation in both instances may be real, but there's an objective difference that should not be dismissed.

It is precisely these differences that are eclipsed by the language we use. When corporations downsize, they fire people, most of them working class. As the gap between those who do the firing and those who get fired grows obscenely wide, we do a disservice both to the people who are suffering the cost of this economic dislocation and to the nation at large when we accept uncritically language that befogs this reality.

Just so, there *is* a working class in America, and its families have suffered the economic shifts of recent decades most acutely. To perpetuate the long-held American fiction that this is a society without class distinctions, that we all have an equal chance at the promise of this bountiful land, helps to keep the working class from a sustained and organized effort on its own behalf. And no agency in the nation has more reason to encourage that effort, nor is there any better equipped to aid and abet it, than a revitalized labor movement.

Notes

1. *Families on the Fault Line* (New York: HarperPerennial, 1995).
2. *Worlds of Pain* (New York: Basic Books, 1976).

4

Intellectuals and Labor
A Brief History

Eric Foner

THE HIGHLY SUCCESSFUL Teach-In with the Labor Movement, which brought academics and trade unionists to Columbia University in October 1996, may well have opened a new chapter in an old and checkered history — the relationship between intellectuals and labor in the United States. There is, of course, nothing new about members of the intellectual community joining with workers in the struggle for progressive social change. But the need for such an alliance is more acute today than at any time in living memory. We live amidst troubling changes in the conditions of life and future prospects of most Americans. In public discourse, the market is persistently invoked as the sole arbiter of economic and social policy. The desire of working people for economic security, health care, and a cushion against the vagaries and inequities of the market economy is today derided as nothing more than a selfish attachment to bloated entitlements, an inefficient drag on an economy that must compete with countries offering their citizens far less expensive social safety nets. While the affluent retreat into gated communities, anything defined as public — mass transit, public housing, public schools, the idea of the city itself as a center of civilization — is progressively being abandoned. In a reversal of trends over a century old, Americans today are working longer hours, for lower real wages, than in the past.

Equally distressing, the country recently witnessed a presidential election campaign in which neither party evinced the slightest interest in addressing fundamental economic and social problems. It is a tragedy that it was left to Pat Buchanan to raise the question of the global economy's impact on American workers. Nearly a century ago, in 1914, Congress felt it necessary and appropriate to declare, in the Clayton Act, that "the labor of a human being is not a commodity." Which of our public leaders would make such a statement today? At such a time, it is organized labor, more than any other institution in the society, that upholds the values of fraternity and comradeship, the idea that human interactions should be governed by justice, not merely profit.

While intellectuals can offer vital services to a revitalized labor movement, it is important to remember that, historically, intellectuals typically have been servants, not critics of power. In the late nineteenth century, academic economics and sociology were dominated by the Social Darwinist view, associated, for example, with William Graham Sumner of Yale, that both unions and state intervention on behalf of workers constituted dangerous intrusions on the "natural laws" by which society functioned. Social stratification, in this view, reflected not an unequal distribution of power, but the superior talent of the rich compared with laborers. These ideas, long since discredited, have risen like ghosts to haunt our own world. Today, for every writer and academic willing to work in cooperation with labor, there are dozens funded by conservative think tanks that churn out treatises "proving" that the unrestrained market is the sole definition of democracy, that efforts to assist the poor, improve the conditions of working men and women, and combat the legacy of racial inequality are counterproductive or pernicious, that government, not the depredations of downsizing corporations, constitutes the leading threat to community stability and social well-being.

Nonetheless, this country has experienced a long history of intellectuals allying with the labor movement, and of labor producing its own intellectuals, who have altered the terms of public debate. Both processes can be traced back at least as far as the American Revolution. For if the struggle for independence established the United States as a sovereign nation, it also unleashed widespread demands for a more democratic, egalitarian society. It was during the Revolution that artisans, journeymen, and others excluded from the Colonial era's "political nation" staked a claim to equal participation in democratic politics, and articulated a vision of an egalitarian society freed from the hereditary privilege and social hierarchy of Europe. In the age of revolution, no one expressed these aspirations for a more just society better than Thomas Paine, who had grown up in England as a working journeyman and emigrated to America shortly before independence was declared. Paine became perhaps our first professional intellectual — that is, a man who earned his livelihood solely by his pen. The leading pamphleteer of the era, Paine was a champion not only of American independence, but of political democracy and the obligation of government to provide for the economic needs of its citizens. Paine's success in America and England relied both on a brilliant literary style, which expressed complex ideas in a language uneducated men and women could understand, and on his deep connections with the artisans and laborers on both sides of the Atlantic.

Two generations after the Revolution, the United States witnessed the birth of the world's first political parties representing the interests of labor — the local workingmen's parties that sprang up in the late 1820s in New York, Philadelphia, and other cities. Among their leaders were labor intellectuals like Thomas Skidmore, a teacher and skilled mechanic, who taught that the political rights of man achieved by the revolutionary generation should be expanded to include access to economic resources. Skidmore developed a penetrating critique of the idea that free competition would produce equitable results for labor. So long as property was unequally distributed, he wrote, efforts to end other inequalities — of educational opportunity, political power, and the like — were doomed to fail, and he called on the government to grant all people (women and nonwhites included) economic "competence" on their reaching adulthood. This same concern for the use of political power to secure workers' economic autonomy motivated George Henry Evans, a British immigrant who became the editor of a series of labor newspapers, including the *Workingman's Advocate*. Every citizen,

Evans wrote, had a right to the soil, and the government, via a "homestead act," should grant land free of charge to settlers in the West. Thanks to Evans and other advocates of the homestead ideal, land reform would remain a key theme in labor radicalism down to the turn of the century.

The early workingmen's parties reflected the anxieties of small producers facing the prospect of long-term economic dependence. By the post–Civil War era, as factory production came to dominate more and more industries, writers, editors, and social reformers joined with the Knights of Labor — the largest labor organization of the nineteenth century — to seek solutions to the impact on labor of rapid industrialization. George McNeill, a shoemaker and wool-mill worker in Massachusetts who became one of the movement's most eloquent writers, insisted that permanent wage labor was incompatible with the economic autonomy required of the democratic citizen. "There is an inevitable and irrepressible conflict," McNeill wrote, "between the wage system of labor and the republican system of government." McNeill's solution was not to return to the days of the small-scale craftsman, but to "engraft republican principles into our industrial system," primarily by replacing privately owned factories with producer cooperatives.

As labor strife spread in the 1880s and 1890s, a flood of books offered solutions to the fundamental economic rifts in American society and the extremely unequal distribution of the fruits of the new industrial technology. Jacob Riis's *How the Other Half Lives* (1890) exposed the terrible conditions in New York's slum tenements. Edward Bellamy's *Looking Backward* (1888) portrayed a utopia in the year 2000, when all would share equally in economic progress. Henry D. Lloyd, in *Wealth Against Commonwealth* (1894), showed how the Standard Oil Company manipulated the market, drove out competition, bribed legislators, and in other ways made a mockery of political democracy and economic justice. Lloyd played a leading role in the abortive effort to create a political alliance between organized labor and the Populist Party in Illinois in 1894.

Most popular of all was *Progress and Poverty* (1879), by Henry George, probably the most influential work of economics ever written in the United States. George's solution to the problem of poverty amidst plenty — a single tax on land — probably did not account for his immense success. More important was his clear, jargon-free exposition of economic relationships, and his powerful sense that something was fundamentally wrong in a society in which economic advance went hand in hand with the exploitation of labor and growing urban poverty. In 1886, labor chose Henry George as its candidate for mayor of New York (he captured 68,000 votes, finishing second to Democrat Abram Hewitt and outpolling the Republican candidate, Theodore Roosevelt).

Of course, not all labor leaders were thrilled to find unions mobilizing behind a newspaper editor whose land program seemed of limited relevance to the problems of industrial society. The slogan of the early American Federation of Labor — "pure and simple unionism" — meant, in part, that nonworkers should be excluded from positions of authority in the labor movement. This was the position of AFL president Samuel Gompers, who became convinced that the nostrums of reform-minded intellectuals — land reform, Greenbackism, the illusion that laborers could be transformed into entrepreneurs — misled workers into thinking that their main task was something other than battling capital for a larger share of the fruits of economic production. Rather than pining for economic independence via land ownership, cooperatives, and the like, workers, Gompers insisted, must accept the fact that they were permanent wage-earners, and that their interests were antagonistic to those of employers. There was little role for intellectuals in the movement, Gompers believed, except to support labor's struggle for higher wages and better working conditions under industrial capitalism.

Gompers's frank recognition that the wage-earning class had become a permanent feature of American life marked a major step forward for labor ideology. But his hostile response to intellectuals did not end efforts at labor-intellectual cooperation. In the Progressive era, a time, like our own, when the rapid concentration of wealth and power posed troubling questions for American democracy, intellectuals worked closely with the labor movement on such issues as child labor, wages and hours legislation, old-age pensions, and ways to introduce democratic decision-making on the shop floor. For the first time, many of the intellectuals with whom organized labor cooperated were women. Social reformers and settlement house workers like Florence Kelley and Jane Addams rejected the traditional view that the poor were responsible for their own fate. From their base at Hull House in Chicago, Kelley and Addams initiated an array of reforms from building and sanitation codes to shorter hours, safer working conditions, mothers' pensions, and the right of labor to organize. Through the National Consumers' League, Kelley helped women mobilize power on labor's behalf, by boycotting goods produced under substandard conditions. The consumer, she insisted, must take an interest in the conditions under which marketplace commodities are produced (a position echoed nowadays in campaigns against barrio sweatshops and overseas child labor factories that produce for some of the most prominent brands in the American marketplace). Above all, Kelley, Addams, and their allies called on government to assume an active role in modern industrial society, challenging the laissez-faire orthodoxy dominant in political and judicial circles.

With the expansion of university education and the professionalization of fields like economics, sociology, and the like, more and more intellectuals were now located at universities, at a social remove from workplaces. Nonetheless, labor relied heavily on statistical studies of poverty, old age, and working conditions by Progressive-era social scientists. James M. Cattell, a psychologist at Columbia, in 1912 put forward what he called "A Program of Radical Democracy," including women's suffrage, progressive taxation, free medical care, old-age and disability pensions, the eight-hour day, and minimum wage laws. Cattell, along with Columbia professors John Dewey, Charles Beard, and E.R.A. Seligman, helped write the Progressive Party platform of 1912, which embodied these demands.

Rarely have relations between reform-minded intellectuals and socially activist unionists been as close as during the Progressive period. This was evident not only in the professors connected with the

Progressive Party, but in intellectuals allied with the Socialist Party and others attracted to the Industrial Workers of the World. Such intellectuals called for even more far-reaching changes in American life — such as workers' control of production or government direction of economic enterprise production — and also sought to combat emerging social attitudes that deprecated the economic and social importance of labor while exalting that of managers and entrepreneurs. Intellectuals of the cultural and artistic avant-garde who congregated in the famous salons of prewar Greenwich Village also saw the rights of labor as crucial to social change. Even as they celebrated the liberated individual free to pursue his or her personal, sexual, and artistic goals, they simultaneously sympathized with the struggles of Wobblies, sweatshop laborers, and factory operatives. The famous Paterson Pageant, organized by the young journalist John Reed, brought striking silk workers to New York's Madison Square Garden to take part in a choreographed representation of their prolonged and bitter strike — a reflection both of how labor's cause appealed to the artistic avant-garde and how artistic acclaim could not substitute for real power at the workplace. The silk strike, after all, was unsuccessful, and some critics felt that the energies that went into planning the pageant might have been more fruitfully employed in organizing in Paterson.

President Woodrow Wilson's decision to bring the United States into World War I shattered many of the connections and alliances that had built up before the war. On the one hand, the AFL and most socialist and progressive intellectuals joined enthusiastically in the war to make the world safe for democracy. Intellectuals on the Committee on Public Information deluged the nation with propaganda portraying Germans as evil incarnate and often calling for "industrial democracy" as a necessary counterpart to political democracy. The war unleashed the most severe period of repression in American history, shattering the Socialist Party and IWW. The defeat of the massive strike wave of 1919 — the year of the Seattle general strike, the great steel strike, and scores of other labor confrontations — ushered in an era of retrenchment for organized labor, in which many of the gains in membership and recognition achieved during the war were quickly reversed. Meanwhile, during the 1920s, many intellectuals retreated from politics altogether, finding refuge in Europe or in universities from a society seemingly in the grip of business conservatism and fundamentalist intolerance.

With the Great Depression and the advent of the New Deal, however, came another period of growth for organized labor, and so too did renewed cooperation between labor and intellectuals. For artists and writers ranging from Edmund Wilson and John Dos Passos to academics like Columbia's Adolph A. Berle and Rexford Guy Tugwell, the Depression opened the possibility of far-reaching social change in which labor would play a pivotal role. Berle and Tugwell were among the architects of the New Deal. Other intellectuals assisted the fledgling CIO. With the Wagner Act, Social Security, the minimum wage, and other measures of the mid-1930s, labor emerged as a critical element in the New Deal coalition that would dominate American politics for two generations. The New Deal inaugurated what one historian has called the "great compromise" between labor and capital, a protracted truce, supervised by the Democratic Party and the national government, that ended the endemic violence so characteristic of American labor relations and for the first time made the industrial worker a partner, albeit a junior partner, in governmental affairs.

Meanwhile, the organization of unions in basic industry via the CIO was powerfully aided both by New Dealers and by intellectuals associated with the Communist Party, then at the peak of its influence on the American left. Communist scholars spent summers instructing auto workers on the history of labor in America — a subject schools and colleges studiously ignored — and on the history of blacks in America, a critical subject, since organized labor for the first time in its history was making an active effort to recruit black workers. In the publications, songs, theatrical productions, and other expressions of the broad left-wing culture of the popular front, a new vision of American culture emerged to counter the nativist and racist view that had come to dominate after World

War I. It stressed pluralism and diversity, not blind conformity, as the hallmarks of American democracy. It was a vision that became the official self-portrait of American society during World War II.

Of course, the relationship between intellectuals and the labor movement has not always been so cooperative as during the New Deal era. In 1961, Harry Van Arsdale, president of the AFL-CIO New York City Central Labor Council, called for a renewal of the "labor-liberal intellectual alliance," which, he claimed, had fallen into abeyance. Relations between intellectuals and labor were paradoxical as the 1960s dawned. On the one hand, unions employed numerous researchers, economists, and educators on their own staffs. On the other, many intellectuals concluded that labor officials had become part of what C. Wright Mills called the nation's power elite, part of the establishment rather than critics of it, an interest group rather than a broad social movement. This sentiment was widely shared within the student movement of the sixties (even though the Students for a Democratic Society, in its earliest days, had close ties to liberal labor unions). In retrospect, the view that labor was now part of the establishment seems greatly exaggerated, but there were reasons for its plausibility. Many unions dragged their feet in coming to terms with the demands of the civil rights and women's movements. The official leadership of the AFL-CIO, moreover, was so tied to official Cold War orthodoxy that it failed to see that the inevitable consequence of America's imperial foreign policy was the globalization of economic enterprise and the export of jobs overseas. While many unions — such as Local 1199 of the Drug and Hospital Workers Union in New York — remained at the forefront of social change, others, especially the AFL-CIO's top leadership, adopted a more conservative course. The New Left rejected both organized labor and the liberal intellectual establishment as models for social change or sources of forward-looking critiques of American society. Ironically, when the sixties ended, a number of New Leftists went to work for labor unions, with a few holding key posts.

Partly because of the abdication of liberal intellectuals and unions in the face of the mounting crisis over Vietnam, by the mid-1960s the torch of radical leadership in America for the first time in our history passed into the hands of students and youth. The war inspired a full-fledged generational rebellion — the counterculture, whose exaltation of sex and drugs and rejection of the work ethic horrified organized labor (although many younger workers fully participated in it). In the 1970s and 1980s, as alumni of the New Left took positions in America's universities, it was inevitable that ill-will between labor and intellectuals generated by the 1960s would linger. Indeed, the rise of the "new labor history" at first widened the breach, for the work of these historians, most of them products of the student movement, tended to neglect the institutional history of unions, which they indicted for racism and conservatism, and stressed the role of mass insurgencies and popular protests outside the workplace in the history of working people.

As progressive-minded intellectuals distanced themselves from the labor movement, and vice versa, top labor leaders in these years courted other intellectuals, neoconservative supporters of the Reagan administration, the most antilabor presidency of the century. The AFL-CIO leadership worked with them in encouraging such movements as Solidarity in Poland. It took time to realize that the conservative intellectuals were more concerned with the rights of labor in communist countries than in the United States. Labor found that ardent support for American foreign policy did not translate into assistance from the federal government as employer after employer abandoned the decades-old "social contract," demanding concession after concession to reduce labor costs or seeking to rid themselves of labor unions altogether. Having hitched its star to the Democratic Party and purged its most militant leaders as part of the Cold War consensus, labor was forced onto the defensive by this assault at the hands of employers, government, and conservative intellectuals, and it has remained there ever since.

Today the AFL-CIO is undergoing a process of revitalization, reflected in the election of John Sweeney as president, and is once again a voice both for the immediate interests of union members and the broader needs of working- and middle-class Americans more generally. It is actively recruiting new members, and reaching out to communities sometimes slighted in the past. At a time when liberal academics often lament their isolation from social movements outside the ivory tower, and when lavishly funded conservative think tanks and foundations frequently set the agenda of intellectual life, labor's new receptivity to constructive engagement with intellectuals is likely to find an enthusiastic response among those who realize that no progressive social change is possible without the participation of a vital, powerful, and inclusive labor movement.

Workers, Eugene V. Debs insisted at the turn of the century, had to think of themselves not just as "hands" hired by a company, but as "heads" as well. "Think of a hand," he said, "with a soul in it." His words were almost indistinguishable from W.E.B. Du Bois's insistence at the same time that African Americans needed and deserved a broad liberal education to prepare them for full participation in public life, and John Dewey's demand for the reintegration of manual and mental labor. For Debs, Du Bois, and Dewey, intelligence — intellect — was a democratic concept, not something for the elite alone. This is the spirit in which labor and intellectuals, working together, can help point the way to a better life for the American people.

5

The People's Flag Is Deepest Red

Richard Rorty

I F YOU GO to Britain and attend a Labour Party rally, you will probably hear the audience sing "The Red Flag." That song begins: "The people's flag is deepest red. It shrouded oft our martyred dead. And ere their limbs grew stiff and cold, their hearts' blood dyed its every fold."

You may find this song maudlin and melodramatic, but it will remind you of something that many people have forgotten: the history of the labor unions, in Britain, America, and everywhere else in the world, is a blood-drenched history of violent struggle. Like the civil rights movement, the labor movement owed its successes to repeated and deliberate criminal acts — acts that we now think of as heroic civil disobedience, but that were brutally punished. To obstruct scabs from entering a workplace into which they are invited by the owners of that workplace is a criminal act, just as it is a criminal act to sit in at a lunch counter after the proprietor asks you to leave. The police who brutalized the strikers thought of themselves as preventing criminal acts from taking place, and they were right.

But, of course, the strikers were also right when they replied that the police were acting as the agents of employers who refused to give their workers a decent share of the value those workers produced. To persuade the American people to see strikes, and violence against strikers, in this alternative way took a long time. Only after an enormous amount of suffering, and very gradually, did it become politically impossible for mayors, governors, and sheriffs to send in their men to break strikers' skulls. Only in recent years has this strategy once again become politically possible.

We are accustomed to seeing labor leaders photographed with Presidents, and officials of GM and of the UAW jumping up and shaking hands at the end of a successful bargaining session. So we think of labor unions as fine old American institutions, built into the fabric of the country. We think of a strike as an accepted and perfectly reasonable method of bringing about a slightly fairer distribution of profits. But we should remember that the early years of labor unions in America, as in the rest of the world, were a history of the skulls of strikers being broken by truncheons, decade after decade. We should also realize that those truncheons have recently reappeared. As John Sweeney reminds us in his book, *America Needs a Raise,* during the last few years they have been used on striking janitors in Los Angeles and striking coal miners in Virginia.

We should also remember that the history of the labor movement is one of heroic self-deprivation. Only after a great many striking mothers had seen their children go hungry were the unions able to accumulate enough money to set up strike funds and to provide a little help. Only because millions of workers refused to become scabs by taking jobs that would have meant food for their families did the strikes eventually succeed. You would never guess, from William Bennett's and Robert Bork's speeches about the need to overcome liberal individualism, that the labor unions provide by far the best examples in America's history of the virtues these writers claim we must recapture. The history of the unions provides the best examples of comradeship, loyalty, and self-sacrifice.

Sometimes American unions became corrupt and were taken over by greedy and cynical crooks. In this respect, their record is no better or worse than that of American churches, American law firms, American business firms, and even American academic departments. But at their best, the labor unions are America at its best. Like the civil rights movement, the union movement is a paradigm case of Americans getting together on their own and changing society from the bottom up — forcing it to become more decent, more demo-cratic, and more humane. The strikers who braved the wrath of the police and the National Guard created a moral atmosphere in which no one was willing to be seen crossing a picket line, be caught wearing clothes that did not bear a union label, or be known to have scabbed. This unwillingness was an expression of the sort of human solidarity that made the year 1989 possible in Eastern Europe and made the Founding Fathers willing to risk their lives, their fortunes, and their sacred honor. The fact that people are once again willing to cross picket lines, and are unwilling to ask themselves who makes their clothes or who picks their vegetables, is a symptom of moral decline.

Most American schoolchildren learn something about the mar-tyrs of the civil rights movement. They at least know how Martin Luther King died. Perhaps they have also heard of Medgar Evers or of Andrew Goodman. But these children usually have no idea of how it came about that most American workers have an eight-hour day and a five-day week. They are unlikely to be taught about the conditions in the sweatshops and factories in which their great-grandparents worked, or about how the unions made those condi-tions a little better for their grandparents and parents. They know nothing of the blood that had to be spilled, and the hunger that had to be endured, in order that unions could be transformed from criminal conspiracies into fine old American institutions.

We should help our students understand that social justice in America owes much more to civil disobedience than to the use of the ballot. They need to know that the deepest and most enduring injus-tices, like the unending humiliation of African Americans and the miserable wages paid to unorganized workers, are always played down by the political parties and by most of the press. They need to remember that the same argument now used against raising the minimum wage — that doing so will discourage economic efficiency and productivity — was once used against the eight-hour day. They need to be able to spot the resemblances between what the politi-cians were indirectly and gently bribed to ignore at the beginning of this century and what they are being indirectly and gently bribed to ignore now. They need to realize that the last hundred years of our country's history have witnessed a brutal struggle between the corporations and the workers, that this struggle is still going on, and that the corporations are winning. They need to know that the deepest social problems usually go unmentioned by candidates for political office, because it is not in the interests of the rich to have those problems discussed in public.

Today our country, like the other industrialized democracies, faces a problem that few politicians, except for scurrilous fascists like Pat Buchanan and Jean-Marie Le Pen, seem willing to talk about: the wages of European and American workers are ridiculously high by world standards. There is less and less need to employ any of these workers, since the same work can be done elsewhere for a fifth of the cost. Furthermore, the globalization of the markets in capital and labor means that no nation's economy is sufficiently self-contained to permit long-term social planning by a national government. So the American economy is passing out of the control of the American government, and thus out of the control of the American voters.

This new situation is fine with the 1 percent of Americans who own 40 percent of their country's wealth. Their dividends typically rise when jobs are exported from Ohio to South China and from North Carolina to Thailand. The strength of the dollar does not matter to them, because investment advisers can flip their money into other currencies at the touch of a button. They have less and less at stake in America's future, and more and more invested in an efficient and productive global economy — an economy made ever more efficient and productive by the constant expansion of the global labor market into the poorer countries. There is little reason to believe that what is good for GM or Microsoft is good for America. The economic royalists whom FDR denounced still had a lot invested in America's future. For today's super-rich, such an investment would be imprudent.

There is much too little public discussion of the changes this globalized labor market will inevitably bring to America in the coming decades. Former senator Bill Bradley is one of the few prominent politicians to have insisted that we prevent our country breaking up into hereditary economic castes. Writers like Michael Lind and Edward Luttwak have sketched plausible scenarios of an America in which the top fifth of the country, the well-educated professionals, carry out the orders of the international super-rich. These people will get paid between $75,000 and $500,000 a year to do so. The remaining four fifths of the country, the portion that now has a median family income of $30,000, will get a little less in each successive year, and will keep on doing all the dirty work. America, the country that was to have witnessed a new birth of freedom, will gradually be divided by class differences of a sort that would have been utterly inconceivable to Jefferson or to Lincoln or to Walt Whitman.

Unless the politicians begin to talk about long-term social planning, Lind and Luttwak argue, economic inequality, and the formation of hereditary economic castes, will continue unchecked. Maybe these authors are too pessimistic, but we shall never know unless the questions they pose are taken up by candidates for public office. The most important single reason for hoping that American labor unions will become much bigger and more powerful than they are now is that they are the only organizations that want to get these questions on the table — to force politicians to talk about what is going to happen to wages, and how we are going to avoid increasing economic injustice. If a revived union movement can get out the vote in the old mill towns, in the rural slums, and in the inner cities, instead of letting the suburban vote set the national political agenda, those questions *would* be on the table.

The whole point of America was that it was going to be the world's first classless society. It was going to be a place where janitors, executives, professors, nurses, and salesclerks would look each other in the eye and respect each other as a fellow citizen. It was going to be a place where their kids all went to the same schools, and where they got the same treatment from the police and the courts. From the days of FDR to those of Lyndon Johnson, we made enormous progress toward the creation of such a society. In the twenty years between World War II and Vietnam the newly respectable labor unions made their presence felt on the national scene and accomplished a great deal. Those were the years in which academics like Daniel Bell, Arthur Schlesinger, Jr., and John Kenneth Galbraith worked side by side with labor leaders like Walter Reuther and A. Philip Randolph.

The Vietnam War saw the end of the traditional alliance between the academics and the unions — an alliance that had nudged the Democratic Party steadily to the left during the preceding twenty years. We are still living with the consequences of the anti–Vietnam War movement, and in particular with those of the rage of the manic student protesters of the late 1960s. These protesters were absolutely right that Vietnam was an unjust war, a massacre of which our country will always be ashamed. But when the students began to burn flags and to spit at returning soldiers, they did deeper and more long-lasting damage to the American left than they could ever have imagined. When they began to spell "America" with a *k*, they lost the respect and the sympathy of the union members. Until George McGovern's defeat, in 1972, the New Left did not realize that it had unthinkingly destroyed an alliance that was central to American leftist politics.

Since those days, leftists in the colleges and universities have concentrated their energies on academic politics rather than on national politics. As Todd Gitlin put it, we academics marched on the English department while the Republicans took over the White House. While we had our backs turned, the labor unions were being steadily ground down by the shift to a service economy and by the machinations of the Reagan and Bush administrations. The best thing that could happen to the American left would be for the academics to get back into the class struggle, and for the labor union members to forgive and forget the stupid and self-defeating anti-American rhetoric that filled the universities in the late 1960s.

This is not to say that those twenty-five years of inward-looking academic politics were in vain. American campuses are much better places — *morally* better places — than they were in 1970. Thanks to all those marches on the English department and other departments, the situation of women, gays and lesbians, African Americans, and Hispanics has been enormously improved. Their new role in the academy is helping to improve their situation in the rest of American society.

Nevertheless, leftist academic politics has run its course. It is time to revive the kind of leftist politics that pervaded American campuses from the Depression through the early 1960s — a politics centered on the struggle to prevent the rich from ripping off the rest of the country. If the unions will help us revive this kind of politics, maybe the academy and the labor movement can get together again and help bring our country closer to the goal that matters most: the classless society. That is the cause for which the AFL-CIO organizers are now fighting, and for which some of their predecessors died.

6

Planning for Our Futures

David Montgomery

OVER THE PAST YEAR labor unions and intellectuals have come together for mutual defense. Now we need to turn our minds toward what it is that we are fighting for: toward a vision of the kind of social and intellectual life we want for ourselves and our children, for our places of work and residence, for our country, and for the world, of which we are all inextricably a part.

By now it is clear what we oppose. For a quarter of a century the material rewards most Americans have derived from their daily work have been in decline. A glance around us at the decaying streets, schools, and subways makes that clear. If family incomes have held steady, it is because more and more of the family members' time has been devoted to earning money. Beggars and gunplay in the streets, the menace of epidemic children's diseases, and the touting of gambling casinos as the way to revive our bankrupt municipalities all remind us of the way life was before the New Deal.

Executives now find their way to the top of the corporate world, not by directing the production of the goods we all need, and not even by guiding their firms toward secure futures with experienced workforces. None of those old-fashioned objectives sends stock prices soaring upward or yields million-dollar salaries and perks for transient chief executive officers. What does rake in quick and boun-teous returns is downsizing, subcontracting, and hiring on a temporary basis. So the prospect for working people has become that of more and more casualization.

I encounter this prospect where I work every day. The administration of my university has enthusiastically joined the campaign to replace experienced, knowledgeable men and women, who have a claim to seniority and benefits, with temporary employees and work crews hired by subcontractors. It has set out to create Valujet University.

The unions at Yale have limited the impact of this effort on the university's maintenance, service, and clerical workers. By means of effective mobilization of their own members and of community support, and with unprecedented assistance from the AFL-CIO, they negotiated new contracts in December 1996 that secure the jobs of current employees, extend union standards and grievance procedures to employees of subcontractors, and marginalize the role of outside firms in university eating facilities. That union success has demonstrated what can be accomplished even under today's circumstances by action that is united, well considered, and tenacious.

Nevertheless, Yale's teaching, managerial, and professional employees, like their counterparts at most universities, have no union contracts to protect them. They have been major targets of casualization at academic institutions throughout the country. The trend of our times is to create a highly paid core of administrators and superstar professors while turning the bulk of teaching over to adjunct faculty in smaller colleges and to graduate-student teachers at major research universities. The abolition of tenure has also come under lively consideration by the trustees at many colleges and universities. So widespread is the casualization of academic employment that the Organization of American Historians devoted the bulk of its November 1996 *Newsletter* to the implications of this trend for the history profession.

This casualization of America's work is accompanied by an all-out political and ideological assault against the public sector and against the opening of the American mind.

That assault crystallized in the Contract with America and in the rapid growth of well-endowed foundations whose explicit purpose is to capture the public mind for the gospel of the free market — for the doctrine that every activity in life should be a source of profits. We are reassured every day that other ways of organizing social life have proven to be abysmal failures. Only by personally racing around the marketplace with credit cards, vouchers, mandatory savings accounts, and flex-dollars can we find happiness.

If we happen to disagree, we may still be able to publish an article in some magazine, as a token "voice from the left." But if we should act together on our disagreement, we can expect ruthless retribution. That was the message of the air-traffic controllers' strike, of P-9, of Caterpillar, of International Paper. That is the fear that haunts every worker entering a bargaining session or deciding whether to join a union. It haunts every student who wonders what the future will bring.

But today we also hear in the factories, offices, streets, and classrooms all around us clear indications that the magic appeal of the free-market mania has already burned out. Political life remains in the doldrums because of the absence of a realistic and compelling vision of what else is possible in today's world. Our mission is to open the discussions that will answer that question and to organize men and women in every walk of life to translate the answer into collective power — into real life.

When we turn our thinking toward the questions of how we got to this point and how to get out of it, we can find some guidance from history (mine is not a useless profession) and in particular from our country's experience during the last half-century. We need to think about much more than just the impact of Reagan and Gingrich on our lives and on our way of thinking. We must also reconsider carefully the failures of Cold War liberalism and the possibilities it suppressed, as well as its social benefits, which are now under attack.

Those of us who were alive and active in 1945 and 1946 cannot forget the high hopes we then harbored for a world without the hunger, book-burnings, wars, and murderous racism that had blighted our youth. The touchstone of our postwar hopes was the industrial union movement, especially the youthful CIO. Massive picket lines in every industrial center won major across-the-board wage increases, turned back employers' concerted efforts to restore authoritarian rule in the factories, expanded the boundaries of trade unionism into the office and the department store, and laid the foundations of comprehensive health care for coal miners and their families, thereby illustrating what could be made available for all citizens.

Union membership reached an all-time peak in the movement's historic strongholds, such as construction (87 percent of all workers), mining (65 percent), and railroads (76 percent). In manufacturing, where "open shop" policies had long cultivated the "loyal employee," 77 percent of the 805,000 workers who voted in NLRB elections during the year beginning with June 1946 cast their votes for unions (more than any other year since enactment of the Wagner Act). Millions of men and women had won a voice in the conditions under which they earned their livings. They no longer faced giant corporations alone and trembling.

That same movement, however, also formulated a vision for our country's future that was very different from what we ultimately got. In 1943 the CIO had demanded a Down-Payment on the Four Freedoms, beginning with democracy in the American South. At its 1946 convention it expanded that vision to demand federal legislation to end racial discrimination in jobs, public accommodations, and political life; to establish single-payer national health insurance and a national network of child-care facilities; to make a meaningful job for everyone the foremost objective of economic policy; and to place public power projects and all nuclear facilities under national ownership, and bomb-building capacities under international control. President Philip Murray also called for the continuation of wartime economic agencies to guide the shaping of a postwar economy. To leave social priorities up to the marketplace, Murray warned, would mean that those with the most wealth would enjoy first claim on the nation's productive capacity, and the pressing needs of working people would stand last in line.

Not one of these proposals became law during the next decade and a half (and most of them never have). They all fell victim to the

Cold War, while the public strength that labor had exercised in the streets and factories was hobbled by the Taft-Hartley Law. Both the legislative demands that had attracted all progressive groupings to the labor movement and workers' power and dignity on the job and in the neighborhoods of industrial America had been swamped by cries for military power that could dominate the world and for ever-rising productivity. The military power, we were assured, would save us from communism. In fact, it made the world safe for run-away shops, shattered popular attempts to democratize economic and political life in the Third World, and bequeathed us the yawning gap in material conditions between industrialized countries and the rest of the globe.

Productivity, unleashed by restoring "management prerogatives" in the factory and office and stimulated by massive research-and-development funding out of the tax coffers, was supposed to resolve all social conflict and political divisions. That belief informed the basic principles of both political parties. Those same principles reduced most of the once-mighty labor movement to a shrinking group of certified bargaining units, each concerned with what it could win for its own members from the individual firm with which it negotiated. When the profits generated by expanded productivity were used to relocate operations around and out of the country, and to shift capital away from the renewal of manufacturing facilities and into speculative financial ventures and leveraged buy-outs, workers were seldom able even to slow down the socially destructive use of the wealth their labor had created, let alone to stop it.

Today our brutal encounter with the Gingrich doctrine tempts us to look back to the 1950s and 1960s as the good old days. We must not fall into that trap. It is true that for twenty-five years the material conditions of the average American improved more rapidly than at any other time in our country's history. But the most important social gains of the Cold War years were won only by new waves of popular struggle *against* the political and economic regime that sustained, and was sustained by, the Cold War itself. Massive civil disobedience smashed legal segregation, a decade and a half after the defeat of the CIO's antidiscrimination program. The systematic subordination of peoples of color that survived the demise of legal segregation, however, tore apart our cities, while the demagogic appeals of George Wallace and Richard Nixon to white voters shattered the electoral coalitions that had been the historic base of liberalism.

During the 1960s a combination of tumult in the streets and liberal lobbying (in which labor played a large and often unacknowledged role) wrung from federal and state legislatures an expansion of social benefits. Widespread and vociferous revulsion against the carnage of Vietnam eventually brought the goal of world military hegemony into question. As the 1970s began, vigorous wage demands from rank-and-file workers, punctuated by far more major strikes than the country had experienced in almost twenty years, shifted the larger share of rising productivity briefly in the workers' direction.

The reaction was fast and furious. Business and government leaders cried out against "stagflation" and "profligate spending." President Nixon instituted wage and price controls and terminated American participation in international agreements to stabilize exchange rates of national currencies. His draconian exercise of state power over the economy proved to be the prelude to the eventual abandonment of the regulatory authority that had undergirded the expansion of the previous decades. Industry began systematically relocating its operations around the globe. Concession bargaining became management's standard approach to the shrinking unions. Productivity continued to rise. Wages did not.

New York City's budget crisis of 1975 signaled the turning point. Secretary of the Treasury William E. Simon then declared that no federal aid should be offered the city unless it charged tuition at its colleges, scrapped rent control, and replaced its city employees with private contractors, especially in health and sanitation.

The public rejected those demands as outrageous. Twenty years later they had become the standard fare of American politics. Simon himself had left Washington to head up the Olin Foundation, which was devoted to changing the shape of American academic and political discourse. A majority of American voters was convinced that government itself was the parasite that sucked up the fruits of their labor and encouraged dissolute behavior. Consequently, the remedy for the problems they faced was to cut taxes and give every man a gun. Everything else was to be turned over to the market. Ronald Reagan and his successors stole a phrase from the 1960s and called that "empowerment."

Now the lesson is sinking home (the hard way): the essential things that make life worth living cannot be bought in the market. The comfort and sustenance people can offer each other, the formation of a child into a human being with a promising future for self and for society, respect and a meaningful voice on the job, safety in the streets, openness of thought and of imagination, and a dignified old age — these things cannot be bought in the discount store. We can secure them only when we think and act together. That is what the public sector is all about. That is what collective action is all about.

In the dismal election campaign we endured last year, there was one speech worth remembering. Jesse Jackson reminded delegates to the Democratic convention that the New Deal was not created by President Roosevelt, and the slaves were not freed by President Lincoln. The struggles of ordinary men and women on the plantations, in their neighborhoods, in the mines and mills, generated the political force and the ideas that pushed even the best of our Presidents into the reforms for which they are remembered.

We need to follow those examples of the past, not by copying the demands of yesterday, and certainly not by returning to Cold War liberalism, but by thinking and working together toward a new vision of our country's future.

That means organizing ourselves to win a strong collective voice. To create that voice we must bring together all working people: the employed, the unemployed, the people on welfare, and those being thrown to the wolves. We must support one another's battles for the best possible conditions. We need contracts that secure the hopes of the new and already casualized workers, along with those of people who have long been on the job. And we must also relearn the lesson that the purpose of organization is not just contracts, but the mobili-

zation of effective struggles, inside and outside the workplace, to
secure a better life for all of us.

It means learning the real and practical meaning of internationalism. As our employers go multinational, so working people must
lend support to one another's struggles across national lines, and
across the Pacific and Atlantic. We cannot and should not set the
goals and standards for people of other lands, but we must support
their efforts to improve their own standards, and solicit their support for our battles. Above all, we must fly to the aid of those who
face death and prison for their part in workers' struggles.

It means recognizing that today, as so often in the past, new vigor
and new ideas are being infused into our country's labor movement by recent immigrants. The mobilization of Latino and Asian
workers in Los Angeles against Proposition 187 brought hundreds
of thousands of people into the streets and shut down eight high
schools with protest strikes. The action reminded me of the massive
mobilization of people of Southern and Eastern European ancestry
against the judicial murder of Sacco and Vanzetti in 1927. Then, as
now, the reactionaries got their way. But the immigrants' protests of
1927 galvanized a new social force that transformed the nation's
political life only half a dozen years later. The Los Angeles protests
of 1994 are also the birth of a social force that will transform this
country's life. The current drive by the Los Angeles Manufacturing
Action Project to unionize that city is propelled by this new vigor
and by the experience and knowledge many immigrant workers
have brought with them to our country.

It is time to loosen up our minds, as the people who rose in
defense of Sacco and Vanzetti did when faced with the Great Depression, and as our precursors did at the end of history's most terrible
war. The problem of our times is not to unleash productivity, let
alone to transfer ever more of our earnings into the hands of corporate CEOs and financial speculators. Since the end of the last century
the already prodigious productive capacity of our people has increased enormously. The first challenge to public policy today is the
same as it has been throughout this century: to create jobs for those
who have been displaced by our technological achievements, not to

drive students, the elderly, and people on public assistance out in search of jobs.

But the flip side of that challenge is an opportunity such as has never before existed in history: the opportunity to do something more fruitful with our lives than grimly pursuing the historic tasks of putting food on the table and getting a table on which to put it. It is now possible to commit our personal and community energies toward the improvement of our health, the expansion of our intellectual and creative capacities, and the enrichment of our private and public lives. Buying and selling have a necessary place in that prospect, but it is only through a new and very different public policy that such a life as is now materially possible can be brought to life, and the proper place of buying and selling can be defined.

That is the vision that should guide us all, whether we are engaged right now in manufacturing or construction, in service work, caring for families, in teaching, research, and publication, or in the brutal quest for employment and income. Simon says we must work harder for less, live in increasingly desolate surroundings, wave our credit cards, and curb our imaginations, because those are what the economy needs. We say it is time to remake our economy and our politics in ways that will make all our lives worth living.

7

Building and Changing
A New Beginning at the AFL-CIO

Robert W. Welsh

I N 1995, in the first contested election in the history of the AFL-CIO, John Sweeney was elected president. During his campaign, he often said the contest was "not about who heads the labor movement but where the labor movement is headed." Indeed, his candidacy emerged from a growing concern among labor activists that the movement was "headed" down, losing membership strength, political clout, and public esteem. At a time when working Americans were suffering stagnant living conditions, it seemed that America's unions were losing the capacity to improve — or even publicly address — their plight.

In the brief time since his election, Sweeney has taken the labor movement in a new direction. History will decide if this direction succeeds. But it is not too soon to conclude that the debate labor conducted in 1995 was essential — and the changes that it began in 1996 and 1997 have started to produce a resurgence in a movement that only recently seemed in irreversible decline.

Labor's Muffled Voice

In 1995, organized labor resembled many large institutions that need to adapt to a rapidly changing environment while maintaining historic goals and values.

For three decades after the end of World War II, American unions built strong national and local organizations and raised the living standards of millions of working Americans. During this period, unions needed to wield power effectively only at the work site, within the firm and industry, and in the political arena. Organized labor's membership strength was sufficient to command the respect of corporate America and public officials. And the nation's labor federation, the AFL-CIO, was an institution designed to wield this power at the national level.

In recent years, this strategy was not adequate to meet the challenge of a changing economy. Union membership stagnated while the workforce expanded and new industries emerged. The deregulation of major industries, the globalization of the economy, and the emergence of new technologies all strengthened employers and weakened workers. And a new generation of workers was interested not only in lifting living standards but in winning a voice in their lives on the job.

As organized labor lost bargaining power and political strength, working Americans — union and nonunion — suffered. During the past twenty years, most working people's real wages have stagnated or declined. And as corporations downsized their workforces and cut health insurance and other benefits, many working Americans felt that their contributions were no longer respected and rewarded.

The reasons for this decline have been discussed elsewhere at great length. At its best, under the leadership of George Meany, the AFL-CIO had been masterful at wielding power, on behalf not only of its own members but of all Americans. Historic advances in civil rights, Medicare, Medicaid, and programs for education, housing, mass transit, and child nutrition, to name just a few, all reflected the power and purposes of organized labor.

But by 1995, the labor movement needed to focus more on building power than on wielding it. And the only way to rebuild the power of working Americans was through a strategy oriented toward organizing and growth. Sweeney understood that everything the labor movement does — from collective bargaining to legislative and political action — must be guided by the need to organize and mobilize working Americans. In order to organize more effectively, labor needs to change in other ways as well — not only by putting more resources into organizing but also by addressing the full range of working people's concerns and by becoming a stronger presence in our communities.

This insight guided the campaign of Sweeney's "New Voice" slate in 1995. And it has informed the efforts of new executive officers and the executive council members who were elected to head the AFL-CIO at the October 1995 convention, when the council was expanded from thirty-five to fifty-four, with the percentage of women and minorities increasing from seventeen to twenty-seven.

Labor's New Direction

From the first, Sweeney and his team set about simultaneously building and changing the labor movement. This build-and-change strategy was crystallized in a program and budget that the AFL-CIO executive council endorsed in December 1996. It set four fundamental goals:

1. *Building a broad movement of working Americans by organizing workers into unions:* For the first time in its history, the AFL-CIO has an organizing department. While most organizing is conducted by individual unions, the AFL-CIO is recruiting and training new organizers, helping formulate successful strategies, building member support for organizing and public support for unionism, and encouraging unions at every level to devote more resources to organizing.

2. *Building a strong political voice for working Americans:* Moving beyond traditional legislative and political tactics, the AFL-CIO is advancing an agenda for all American working families, building a broad progressive coalition, and educating working Americans on the issues that shape their lives.

3. *Changing unions to give voice to workers, from their job sites to the global economy:* The AFL-CIO is helping unions widen their focus from negotiating and servicing collective bargaining agree-

ments to giving workers a say in all the decisions that affect their lives — from capital investments, to the quality of products and services, to how work processes are organized.

4. *Creating a new voice for workers in their communities:* The AFL-CIO is revitalizing its local and state labor councils — the movement's grassroots — to help working Americans make their voices heard in their communities, and advocating more aggressively on behalf of working families in all our communities, from local to international.

This program amounts to a challenge to the labor movement at every level — from the workplace and local union hall to local and state labor councils, to national unions and the AFL-CIO itself.

Rebuilding the Movement by Organizing

At the heart of our effort is a challenge to local and national unions to move significant resources into organizing. The AFL-CIO is devoting 30 percent of its budget to organizing — and is challenging unions at every level to do the same.

In recent years, one of the most effective efforts to promote organizing has been the Elected Leader Taskforce — an informal gathering of local and regional leaders who are shifting their own unions' resources toward organizing. These leaders represent a cross-section of the labor movement: nurses in New Jersey, health care workers in Ohio, state and local government employees in Illinois, retail workers in Michigan, hotel and restaurant workers in the West, and clothing and textile workers throughout the South. They have proved that it is possible to restructure local and regional unions to put more resources into organizing and to use these resources to recruit new members.

In 1997, the Elected Leader Taskforce was expanded, holding four two-and-a-half-day conferences instead of the one that had been held in each of the preceding two years, and attracting new heads of large local unions. Taskforce members' experiences are summarized in an educational booklet, "Organizing for Change: Changing to Organize," which is available from the AFL-CIO. At the heart of the message are four principles. Changing to organize involves shifting resources to organizing, hiring talented organizers, developing a solid strategic plan, and involving present members.

Under the new leadership, the AFL-CIO reached out directly to the thousands of locals that are needed to take responsibility for organizing in the Changing to Organize program. More than a dozen regional organizing conventions were held across the country during the spring and summer of 1997.

The AFL-CIO also broadened its capacity to organize by expanding the Organizing Institute's recruitment and training program to prepare and place more new organizers than ever before. One of the important areas of greater focus is the training of member organizers. In addition, the institute has sought to provide more campaign managers, capable of organizing on a large scale, and more organizers at the top level who can run small campaigns and direct others.

In 1997, the federation doubled its organizing fund to $10 million, to leverage national union spending on organizing campaigns that could become models for labor movement growth.

The federation targeted the fund in two ways. First, it supported national industry-wide campaigns, or campaigns in defined market sectors, that could create power for workers in each of the industries. The idea behind these campaigns is that it's not enough to spend money on organizing or even to win; the need is for building the power to negotiate contracts and improve standards and conditions. For example, the national strawberry workers' campaign, in which the AFL-CIO is a partner of the United Farm Workers, has targeted twenty thousand strawberry workers across the entire industry so that growers that become organized cannot just plow under their fields, as many did in the past, or cry "noncompetitive" with nonunion growers. Similarly, the AFL-CIO helped fund a historic campaign that brought together fifteen building trades unions in Las Vegas to organize the entire construction industry in that city.

Second, the fund supported geographic campaigns — campaigns in a handful of cities to create new models of cooperative organizing by many local unions in different occupations in order to build momentum and shared power.

In 1996 the AFL-CIO's membership decline stabilized as unions began to add new members and even won some major organizing victories. Almost eighteen thousand state employees in Maryland voted for union representation. Some eight thousand workers at hotels in Las Vegas won the right to be represented by the Hotel Employees and Restaurant Employees after the MGM Grand and Main Street Station Hotels agreed to recognize the union because a majority of the workers had signed authorization cards. And in New York City, the Laborers successfully organized fifteen hundred workers in asbestos abatement and a thousand demolition workers. Nonetheless, the challenge facing organized labor is substantial: we must grow by 300,000 workers every year just to maintain our current percentage of the workforce. To grow by only 1 percent, we must add a million new members.

Meanwhile, the AFL-CIO is launching a highly visible campaign to build public support for workers' right to organize. Through a program of media and community outreach, the Right to Organize Program is educating Americans about the need for unions and the difficulties workers face in forming unions in the face of antiquated labor laws and brazen employer rebuffs of workers' rights. More than ten thousand workers a year are fired illegally, according to Harvard law professor Paul Weiler, just for trying to organize in order to have a voice at work and improve their lives. Even without breaking the law, employers have found limitless ways to circumvent workers' attempts to organize, from old-fashioned intimidation to new job structures, such as making full-time jobs into contract positions. Until recently, organizers were trained to brush off firings lest they be allowed to dispirit workers trying to organize or interfere with campaign timing. But now, the AFL-CIO is encouraging local unions to organize mass demonstrations when workers are fired, and to encourage other local union members and community allies to support the workers seeking to form a union. Our aim is to establish the right to organize a union as a basic and inviolable civil right. We are asking AFL-CIO local labor councils to get local governments to codify organizing rights as a condition of being awarded public contracts, and encouraging local unions to insist that elected officials and candidates for office at all levels sign pledges to support workers' rights to organize. This campaign will lay the groundwork for an eventual effort to reform the nation's labor laws.

We are also leading a campaign — Working Women Organize — to demonstrate that working women need unions to address the economic pressures their families face. We are reaching out to working women through surveys and work-site visits and a national meeting for women who are organizing into unions.

And we are reaching out to the next generation of workers. In 1996, more than twelve hundred students and young workers participated in Union Summer, joining in efforts from organization drives, to contract campaigns and public education on working family issues. In 1997, Union Summer was repeated, and a new youth program for the AFL-CIO was launched to maintain and expand campus support for unionism.

Building a Political Voice

If any event spurred the movement to transform the AFL-CIO, it was the Republican victory in the 1994 congressional elections. It seemed that working Americans had come to a critical point — with corporations downsizing, wages stagnating, unions declining, and our enemies seizing control of Congress.

The fault was not only in our times but in ourselves. Too often, our legislative and political action had dwindled into writing checks to political candidates and party organizations, lobbying members of Congress, and, just before Election Day, sending mailings to union members informing them of our endorsements.

Labor's new leaders decided to pursue a different form of political participation: building an independent movement that mobilizes working people, raises their issues in public debate, and brings their concerns before public officials every year and all year round. Now, the labor movement is doing what union members have asked of it in countless surveys: keep them informed about what public officials are doing, or failing to do, on such issues as jobs, wages, Social Security, health care, and education and training. Armed with that information, union members can make informed decisions at the polls.

That is why, in 1996, the AFL-CIO conducted an unprecedented effort at public education on issues important to working families:

- First, we held a series of town meetings in thirty cities on why America needs a raise. Working women and men discussed their economic plight and the growing gap in wages and wealth between working families and the wealthy.
- Second, we raised working families' issues over the nation's airwaves, with television and radio advertisements. These messages answered the attack on working families by the new majorities in Congress who were trying to cut Medicare, Medicaid, education, job safety, and health and pension protections while giving new tax breaks to big business and the rich.
- Third, we zeroed in on raising the minimum wage. During the congressional recess in the spring, the AFL-CIO broadcast TV and radio ads in some thirty congressional districts where representatives from both parties hesitated to support an increase. The effort paid off. Public opinion surveys showed that three quarters of all Americans wanted to raise the minimum wage, and the measure passed both houses of the Republican-controlled Congress and was signed into law by President Clinton.
- Fourth, during the fall, organizers fanned out through congressional districts with large numbers of union members — and representatives with poor records on working families' issues. In these districts, hundreds of union members donated their time to keep their co-workers informed about the issues in the elections. On Election Day, eighteen representatives with poor records on working families' issues were defeated. More important, labor's effort set the terms of debate in many 1996 elections for Congress, focusing attention on Medicare, education, and pensions.

In 1997 and beyond, the AFL-CIO is stepping up the effort to help working Americans make their voices heard in public debate:

- The AFL-CIO is aggressively advocating an American Working-ing Families' Agenda, including public policies and specific legislation that advances their interests and values. With five broad headings — Good Jobs, Secure Families; Education; Health Care; Social Security and Pensions; and Fair Tax, Trade, and Economic Policies — this agenda sets up a range of policy issues, from defending workers' rights to organize, to eliminating the tax breaks that encourage multinational corporations to move American jobs overseas. It also includes a platform of four grassroots action components: (a) inform, educate, and mobilize working families for national issues debates; (b) hold elected leaders accountable through activism around issues; (c) renew ties with community allies around a shared agenda; and (d) increase voter rights and participation and recruit candidates.

- We are continuing to involve working people in the political process by forming networks of activists in local communities. And through the National Labor Political Training Center we are also recruiting and training union members to run for public office themselves.

More Power from the Workplace to the World Economy

The AFL-CIO is striving to transform unions in other ways as well. In the past, it may have been sufficient to negotiate and enforce collective bargaining agreements. In the new economy, unions must enable working people to make their voices heard in all decisions that shape their lives, from their workplaces to the boardrooms of multinational conglomerates. Helping working Americans amplify their voices is the common purpose behind these initiatives:

- We are conducting an Economics Education program to help working people better understand their interests in the rapidly changing global economy and the real causes of their problems at work. The project has produced tools and templates that are ready to be used by local unions, national unions, and our community allies — especially intellectuals and academics. And, through the Corporate Accountability Project, the AFL-CIO is speaking out against short-term speculation in capital markets, "low-road" corporate strategies, and government policies that encourage corporate irresponsibility.

- Through the Center for Workplace Democracy, we are supporting national unions in workplace democracy initiatives, studying the best programs, and training union members, leaders, and staff to participate in these efforts. At their best, these efforts build more successful businesses and stronger unions, enhancing worker safety and satisfaction.
- Through the Capital Strategies for Labor effort, the AFL-CIO is helping organize workers' financial assets to better serve their interests. The federation is cataloguing worker assets and developing investment programs to make sure they contribute to worker-friendly economic development.
- The federation is monitoring, analyzing, and reporting major collective bargaining trends and sharing the most effective strategies for dealing with major national and multinational corporations. And through the Global Education and Bargaining Project, we are working with labor movements throughout the world to coordinate our efforts at the industry and corporate level, developing global strategies for organizing and bargaining.

Providing a Stronger Voice in Our Communities

Finally, the labor movement is strengthening its voice throughout grassroots America — in our cities, suburbs, and small towns.

The AFL-CIO is launching a Union Cities program to build strong community labor councils. These councils are redefining themselves around the labor movement's new priorities: helping local unions put more resources into organizing, helping workers organize unions, building community support for workers' struggles, building political and legislative networks, and advancing progressive economic development initiatives.

On the local level as on the national scene, labor is reaching out specifically to working women and is forming new partnerships with allies, including religious, civil rights, consumer, and environmental activists. And the AFL-CIO is training union and community leaders for action on our common goals.

Looking Forward

The new AFL-CIO agenda reflects the need to build power as well as to wield it. Most important, it is focused on building membership strength through organizing — and on transforming unions at every level into institutions with the will, the skill, and the resources to organize effectively. In the political arena, in the communications media, and in our communities, labor's new agenda is also oriented toward amplifying working people's voices and addressing the issues that determine their lives and livelihoods. In everything we do, labor's new agenda is geared not only to strengthen institutions but to energize and mobilize the members — as organizers, political activists, community leaders, and media spokespeople.

American labor is taking a new direction not only in rebuilding our power but also in addressing new and wider concerns. From the organization of work at the job site to investment decisions on the global level, we are building the strength and the skill to help working Americans make their voices heard.

In the long run, three challenges will determine what place the new leaders of the AFL-CIO will hold in the history of American labor.

First is the simple question of survival. Will labor's new emphasis on organizing enable it to rebuild the membership strength it needs to remain a force in our nation's economic, social, and political life?

Second is the issue of activism and inclusion. Will we succeed in motivating and mobilizing union members and working people outside our ranks to participate in our movement? Will we represent all working people? Will our vision inspire allies and others who can help shape a progressive society? After all, the labor movement is an institution of women and men — not bricks, mortar, and bank balances — and its vitality depends upon the involvement of our nation's working people.

Third is the issue of courage and imagination. Labor's new leadership and its new agenda emerged from a process of rethinking and debating the future. This process must continue, even as the labor movement does what it must to survive its current challenges. The only certainty is that new changes and new challenges will emerge.

If American labor enters the twenty-first century determined to anticipate and answer change, and to solicit and embrace criticism from intellectuals and others who share our goals, then working Americans, our economy, and our democracy will all benefit.

8

Education for Worker Empowerment

José La Luz

Introduction:
Beyond the Limits of Traditional Labor Education

The election of a new leadership team in the AFL-CIO has generated waves of hope, vigor, and enthusiasm among hundreds of union activists across the country who have been fighting consistently over the years for substantive and profound changes in America's house of labor. I am one of many union activists who, having devoted lots of time, energy, and passion to the transformation of labor, feel strongly that organized labor must develop a new educational strategy for union members, officers, and staff in order to become an effective vehicle for collective action and worker empowerment in this day and age.

There is a recognition by the new leaders of the AFL-CIO, the only federation of unions in the United States (most other countries have several confederations), that, as an institution, organized labor has become increasingly weak and powerless. The consequences of this decline have left American workers at the mercy of powerful forces in business and industry that are seeking to undermine and ultimately wipe out most if not all of the gains, rights, and benefits obtained by workers through decades of collective action and struggles.

Along with a massive redistribution of wealth from the bottom to

the top of the American economy, we have witnessed a huge redistribution of power from workers and their families to those who own
wealth and privilege. It has reached a point where the country's
democratic principles and practices should be called into question.

Therefore, changing the house of labor itself, as well as the unions that are affiliated with it, is essential to give workers in the
United States a new voice and power that, collectively as a class, they
have not exercised for decades . . . and perhaps for a entire generation.

What I am proposing as a new education strategy is *not* more of
the same kind of education programs that are now being conducted
by most unions. These programs are, for the most part, designed in
isolation from the various unions' strategic objectives. They are not
part of the permanent, systematic process, and are conceived only in
terms of classroom learning. Their structure is not designed to mobilize people to action, nor are they empowering. Their methodology
is based on the transmission of information by expert knowledge,
not on the collective construction of knowledge by both the teachers
and the learners.

The kind of education I propose is not based only on experiential
knowledge as it is practiced in adult education, as important as this
is in the pedagogical practices in the field of labor education. Nor
does it have to do exclusively with the use of techniques that are
participatory, interactive, inclusive, and democratic. Furthermore,
the kind of education for workers and trade unionists I propose is
not even new. Indeed, it has been developed and practiced by scores
of labor and popular educators inside and outside unions in places
like Brookwood Labor College, the Highlander Center, and, in spo-
radic and short-lived instances, in some industrial unions.

In fact, it has been practiced in many South American and Brazilian trade unions and in dozens of worker co-ops and community-
and neighborhood-based organizations throughout the Americas. It
is often referred to as popular education or as liberator education
and in some academic circles is known as critical pedagogy.

The single most important distinguishing feature of this kind of
education is that workers are not just recipients of information that

reproduces the values, knowledge, and skills to maintain the existing relations of power in the society. Instead, they will be able to create new knowledge as they reflect on and analyze their own experiences. They will learn to develop strategies to change existing conditions in their workplaces, neighborhoods, and in their unions. And they will understand how to organize and mobilize themselves and others for action as they evaluate and learn together.

This methodological framework requires that the union become a teaching organization that conceives of education as an uninterrupted and permanent, systematically planned series of learning experiences.

Every action of the union, such as bargaining for a new contract, resolving a grievance, or conducting a job action, becomes a learning experience that, in practice, demonstrates how organizing, mobilizing, and educating are all aspects of the same effort.

The Union and the Workplace as Schools for Learning about Change: The NAFTA Campaign

In the late spring of 1992 tens of thousands of American workers, mostly union members, mobilized to fight against the proposed North American Free Trade Agreement. The AFL-CIO and its affiliated unions were energized with the rising militancy of workers who were alarmed by the massive offensive, launched by powerful interests in business and industry, to convince policy-makers in Washington that their programs to liberalize trade and lower investment barriers were good for America. The presidential race was also heating up, and it was becoming clear that organized labor's most likely choice, Bill Clinton, would also be supporting NAFTA. In fact, Clinton had proposed some revisions regarding labor and environmental standards that were to be negotiated as parallel side agreements if he was elected.

Most union members, particularly those in industrial unions, were afraid that their jobs and their wages were now in jeopardy. They had for years experienced a decline in their standard of living. My union at the time, the Amalgamated Clothing and Textile Workers, was engaged in an intensive effort to educate and mobilize its rank-and-file membership not only to fight trade and investment policies contained in the proposed agreement but to put forth a new and different vision of trade and economic integration that would benefit workers in the United States, Canada, and Mexico.

Our fight was no longer to "Stop Imports, Buy American," which for decades had been the slogan of the union in its struggle to restrict the importation of garments manufactured overseas. That kind of protectionist approach had proved to be ineffective before, and, more important, was inadequate to address the new challenges posed by the process of regional and hemispheric economic integration.

As the person responsible for designing and administering the union's educational programs, I had the opportunity to shape a program that would go beyond the scope and the experience of traditional labor education. The choices I had to make in terms of program development did not have much to do with how the "correct view" about NAFTA and its consequences was to be transmitted to our union members. That was a task for communications specialists and experts. As a worker and popular educator I saw the opportunity to create new knowledge that would lead to action that might transform the relations of workers and those making the decisions that affect the country's working majority.

I thought a basic question to be raised was as follows: If this trade agreement is so good for the country and its people, why have workers and their unions not been invited "to sit at the table" and participate in the process the same way CEOs and their companies were asked to do?

The challenge seemed to me much larger than transmitting facts and figures from the experts in the subject to our members and providing them with already accumulated knowledge. I was convinced that for workers to understand everything that was wrong with NAFTA, they had to be aware of what was in it and who was pushing it, and also understand that Mexican workers were not their enemies because they would be "taking jobs away from us Americans."

With the full support and cooperation of the southwest regional director of the union and her staff we decided to conduct an educational experiment and invited a group of women workers employed in the Maquiladoras on the Mexican side of the border to participate in a workshop in southern Texas with members of our union. But rather than asking the national president of the union to deliver a speech about the perils of NAFTA or have our leading labor economist give a lecture on the correct view of economic integration, we chose another course of action.

We organized a large group discussion about the state of our industry and the tremendous effect of trade on the garment and textile workers. Among other things participants wanted to know was why NAFTA was being negotiated now, by whom, and for what purpose. Factories were being shut down, and thousands of jobs lost, because companies were already investing capital in other countries, including Mexico. What made NAFTA different from other trade policies?

One of the themes that emerged from the group discussion was that trade in itself is not necessarily bad for working families. To me, that was a critical moment in the discussion. Given that workers and their unions in the three countries had been systematically excluded from the negotiating process, now that we had several Mexican workers with us, perhaps we could turn the tables a little.

The large group was divided into smaller groups, each of which included one or two of our Mexican guests. Every group was asked to negotiate a trade agreement that would raise the standard of living of the workers in all three countries.

What came out of the discussions resembled many of the provisions that could have been contained in, but were missing from, the proposed NAFTA. In the course of their dialogue, the participants were creating new knowledge collectively and, more important, were discovering that they had common interests and aspirations. The logical question was what we as workers could do to prevent all of us from being hurt. The participants observed that for the trade agreement to be improved, the silenced voices, those of workers and their unions, would have to be heard.

I became truly excited as the participants began to develop action strategies. At the end, when most of our members embraced our Mexican guests (our presumed enemies), I could not contain my tears of joy. My dream of international solidarity among workers, which had remained so elusive, became real at least for those few moments in the process of critical learning.

When I told this story at one of the union's leadership retreats, the national president, Jack Sheinkman, asked me whether I had taped the meeting. I confessed that I had not, but could not help wondering what would have happened had the participants known that the learning exercises were being videotaped. Would they have modified their behavior? To this day I do not know the answer.

I was pleased that our educational experiment eventually led to many similar experiments, including cross-border exchanges that laid the foundation for a transnational organizing project in Mexico and the Dominican Republic.

My years as the educational director of a union with a great intellectual tradition, beginning with one of its founders, Sidney Hillman, and the educational legacy of many outstanding labor educators who preceded me, helped crystallize my views on the kind of empowering education for workers that I have long advocated.

Education for Union Transformation: Learning About the Sources and Uses of Power

One of the many important lessons I learned during my years with ACTWU is that the process of educating — and learning with — workers who choose to participate in the life of the union — that is, union activists — is crucial to the success of any worker-education strategy.

For the union activists, the union is often a central educational experience, because their participation in building it makes the institution a meaningful and dynamic experience for them. The union is not an empty hall located on Main Street, nor is it the occasional visit to the workplace by a union staffer, as it may appear to those workers who do not participate in shaping it. Often unions are led in ways that discourage participation and ownership by its members. The same group of elected union officers and staff that has been deciding everything for the past twenty years blames the members for being apathetic and disconnected from the union. "They don't come to meetings" is a frequent complaint of many of these leaders, as if the life of the union was centered on attending what most often can be described as boring and uninspiring meetings.

This kind of union behavior and practice has been referred to as "the bureaucratic insurance agent form of unionism" and as the "servicing model of unionism" by veteran union activists and labor educators, all of whom have spent years experimenting and analyzing the outcomes of different approaches to revitalizing unions. While their contribution to the growing debate is important, their emphasis has been mostly on strategies and tactics designed to organize, recruit, and mobilize workers who are either union members already or who should be "targets" of union recruitment efforts.

Instead of focusing on what the union leaders fail to do to increase membership involvement, I want to focus more on how unions can become the organizations where workers learn about the sources and the uses of power. Unions can often be laboratories for collective action when a contract is being negotiated, or a strike or other job action is being executed, or when new members are recruited in an internal or external organizing campaign. But very seldom have unions encouraged workers to analyze their collective and individual practices and thus create new knowledge about ways to increase their power.

How can the union's activities provide the opportunities for teaching how to empower workers? Can educational programs promote change? In describing the educational experiment during the NAFTA campaign I tried to outline several key elements in developing such an approach to learning. One of the basic principles is that workers are understood to be the subject, not the object, of the learning process. This means that the education begins with the knowledge they already have. In the NAFTA "case study," we didn't begin by lecturing workers about the provisions contained in the trade agreement and how bad they were for workers and their families. Rather, we first discussed what was happening in the workplace and then in the industry, and eventually the question of trade and what it means emerged in the discussion. Our discussion and analysis went from the particular to the general aspects of the problem.

Another basic principle is that education is not neutral. In discussing NAFTA and its implications for workers, the emphasis was not on the participants' acquiring "facts" by transmission of information but on raising the questions about who was conducting the NAFTA negotiations and who was to benefit from them.

Action to change the present conditions or to resolve problems is yet another basic principle. What can be done and how do we go about implementing it? Empowering education leads not to contemplation but to transformation. If NAFTA, as it was being negotiated, would not benefit workers, what actions could be taken to alter it?

Finally, we have to learn collectively and individually from our actions. The purpose is not only to find out what was effective or whether our goal was accomplished, however important these are in our evaluations. More important is what we learned about the union and its members, about the captains of industry and their ways of doing business, about the government and whom it serves, and what it would take to win our struggle.

This process is what those of us in empowering education call the collective construction of knowledge. Once again the basic premise is that education begins with the knowledge that the workers already have. They will learn to use their accumulated knowledge and, most important, how to analyze and assess this knowledge.

This kind of education is not only participatory and democratic; it is critical and inclusive. Its practice requires a careful examination of the relations of power in the workplace and in the industry. The union can view the nation and the world as laboratories for change. It can be a vehicle for teaching how to transform the existing power arrangements in order to improve the lives of working men and women.

Bibliography

Arnold, Rick; Burke, Bev; James, Carl; Martin, D'Arcy; and Thomas, Barb. *Educating for a Change,* Toronto, 1991.

Banks, Andy, and Metzgar, Jack. "Participating in Management: Union Organizing on a New Terrain," in *Labor Research Review* 14, Fall 1989.

Fletcher, Bill, and Hurd, Richard. "Beyond the Organizing Model: The Transformation Process in Local Unions," in *Organizing to Win,* Cornell University–ILR Press, forthcoming 1997.

Horton, Myles, and Freire, Paulo. *We Make the Road by Walking: Conversation on Education and Social Change,* Temple University Press.

La Luz, José. "Creating a Culture of Organizing: ACTWU's Education for Empowerment in Labor," in *Labor Research Review* 17, Chicago, Spring 1991.

A New Voice for American Workers: Rebuilding the American Labor Movement, Washington, D.C., 1995.

9

Globalization and the American Labor Movement

Ron Blackwell

I T IS commonly observed that, among the challenges to the American labor movement in the late twentieth century, none is more serious than the globalization of economic activity.

The term *globalization* carries so many meanings, however, that it serves only poorly to explain the complex changes under way in the world economy. To some, globalization means international trade, and increasing globalization means increasing trade. No doubt international trade is an important dimension of globalization and has expanded rapidly over the past two decades, more rapidly than economic activity in general. Indeed, as a result of increasing trade, the United States economy is twice as open as it was in 1979, as measured by the proportion of Gross Domestic Product represented by imports plus exports.

Together with this increase in trade came the loss of millions of jobs in United States industries that compete with imports. This loss of jobs occurred first in apparel in the late 1960s, followed quickly in electronics, steel, auto, and now virtually all manufacturing industries.

Of course, exports also grew, but not by nearly enough to balance ballooning imports. As a result, the United States experienced a traumatic deterioration in its international trade balance. A series of trade deficits of historic magnitude, particularly after the appreciation of the dollar in the early 1980s, transformed the United States from the world's largest creditor nation into the world's largest debtor.

Massive job loss to imports produced a powerful protectionist reaction among unions attempting to stanch the hemorrhaging of jobs and members. Important battles over imports in specific industries were won — most notably with the establishment of the managed trade Multifiber Agreement in the apparel and textile industries. Nevertheless, the labor movement's efforts to meet the challenge of globalization on the international trade front alone are not succeeding. Such trade continues to grow at a faster rate than the entire economy, and as a result, our economy is increasingly open. The rules of international trade and investment, as they affect the interests of capital and the concerns of workers, are more and more unbalanced.

As the United States registers trade deficits of $100 billion a year, administration economists continue to extol exports as the leading source of jobs for tomorrow's American workers. They lecture working Americans on the necessity to improve their skills as the only way to adapt to the inexorable logic of the global economy. Indeed, the United States trade representatives propose to extend the North American Free Trade Agreement to Chile and other countries in Latin America, push the pace on an Asian regional free trade agreement, and prepare to support China's efforts to join the World Trade Organization.

Meanwhile, many of the protectionist alliances between industry and labor have weakened as more companies, even entire industries, have embraced the new global reality and abandoned commitments to their American employees, to the communities in which they were founded and grew, and to the national economy.

Increasingly isolated and embattled on the trade front, many in the labor movement have come to understand that international trade is only one dimension of globalization and, in any case, is not the source of the serious challenge posed to the American labor movement by globalization.

In fact, globalization has at least three fundamental aspects. The first is the international movement of goods and services — trade. The second is the international movement of capital — investment. And the third is the international movement of people — immigration.

These three forms — trade, investment, and immigration — are weaving together the economies of the world, meshing the fortunes of the world's workers and all the world's people. To understand and answer the complex challenge of globalization, the labor movement must understand trade, investment, and immigration as distinct issues — and also as related aspects of a much larger reality.

Understanding globalization also requires that we inquire more deeply into its causes. Conventional wisdom holds that the driving force of globalization is technological — the innovations in information, communication, and transportation technologies symbolized so powerfully by the role of the computer in modern life. While these technologies are essential to globalization, by making possible the organization of economic activity over great distances, they are not its driving cause.

So what is the ultimate cause of globalization in all its forms, the force that propels the international movement of goods, capital, and people, that develops and harnesses new information, communications, and transportation technologies for its own ends? It is the modern corporation — especially the multinational corporation — that is coming to dominate much of the world's economic activity. To understand and address the challenge of globalization, we must develop effective means of responding to the multinational corporation.

At the end of the Cold War and at the edge of the new millennium, the modern corporation stands as the most important and powerful institution in the world. It is the most important because the private corporation controls the productive processes of world civilization, particularly with the collapse of communist and socialist alternatives. It is the most powerful not only because of its size and enormous resources but also because no other institution can equal the reach of its activities or serve as a counterweight to its influence, economically, socially, or politically. Many governments cannot command the resources of the largest corporations, and no government can exercise its sovereign authority without considering the reaction of the world's largest corporations.

As corporations internationalize their operations, they are redefining the operation of the world economy. No longer do the largest corporations compete in national markets under rules of local and national governments to ensure that the results of competition are fair and the benefits widely and equitably distributed. Multinational corporations internationalize their operations, and particularly their productive processes, to gain access to new markets, to obtain resources unavailable at home, and to hire workers at a fraction of the cost of employees in the United States. This last motivation — low wages — poses the most serious challenge to the American labor movement, as corporations scour the globe in search of the most impoverished and oppressed workers to exploit.

Whether their motivation is markets, resources, or exploitable labor, the capacity of multinational corporations to operate internationally expands their bargaining power, at the expense of workers, unions, and national governments. It is this dual shift of power — from workers to their employers and from governments to corporations — that poses the fundamental challenge of globalization. Without countervailing power from other social forces or effective governmental regulation, there is no way to make private corporations fulfill their public responsibility to provide the widely shared economic opportunity necessary to maintain stable societies and support democratic political systems.

Without effective regulation, corporations pursue profit with no regard for the wider social or environmental impact of their activities. Rather than pursue high-road competitive strategies that benefit society while building successful businesses, corporations choose, or are forced, to travel the low road — enriching their shareholders and chief executive officers, at least in the short term, but leaving everyone else behind. Unchecked and unaccountable corporate power is shunting the entire world economy onto the low road, benefiting a privileged few as never before and forcing the majority of the world's people to accept lower living standards. As we say at the AFL-CIO, where once as a society we grew together, today we are growing apart — economically, socially, and politically.

Working Americans, along with working people throughout the world, have suffered from the complex processes of globalization. The source of these problems, however, is not globalization itself but the irresponsible actions of corporations in regard to workers, unions and other social movements, and to governments as they pursue competitive strategies that, even when successful, benefit only a minority. The problem for workers is not international trade, nor international investment, nor immigration. The real problem is that these international movements are driven by powerful private corporations that, operating internationally, are intent on enhancing their own power and pursuing competitive strategies that, when they succeed, do so at the expense of the rest of society and the natural environment.

The challenge to the American labor movement is not to stop globalization but to restore a balance of power between workers and their employers and to make corporations accountable again to government and the people. The challenge today recalls the challenge at the end of the last century in the United States, when national markets were forming and previously local businesses were "nationalizing" their operations. Then, as now, the geographical range of emerging national corporations grew beyond the authority of state and local governments. Then, as now, bargaining power shifted from employees and from government to private corporations that had the option to locate elsewhere. Then, as now, corporations used their power to redistribute income from employees and the public at large to the benefit of a small corporate elite.

These problems spawned movements aimed at restraining corporate power and easing social and economic inequalities. At the end of the last century, the Populists gave voice to agrarian anger at the new economic order. By the turn of the century, the Progressive movement, with strong support from the middle class, promoted initiatives to regulate corporations, taking aim at the trusts and unfair or unsafe business practices. But not until the 1930s, with the growth of industrial unions and the emergence of the New Deal, did institutions such as the modern labor movement and an activist national government prove capable of protecting workers and consumers against corporate power.

Today, the situation is similar to that of the last century. In order to defend ordinary people against multinational corporations, we need to do more than rebuild the American labor movement and renew our government's capacity to promote corporate responsibility and assist working people. We must also build international solidarity with working people and their unions around the world and create international mechanisms for regulating multinational corporations and defending workers' rights. Now, as in earlier eras of reform, the labor movement and other social movements must work together to balance the power of corporations that, because of their mobility, have escaped the reach of public authority and are pursuing their private objectives at the expense of the rest of society.

But there are ways in which our labor movement and workers and their unions around the world can and must take the lead. In the remainder of this essay, I will briefly present three case studies of campaigns in which American labor has responded to the challenges of international trade, international investment, and immigration.

Defending the Rights of Workers to Organize in the Global Economy: The Gap

There is no industry more trade sensitive than apparel. Over half of all apparel sold in the United States is produced abroad, much of it in so-called free trade zones in the developing world. Over 60 percent of all apparel produced for export in the developing world is imported into the United States. Millions of textile and apparel workers in this country have lost their jobs as multinational companies moved operations overseas in search of cheap labor.

In the early part of the twentieth century, low-wage competition from the Southern states destroyed textile and apparel jobs in New England, the early home of these industries in the United States. Today, the challenge to jobs and wages comes from the "New South" surrounding the Caribbean — Mexico, Central America, and the Dominican Republic.

In the earlier period, the strategy of the unions — the ACTWU and the ILGWU — was threefold. First, the unions "followed the work" in these notoriously footloose industries and organized the new workers: the daughters of farmers in New Jersey, immigrant women in Philadelphia, or white and African-American women in the South. Second, the unions worked with employers when they could — or fought them when they had to — to compete with each other in ways that did not depend on exploitation and oppression. Production was formalized, and the piece rate (then a workplace advance) was established. Finally, the unions fought to change the rules of interstate commerce to take sweated labor out of competition. The Fair Labor Standards Act, which regulates minimum wages and conditions of work, covers only those goods which enter interstate commerce. A national minimum wage and other minimal labor standards limited the ability of states to compete among themselves by using substandard labor conditions to attract nationally mobile corporations.

A similar strategy to deal with work running away to the New South was adopted by these two unions at the merger convention called to establish a new union, UNITE, the Union of Needletrades, Industrial, and Textile Employees. Working with the National Labor Committee, UNITE introduced two young apparel workers from Honduras who were attempting to form a union in a plant producing apparel for the Gap, a major U.S. apparel retailer. These two workers were able to convey to UNITE members the reality of globalization in the apparel industry, the abominable conditions of free-trade-zone workers in the Caribbean, and the need for concerted action.

UNITE and the National Labor Committee launched a national

campaign focused on the Gap, demanding that it (1) recognize and accept responsibility for the conditions under which their clothes are produced; (2) remain in Honduras rather than flee, and correct the problems there of child labor, physical abuse, and suppression of unions; (3) translate and post the company's "code of conduct" with all its offshore contractors; (4) develop a system of independent monitors to ensure that the terms of its code are enforced.

The campaign spread across the United States and Canada and sent hundreds of delegations of workers, students, church members, and others to Gap stores to challenge the company at its most sensitive point — the stores where the company meets its customers. Like other apparel companies, the Gap — which is, in fact, among the more socially responsible apparel retailers — realized a serious contradiction in its business. The standards of competition in today's global apparel industry require companies to engage in labor practices that are obnoxious to its customers. When customers learn of these practices, the value of a brand name and the good will engendered by advertising and publicity efforts, which may have cost hundreds of millions of dollars, can all be destroyed. In this sense, exploitative practices are not just socially irresponsible; they are economically reckless.

The pressure brought to bear on the Gap by the campaign, which seemed to feed on its public relations efforts, finally convinced it to negotiate with the union and representatives of the religious and human rights community. Eventually, the company accepted all the campaign's demands: it remained in Honduras; it narrowed its base of international sourcing to fewer countries, allowing more responsible monitoring of labor conditions; it translated its corporate code into the languages of the workers who produce the clothing; it forced the Honduran contractor to rehire the workers fired in the local union's organizing drive; and, perhaps most important, it initiated the first system of independent monitoring in the United States apparel industry. Today, the Gap is among the leaders in the still early effort to reform the global apparel industry to once again "take oppression out of competition."

Defending Workers' Right to Strike at a Foreign-owned Company: Bridgestone/Firestone

In 1988, the Tokyo-based Bridgestone, Incorporated, the world's largest rubber company, acquired the United States–based Firestone Tire and Rubber Company.

Bridgestone initially cooperated with the union representing Firestone employees, the United Rubber Workers. But early in 1994, the company radically changed course, demanding massive contract concessions designed to give Bridgestone an unfair advantage over its competitors and to destroy the union. More than four thousand workers in four cities — Des Moines, Iowa; Noblesville, Indiana; Decatur, Illinois; and Oklahoma City, Oklahoma — were forced out on strike.

Soon after the strike began, Bridgestone/Firestone committed a series of unfair labor practices. It cut off accident and sickness benefits to sick and injured employees who never joined the strike and fired strikers for lawful picket-line conduct. In January 1995, the company announced that it was hiring "permanent replacements" for thousands of strikers. Eventually, the National Labor Relations Board issued a complaint against Bridgestone/Firestone, alleging that the strike was an unfair labor practice strike and that the company had unlawfully discharged over two thousand employees, whom it falsely claimed to have permanently replaced. The union declared an unconditional end to its strike in May 1995, but Bridgestone/Firestone refused to reinstate many of the strikers at the expense of the replacement workers.

Meanwhile, the United Rubber Workers had merged with the United Steelworkers of America (USWA). In response to the multinational corporation's assault on its employees, the USWA launched an international "Don't Buy" campaign against Bridgestone/Firestone products and services, a campaign aimed not only at individual consumers but at large purchasers as well — from auto companies and heavy-equipment manufacturers to state and local governments and school boards. Among the large purchasers that eventually refused to buy Bridgestone/Firestone tires were the Saturn Division of

General Motors, the cities of Atlanta, St. Louis, Minneapolis and St. Paul, and the government of Lake County, Indiana.

In May 1995, the union dramatized the campaign by disrupting Bridgestone/Firestone's marketing strategy for the Indy Car racing. The union used the theme of "black flagging" Bridgestone/Firestone — in auto racing, a black flag means immediate disqualification for a serious violation of the rules. The USWA first used the black flag theme on Memorial Day 1996, at both the Indianapolis 500 and the rival U.S. 500 race in Michigan. More than a thousand Steelworkers demonstrated on the day of the race in Indianapolis, distributing thousands of small black flags to race fans. And the slogan was also used in radio and newspaper advertisements in strike cities, Indianapolis, and New York.

Meanwhile, the union organized support for the strike throughout the world. On the weekend of July 12–14, 1996, the second anniversary of the strike, labor organizations on several continents rallied to the Bridgestone/Firestone workers' cause. In other expressions of global solidarity, unions held demonstrations in Japan, Turkey, Belgium, Spain, and Italy. In March 1996, a World Conference on Bridgestone was held in Nashville, with Bridgestone workers from fifteen countries supporting the American strikers' cause. And the USWA filed a complaint against Bridgestone/Firestone with a respected international body, the Paris-based Organization for Economic Cooperation and Development.

Facing pressure in the United States and throughout the world, Bridgestone/Firestone reached an agreement with the union in November 1995. In a major victory for the union, the agreement provided the first across-the-board raise in the tire industry since 1982 — and $15 million worth of supplemental bonuses for illegally replaced striking workers. The striking workers ratified the agreement on December 12, 1996.

Defending Immigrant Workers: The Strawberry Campaign

California strawberry workers are an example of a severely exploited, mostly immigrant, and largely Latino workforce. They work as stoop laborers under horrendous conditions, and many of them live with two and three other families in an apartment. Some live in cars and others in makeshift shacks. They work ten- and twelve-hour days, average only $8000 a year, often are paid less than the minimum wage, and are cheated out of overtime and other benefits.

Their employers are 270 "growers" in the Central Coast of California. These are essentially intermediaries for the shipping and packing houses — "coolers" — that really control the workers' conditions. While the cooler doesn't employ the strawberry pickers, it has captive strawberry growers who get their plants from the cooler, are paid by the cooler, and have their product shipped and marketed by the cooler under the cooler's label. All in all, California strawberries are a $600 million industry.

To help strawberry workers win a better deal, the AFL-CIO and the United Farm Workers have launched an ambitious organizing campaign. The goal is to put pressure on the strawberry industry through a combination of job actions, consumer support efforts, and corporate activity. A big part of this effort is a national consumer campaign to support the strawberry workers, with state and local central labor councils mobilizing union members, sympathetic organizations — including religious, civil rights, and political organizations — and the general public.

For instance, in New York City, the Central Labor Council hosted a coalition support meeting and press conference that included the Council of Churches, the Board of Rabbis, Catholic Charities, community and political leaders, and leaders of major unions. The City Council passed a resolution endorsing the campaign, as did the chief executive officer of Red Apple Supermarkets.

Just getting under way, the strawberry workers' campaign is an example of how the labor movement can reach out to Americans of good will and fight to improve conditions for immigrant workers. The campaign recalls successful organizing drives decades ago for earlier immigrants in other industries, and it is a model for future efforts to organize the new immigrant workforce.

The Gap campaign, the Bridgestone/Firestone strike, and the

strawberry workers' campaign are examples of how the labor movement can answer the challenges of trade, foreign investment, and immigration through direct action focused on the organizing and bargaining needs of the labor movement, directed at multinational employers, and employing creative nontraditional strategies.

The success of the labor movement's new strategies is constrained, however, by rules of international trade, investment, and immigration, which have been constructed to buttress the power of multinational employers in relation to workers internationally. Without exception, so-called free-trade agreements carefully protect the intellectual property rights of multinational corporations while ignoring the human rights and social and environmental concerns of workers.

Until trade and investment agreements condition international commerce on respect for the fundamental rights of workers — especially their collective rights to organize and bargain collectively — the power of multinational corporations with respect to workers will remain unbalanced, and the international organizing and bargaining efforts of unions will be limited. Therefore, to direct action internationally to achieve their organizing and bargaining objectives, unions must aggressively pursue a political strategy in every country to ensure that the international trade and investment agreements recognize the protection of human rights as an essential condition to participation in global trade and investment.

The combination of creative organizing, bargaining strategies, and political action to reform the trade, investment, and immigration regimes is the only route to restoring a balance of power both between multinational corporations and workers and between those same corporations and national governments. Only when such balance is achieved can the process of globalization be transformed from a race to the bottom into a campaign to lift the world's workers to the top. And only when globalization is changed in this way will it promise a more just and sustainable future for all people.

10

The New Reserve Army of Labor

Frances Fox Piven

ORGANIZING THE UNORGANIZED," the old union refrain, is the rallying cry of the new leadership of the AFL-CIO. The reasons are clear. Unions cannot recover their strength in numbers, treasuries, and organization unless they organize aggressively, especially among workers in the growing service sector. But the challenge is even bigger. If the reviving union movement is not to be cut off at the knees, it must also organize the millions of poor people who are being disgorged into the labor market as a result of the policies called "welfare reform."

One of the anomalies of the moment is that, while official unemployment is at a historic low, wages are not rising. Part of the explanation is that many people anxious for work or income are not counted in official unemployment rates. This includes the enlarging numbers of "contingent" workers — involuntary part-timers and temporary employees — and those forced by irregular employment to move from job to job or in and out of the labor force. And it includes the millions of people who until recently relied on public benefits that are now being slashed or eliminated. These groups, taken together, constitute a new reserve army of labor. The significance of the growth of this reserve army is starkly clear. Worker bargaining power depends on tight labor markets, which give workers leverage over employers. And tight labor markets are inevitably jeopardized when legions of insecure people are available to under-bid the wages and working conditions of existing job holders.

The growth of the reserve army is partly the result of a downward spiral of perverse effects initiated by labor market restructuring and declining wages.[1] Thus, jobs are lost through outsourcing, down-sizing, or through the spreading corporation practice of "renting" temporary employees to fill what were once stable jobs. A surplus of unemployed or insecure workers, in turn, drives down wages for other workers, especially when unions are weak and on the de-fensive. This helps explain why most workers have suffered wage cuts over the past twenty years. Declining wages, in turn, have had the ironic effect of further increasing the supply of labor, as more workers are driven to accept overtime or a second job to shore up falling household incomes, and more women raising children are driven into the labor market, where they work at check-out counters or computer terminals to supplement household incomes. And, as more people bid for more work because declining wages cannot sup-port customary levels of consumption, wages decline further, forcing more people into the competition for work and wages.

Of course, insecurity about work has been a perennial feature of capitalist labor markets, interrupted only by brief periods of boom employment. Now, however, the effects of job competition are heightened by the widespread belief that an epochal transformation has occurred, and the hope of stable lifetime employment is a thing of the past. The transformation is widely attributed to the globaliza-tion of production, trade, and investment, combined with the tech-nological changes in production, communication, and transporta-tion that make globalization possible. This view now constitutes the taken-for-granted premise in most discussions of the economy, on both the right and the left. The familiar argument is that capital and goods spin about the globe searching for the lowest production costs and the highest sales profits, thus pitting American workers against low-wage workers everywhere. The persuasiveness of the argument rests in part on its having some reality, as American consumers find when they shop for Japanese VCRs or Italian shoes or Brazilian umbrellas. But even more influential than this confirmation in experience is the constant reiteration of the globalization argument in think-tank reports, on talk shows, and in every political campaign and labor dispute.

However, neither the visibility of Japanese VCRs nor endless reiteration makes the analysis true. By almost any measure, the United States economy is less integrated into global markets than are the economies of Europe and Japan. Internationalism certainly cannot explain, therefore, why American workers, especially lower paid workers, now earn much less than workers in Europe and Japan, or why more American children are poorer than children in other rich countries, or why workers here work longer hours, receive fewer public benefits, and so on. Indeed, the globalization thesis is so exaggerated, and used so wantonly to explain job losses and wage cuts and public program rollbacks, that it is better understood as ruling-class propaganda than as serious analysis.

It is propaganda that is devastating for worker power, however, both in the marketplace and in democratic politics. The idea that investors now operate on an international scale seems to bring American workers into direct competition with legions of low-wage workers across the globe. It also creates the illusion that markets are now beyond the control of national governments. Either way, the implication is clear: workers no longer have much leverage over employers, and governments are also helpless to control economic conditions. The ideology of international laissez-faire thus makes the real threat of job competition more acute. It also veils the role of business interests in creating and enlarging the reserve army to deploy against all workers, and especially against unionized workers.

The definitive evidence is in the major role that public policy — and the politics that shapes public policy — is playing in systematically increasing the numbers, and the desperation, of the reserve army. A business-dominated national government is apparently determined to push ever more people into the labor market and to heighten the vulnerability of those already in the market. For example, when the Social Security program was created in the mid-1930s, it was with the goal of *removing* older people from a labor market that treated them badly and put them in competition with other workers for jobs. Now, however, the direction of policy has been reversed. The age at which people become eligible for Social Security pensions is already being gradually raised, from sixty-five to sixty-seven, with talk of eligibility at age seventy in the future, thus ensuring that many millions of older people will continue to work. Meanwhile, those currently receiving benefits are encouraged to remain in the labor market by new regulations that reduce the penalties on earnings. So far, these changes have attracted little attention, because they are being implemented gradually. There is the looming prospect, however, as talk of the so-called crisis in Social Security financing becomes more strident, of additional major rollbacks, including downward revisions in benefit levels and upward revisions in the age of eligibility,[2] as well as the privatization of at least a good part of Social Security savings (a prospect that excites much interest in the financial markets, since it entails a windfall of new investment).[3] Together, these changes would result in a flood of many millions of pensioners and erstwhile pensioners bidding for jobs, especially low-wage jobs.

What is more immediate and more urgent are the draconian provisions incorporated into the Personal Responsibility and Work Opportunity Reconciliation Act of 1996 (the so-called welfare reform). Each of the major measures included in the act will have a heavy impact on the reserve army. First, legal immigrants will no longer be entitled to Medicaid, food stamps, or cash assistance. Much of the public seems to go along with these exclusions, presumably because they don't think immigrants should enter the country unless they can support themselves. But no informed observer believes that denying these benefits will actually be a significant deterrent to immigration. Indeed, the conservative think tanks and business lobbyists that backed the benefit cutoffs, and the congressional bloc that pushed them through, also worked strenuously to defeat other legislative proposals to tighten restrictions on immigration. The objective, apparently, is not to keep immigrants out, but to bring them in and keep them vulnerable. Denying benefits ensures that, once here, they will be without any protection to tide them over periods of adversity or to supplement low wages.[4]

Or consider the cutbacks in food-stamp benefits, by almost 20 percent, reducing the average benefit per meal from 80 cents to 66 cents.[5] These cuts will affect not only welfare recipients and the elderly, but the working poor. Indeed, one of the especially harsh provisions limits unemployed adults without children to three months of food stamps during any three-year period of unemployment. Again, the likely effects seem clear. Public benefits were intended in part to help the unemployed weather a stint of joblessness without being forced to accept sharply lower wages and poor working conditions. The withdrawal of those benefits inevitably will have the reverse effect.

Or consider the radical overhaul of Aid to Families with Dependent Children (AFDC), the program that provides cash assistance to impoverished single-parent families. Most of the extended and heated debate about "welfare reform" was, in fact, directed at the AFDC program. It has now been abolished, replaced with lump-sum grants to the states to run their own programs. It is already evident that most of the states will lower benefits and impose tight time limits on their receipt. States inclined to be more liberal will be constrained by requirements in the new law to put recipients to work within two years (simply dropping mothers from the rolls counts as a work placement).[6] The federal law also imposes a lifetime limit of five years on the receipt of benefits.

Even before the new law took effect, the states were reporting dramatic reductions in the rolls. Some of this was no doubt the result of an improved economy, which allowed mothers to leave welfare for work. But experience suggests that a good part of the drop reflected harsher administrative practices bred by a years-long campaign against welfare. The *New York Times,* after interviewing dozens of state officials, described the new attitude: "the goal is to put people in jobs, any jobs . . ."[7] Virginia has even decided to link the campaign against immigrants to the campaign against welfare recipients with a plan to offer an immediate pool of welfare recipients to employers who are raided by the Immigration and Naturalization Service.[8]

Taken together, these changes will result in several million desperate mothers scrambling for whatever work they can get. This will be hard on them. It will also be hard on the low-wage workers with whom they will be competing. The Economic Policy Institute estimates that wages among the lowest paid 30 percent are likely to fall by about 12 percent when the cutbacks are fully implemented.[9]

The mandatory work requirements for welfare recipients are also giving rise to a virtually indentured labor force of welfare recipients who will augment the ranks of the reserve army. While we have had such welfare work programs in the past, the new ones will affect many more people, and they are harsher. The education and training activities that often counted as work in the past no longer do; there are fewer exemptions allowed; and the work rules have been stiffened by provisions that specify the overall work-participation rates the state must achieve in order not to lose a portion of their federal grant. By the year 2002, 50 percent of the people on state caseloads must work a minimum of thirty hours each week.

To meet this requirement, states with larger caseloads are creating "workfare" programs, in which recipients are assigned to some kind of job in exchange for their grants. Previously, federal law stipulated that such work assignments be limited to jobs with a public purpose. That stipulation has now been removed. The new legislation is silent on the question of whether these recipients are in fact "employees."[10] And it is silent on the question of whether these work recipients are entitled to the minimum wage or to overtime pay. Similarly, we do not know whether they are covered by state labor laws, by the protections of the National Labor Relations Act (assuming they are placed in the private sector jobs to which the NLRA applies), or by the Occupational Safety and Health Act. In other words, for these workers, half a century of labor protections may well have been wiped away.

Finally, the new legislation, by turning funds over to the states with minimal federal requirements, appears to have smoothed the way for the privatization of state welfare programs. To be sure, some states had already contracted with private companies for the conduct of particular welfare functions, such as the collection of child-support payments and job-placement activities. Now, however, we are likely to see far more sweeping forms of privatization, including privatization of the massive workfare programs that will be created. Already some of the biggest corporations have joined in the scramble for contracts, including Lockheed Martin IMS and Electronic Data Systems. A major conference on "Welfare Privatization" was organized in March 1997, under the aegis of the Reason Foundation, with the cooperation of the Cato Institute and the Heritage Foundation. Among other features promised by the conference promotional material was instruction in how private industry could "gain a leading edge in the market while it is in its early stage." And since privatization raises the specter of a frontal assault on the unionized public services, the conference planners also promised to provide "vital information to manage union opposition."[11]

Will the unions meet the challenge of this large and growing reserve army and the government policies that are creating it? Certainly, the developments are ominous. Nevertheless, the union answer is by no means clear. The AFL-CIO was on record as opposing the new welfare legislation, and so were the main public sector unions. Still, during the months and years that welfare cutbacks were debated in Congress, the unions were largely invisible, confining their opposition to insider negotiations with their friends in the White House and Congress. Apparently the welfare issue was not considered important enough to justify investing real political capital.

That was a big mistake, and it forces a retreat. Now the fight over welfare policy has shifted to the fifty state capitals, where business wields even more leverage than in Washington. Still, the states have options under the federal law. They can decide, for example, to opt out of a requirement that recipients be assigned to some kind of work activity after only two months instead of two years; they can decide to exempt parents of very young infants from work requirements; they can allow legal immigrants already in residence before the federal law was passed to continue to receive Medicaid, food stamp, and cash benefits; they can request exemptions from the three-month limit on food stamps for the childless unemployed when local unemployment levels are high; they can exempt mothers of young children from work requirements when decent child care is not available. States have always set the level of cash benefits for families, and have always set them low, but now they are responding to the punitive mood encouraged by the new law with dramatic new cuts, despite the fact that the lump-sum grants are turning out to be a fiscal bonanza.[12] There are local coalitions of advocacy groups that try to influence state decisions on behalf of the poor, but they are frail, their member organizations usually small and underfunded. The unions might make a difference if they were to throw their weight behind them.

Confronting the challenge of the reserve army also means mounting a broader defense of the social programs. The effort to restructure the Social Security system is obviously a major concern. The way has been prepared by years of argument to the effect that the program is financially unsound and is certain to collapse as the baby boomers reach retirement age. In fact, modest adjustments in tax levels would solve most of the problems until well into the twenty-first century.[13] The guiding principle of a union fight to preserve Social Security — and it will be a fight — ought to be the conviction that economic security for older people is also security for working people. If Social Security benefits are rolled back, workers in their prime will again have to shoulder much of the burden of caring for aged parents, as they once did or tried to do. And when Social Security benefits are rolled back, older people will again compete in the labor market, on unfavorable terms.

Similarly, the federal safety net for the very poor, already badly torn, is likely to be the target of renewed assaults in the future. The Medicaid program is an especially attractive target, since there is much more money at stake here than there was in welfare. The unions could be in the forefront of future efforts to defend what remains of the safety net and be ready to lead future campaigns to restore the damage already done. Again, the issues are clear. Public income supports for people who are at risk in the labor market are important not only because large principles of social justice and a caring community are at stake. They are also important to workers and unions for the very practical and self-interested reason that these programs constitute a floor under wages and thereby reduce the reserve army of labor.

Finally, and urgently, the unions should take the lead in organizing the hundreds of thousands, and potentially millions, of people forced into workfare programs under the new welfare law. These people, most of them poor mothers, are already being hurled like hostages into the front lines of the campaign against workers. The plan is simple, bold, and big, and could be devastating to the affected unions. Workfare recipients can replace regular workers at little or no cost to employers, and they are given none of the job-related protections won by labor over the years. This is a reserve army of totally vulnerable people; if they lose their workfare assignment, they do not even have welfare to fall back on. Moreover, if the unions do not take the lead in an organizing campaign to defend workfare recipients, the potential for rancor and division is enormous. Regular workers will view workfare recipients as threatening their jobs and their hard-won job protections. For their part, workfare recipients will bitterly resent the privileges enjoyed by workers who do essentially similar work. This augurs a festering war of resentment between workers and the poor.

There is at least a chance of averting this calamity. The unions could launch a campaign to organize workfare recipients, offering them solidarity, organizing resources, and the ability to advance the loud and compelling demand that all workers who do the same work should be treated alike. It is hard to see how this can be done without the unions, because only they have the reach and the resources to organize on the scale of the workfare armies that are being raised. If the unions enter the fight, with troops and dollars and enthusiasm, they may be able to put a halt to at least this part of the deliberate expansion of the reserve army of labor. They may also succeed in building alliances across the racial, gender, and class divides that have often defeated American labor.

New York City, with its large recipient population, is a kind of pilot site for massive workfare programs, and it reveals some of the dangers, both to recipients and workers. Even before the passage of the federal law, implementation of workfare for recipients in the state and locally run "home relief" program was already under way in New York. The reason for the rush was not mysterious. New York City has been under crushing fiscal strain for many years, largely as a result of the steady erosion of federal and state aid. Budget short-falls mean cutbacks in city payrolls, a process that has continued relentlessly for years, with the result that the numbers of workers in the municipal unions have also shrunk. Now workfare recipients do the work that union workers once did, and they do it without the employment status or wages or benefits that municipal workers have, unprotected by national or state labor laws or by the job-re-lated regulations that protect regular workers. And workfare will grow. Indeed, if the program is not checked, workfare recipients could become the main source of municipal labor, overwhelming the numbers of regular employees left on the city's payroll. Some fifty-thousand recipients are already at work, mainly cleaning the parks, streets, and subways, doing the work that union members once did. The numbers will at least double by the end of the century, as four to five thousand AFDC recipients are added to the program each month. Meanwhile, workfare recipients complain bitterly of their inferior treatment, ranging from the denial of proper clothing and equipment for the work they do, to the lack of such elementary conveniences as lockers and bathrooms, to the cavalier disregard with which they are sometimes treated by union workers.

But if the challenge to the New York unions seems clear, their response is not clear at all. For months, the leaders of the city's public sector unions have vacillated. Stanley Hill, executive director of District Council 37, the umbrella AFSCME union, first called for a moratorium on workfare, then backed away when the mayor offered conciliatory but vague promises to consider hiring an unspe-cified number of welfare recipients as city employees. The Transport Workers Union agreed to allow workfare recipients to fill jobs elimi-nated by attrition after being threatened with big layoffs. And they tried to cope with the anger between workers and recipients by securing a contract agreement that work schedules be designed to avoid contact between union members and welfare recipients, in order to ensure the union that it will "not be embarrassed." Meanwhile, both unions also won protections for existing workers for the life of the contract.

The calculus is clear. The New York unions are trading in the prospects of the poor, and of the public sector workforce, for short-term protections for current workers and, by extension, incumbent union leadership. That may help union leaders ride the tides for a while, but it will lead in the longer term to the erosion of wages and worker rights, and to the steady loss of union members and union power. And it will contribute to the bitter divisions that are growing in American society.

The AFL-CIO is committed to organizing the harder-to-organize workers of the contemporary American economy: the huge numbers in the service sector, from university clericals and faculty to fast-food workers to janitors and cleaning workers, to workers in the new industries — the sweatshops and chicken-processing and garbage-recycling plants — both in the Sunbelt and the old cities. And as labor market restructuring continues, organizing the unorganized is likely to entail the tough challenges of organizing part-time and temporary workers. All this is obvious.

It is only a little less obvious that organizing the unorganized in the late twentieth century should also mean organizing the new reserve army of labor. This is partly a practical matter of union survival. It is also a matter that speaks to the moral standing of the unions in American society. The unions can try to hold on, to slow their decline of the past decades by concentrating on building membership, collecting dues, and protecting collective-bargaining contracts while ignoring the reserve army that undermines these efforts. Or they can become a voice for social justice by extending themselves in solidarity to all working people, including the poorest working people.

Notes

1. See Richard B. Freeman, "Solving the New Inequality," *Boston Review,* December 1996–January 1997. Freeman reports that labor force participation in the United States has risen from 65 to 71 percent of the population since 1974. This trend is usually ignored by analysts on the left, who fasten on the scarcity of jobs rather than the surfeit of job seekers. The comparable figures for OECD countries show a decline from 65 to 60 percent.

2. See, for example, Peter G. Peterson, *Will America Grow Up Before It Grows Old? How the Coming Social Security Crisis Threatens You, Your Family, and Your Country* (New York: Random House, 1996). Since Social Security recipients are numerous and well-organized, benefit cuts run the risk of serious opposition. The stratagem being floated now is a statistical sleight-of-hand where benefits would be lowered by reducing the official rate of inflation, which is the basis for calculating annual cost-of-living adjustments. One estimate is that in high-cost areas of the country, a 1 percent reduction in the cost-of-living formula over ten years would reduce real benefits by 10 percent. See Lars-Erik Nelson, "Gingrich's Stealth Tax Hike," *New York Newsday,* January 19, 1995.

3. If the entire Social Security fund is invested in private markets, experts estimate that $2 trillion in new money will flow into the stock market. This prospect has stimulated a major lobbying effort by financial interests, spearheaded by the Cato Institute. See Leslie Wayne, "For Interest Groups, Battle Lines Form in Debate Over Social Security," *New York Times,* December 30, 1996.

4. American employers have in fact always lobbied for a policy of open borders for immigrants and closed borders for goods. On business opposition to restrictions on immigration in the current period, see Eric Schmitt, "Milestones and Missteps on Immigration," *New York Times,* October 26, 1996.

5. The estimate is from Douglas Henwood, "Demote the General Welfare," *Left Business Observer,* no. 74, October 7, 1996.

6. Unless the states elect to opt out, the law also requires some "work activity" within two months of receiving aid.

7. Peter T. Kilborn, "Previously Reluctant States Moving on Welfare Changes," *New York Times,* December 16, 1996.

8. Jon Jeter, "Va. to Turn INS Raids Into Welfare Job Leads," *Washington Post,* November 1, 1996.

9. See Lawrence Mishel and John Schmitt, *Cutting Wages by Cutting*

Welfare: The Impact of Reform on the Low-Wage Labor Market
(Washington D.C., The Economic Policy Institute, 1996).

10. The legislation does specify that people required to work as a condition
    of receiving food stamps receive the same benefits as employees per-
    forming comparable work.
11. These quotes are from the conference brochure, entitled "Welfare Pri-
    vatization," produced by the World Research Group and officially
    sponsored by the Reason Foundation.
12. State grant levels are set by the 1994 level of federal spending. Since the
    rolls have plummeted, the states will get substantially more federal
    money than they would have under the previous grant-in-aid formula.
13. See Richard B. Du Boff, "Thurow on Social Security: The 'Left' Strikes
    Again," *Monthly Review,* October 1996. See also Jeff Madrick, "Social
    Security and Its Discontents," *New York Review,* December 19, 1996.

11

Seizing the Time
Because the Time Is Now

Welfare Repeal and
Labor Reconstruction[1]

Bill Fletcher, Jr.

THE DILEMMA confronting organized labor in the wake of welfare repeal[2] brings to mind several points raised by W.E.B. Du Bois in the initial chapters of his monumental study *Black Reconstruction in America*. Laying the basis for his discussion of the dynamics of the post–Civil War Reconstruction period, Du Bois sets the stage by addressing the character of slavery in the United States. He pointed out that with the rise of the early U.S. labor movement — during the period of the so-called Jacksonian Democracy (1820s–1830s) — there also erupted a major struggle regarding the attitude of the labor movement toward the slavery question. Specifically, the question was whether organized labor should unite with the Abolitionists in opposition to slavery, should support slavery, or should remain essentially agnostic. On this question, the movement split.

The nature of the split was actually quite profound. Each point of view had identifiable partisans who articulated substantive points of view. The essence of the matter, however, was the question of job competition. Would the white section of the working class, that section which was beginning to organize into trade unions, be dragged down by slavery, constantly undermined at every turn, or was the greater danger to be found in liberating the slaves and thus competing with a mass of free black labor?

The division was, from the standpoint of history, quite fascinating, though at the time it held immense consequences. Organized labor had, within its ranks, otherwise militant leaders who were prepared to support slavery, or at least not openly oppose it. They saw, with the possibility of the liberation of the slaves, the further growth of industrial capitalism and the horrendous conditions associated with it.[3] At the other end of the spectrum were equally militant leaders who saw either a proslavery or agnostic position as antithetical to the essence of trade unionism. On mere practical terms, they argued, the existence of a large mass of enslaved labor would always present the possibility of the undermining of any victory won by organized, free labor.

The pre–Civil War labor movement was never able to cohere as a force. There were various contributing factors, but it is clear that the division on the slavery question was one of the most profound. This split actually foreshadowed, and soberly illustrated, a recurring division within the ranks of organized labor in the United States. It can be described as the rift between the exclusionist wing and the inclusionist wing of organized labor. The division has taken many different forms, with race perhaps the paramount form but not the only one. Divisions based on gender, national origin (immigrant versus so-called native), craft, and skill have all torn apart organized labor in this country.

There are numerous examples of the inclusionist versus exclusionist contradiction. One need consider only the history of the American Federation of Labor. Although its original constitution proclaimed its intent to include all workers, it quickly became clear that one could not use the word *all* too loosely. By definition, the bulk of the unions constituting the AFL were craft-based; the entire philosophy of the AFL was to organize workers according to craft. It opposed the notion of industrial unionism, particularly as articulated by the Industrial Workers of the World (IWW) in the early twentieth century. The aim of the AFL was, in essence, to narrow the possibility of job competition by opening the ranks of its constituent unions on a selective basis. Flowing from this foundation came the exclusion of women, unskilled workers, and, increasingly, workers of color.[4] Many of the craft unions of the AFL never developed the capacity to organize unorganized workers on any scale, a fact that haunts the descendants of many of these unions to this day.

In contrast to the AFL, and in competition with them, arose various formations, the IWW among the best known.[5] One could describe the opposition as representing the inclusionist wing of organized labor. Characteristic of the IWW was its vehement antiracism. Along with its intense organizing spirit, the IWW would not capitulate to Jim Crow, even when described in cultural terms, as it often was in the South.

Although the IWW was destroyed largely by an alliance between the federal and state governments, along with the employers (sometimes in open collaboration with the AFL), the inclusionist wing continued to exist, even within the AFL itself. Unions such as the International Ladies Garment Workers Union (ILGWU — which eventually merged with the Amalgamated Clothing and Textile Workers Union to form the Union of Needletrades, Industrial, and Textile Employees — UNITE), the United Mine Workers of America (UMWA), and, with its founding in the 1920s, the Brotherhood of Sleeping Car Porters (BSCP) were among those which stood firmly for industrial unionism. The split in the AFL, in 1935, leading to the formation of the Congress of Industrial Organizations (CIO), was perhaps one of the more dramatic illustrations of the contradiction after the demise of the IWW. Subsequent to this split, the inclusionist-exclusionist contradiction has been replicated on countless occasions.

This contradiction, and the dilemma associated with it, is seen again today in the issues surrounding welfare repeal. Before examining labor's dilemma, it is important to examine the context. Welfare repeal takes place in an era dominated by a tendency the world has come to know as "neoliberalism." Neoliberalism speaks not so much to a partisan political tendency — for example, New Deal liberalism — but rather to an economic philosophy with many political implications. The essence of neoliberalism is the notion that any and all impediments to the so-called free market and the maximum accumulation of profit and wealth must be removed by any and all means.

Neoliberalism has swept the world, particularly in the aftermath of the Cold War. Taking many forms, it is manifested in the countries of the "South" (the so-called Third World) and in many of the countries of the former Soviet bloc, by so-called structural adjustment programs. Such efforts, particularly as advanced by the International Monetary Fund and the World Bank, aim at denationalizing or privatizing many institutions once run by governments. Airlines, telephone-telegraph, power, even water systems are being forced into the private sector as a condition of assistance to hard-pressed nations in Africa, Asia, and Latin America.

Beyond denationalizing various institutions, neoliberalism represents an assault against the public sector as a whole. For many Republicans, for instance, the neoliberal orientation can be found in the privatization efforts of several state services. The removal of state governments from the provision of mental health services, or even the control of roads and highways, represents the specter of neoliberalism. At its charlatan best, neoliberalism articulates the view that government should not provide services but should ensure that services are provided. Let the private sector reign! The problem is the decay of mechanisms for accountability in service provision as well as in the level of the services themselves.

Neoliberalism has an even more ominous side, one often hidden from public view or rationalized away. This is the war against the poor and the working class generally. Structural adjustment programs have insisted that service provisions in countries of the Third World be cut and trade unions (and other popular organizations) restricted as an additional condition for assistance. Multinational corporations have set up shop in various countries and essentially blackmailed the local governments into providing concessions in order for them to remain. Wages are extremely low, and conditions are abominable. Alongside this is increased poverty, massive and unprecedented migrations (from the countryside to the urban areas, and from nation to nation), homelessness, and large-scale unemployment. Following the neoliberal approach to poverty to its logical and extreme conclusion, one witnesses the attempts at the extermination of homeless youth in Brazil by right-wing death squads. (If one cannot eliminate the problem, then eliminate the people.)

The antipoor spin to the attack on welfare and welfare recipients was, therefore, neither accidental nor particularly American in its nature. The political right, in advancing a procorporate agenda, has taken every opportunity to further degrade the working conditions and living standard of the working people of the United States as part of what the economist Bennett Harrison calls the low-road approach to globalization and economic competition. Driving the living standard down and disorganizing the working class clears the way for greater control by the corporations, a greater profit margin, and less chance of popular resistance.

The stigmatization of the poor was facilitated by an attempt to divide the poor into two nearly mythological categories: the deserving poor and the undeserving poor (with racial implications for both). The deserving poor are the so-called working poor. These are the individuals who seem to come from a Dickens novel. Having little of their own, working at minimum wage, rejecting government "handouts" or accepting some — but working every day — these are the people attempting to work their way out of poverty. Some immigrants are put into this category (Cubans, Irish, East Europeans, some Asians), rural whites (if anyone remembers that they still exist), and some African Americans, particularly those who accept conservative social messages.

The working poor are to be contrasted with the nonworking poor. This is the category of the "welfare queens," the alleged generations of welfare recipients, the people who refuse to go to work. This category is largely African American and nonimmigrant Latino. It is the section of the poor to be despised, the group that exists as parasites on real, hardworking Americans.[6]

The political right has so developed these caricatures that they have become part of accepted reality for too many working-class and professional people. By creating a category of undeserving poor and placing the problem of poverty on the poor themselves (rather than on the system that promotes poverty), the political right has succeeded in undermining any legitimate notion of a social safety net, replacing it with the reality of forced labor. The particular irony here is that abject poverty for the bulk of working-class people is little more than two pay checks away. Yet the political right has successfully developed the schism in such a way that one section of the working class is unable to recognize another. This distinction, it should be noted, is not limited to welfare. In the arena of disabilities, one also finds a distinction manufactured by the right between deserving and undeserving disabilities. A case in point is the manner in which drug and alcohol abuse has become a centerpiece of the category of undeserving disabilities, with the focal point being its criminality. This can be contrasted with more acceptable forms of disability.

One means of deepening the schism was to stress that the distinction between the deserving and the undeserving poor was colored by color. The political right successfully used the "race card" as a means of making socially acceptable a repressive policy and practice. Such a practice has a long and unsettling history. As Du Bois pointed out in *Black Reconstruction,* the ruling class in the antebellum South was immensely successful in turning the South into a well-armed camp, armed ostensibly to prevent slave rebellions but actually as a means of maintaining total social control. This was done through the use of the race card.[7]

Accompanying the notion of two sectors of the poor is the notion that "something had to be done" about the welfare system. This was the view that the system was in crisis. In a very real sense there was a crisis, but not as the political right portrayed it. The crisis was for the recipients. The conditions under which they had been living were anything but luxurious. As many welfare rights advocates have pointed out, welfare recipients often held other jobs just to make ends meet, not in order to buy a Lexus. And the jobs that could provide a decent living standard for unskilled workers have been evaporating for twenty years, making alternatives to poverty less possible. The crisis did *not* exist at the level of a problem for the federal budget; Aid for Families with Dependent Children (AFDC) accounted for less than 1 percent of the budget.

By declaring a crisis, the political right advanced a corporate agenda to make more palatable the notion of forced labor. Welfare recipients, now more properly referred to as either Temporary Assistance to Needy Families (TANF) recipients or workfare participants, have been moved into a niche not dissimilar from that of the nineteenth-century slaves or twentieth-century chain-gang workers. In thrusting large numbers of unskilled and semiskilled workers into the labor market at wages below standard, welfare repeal accomplishes the same thing these two other institutions did. Instead of laying down a floor, beneath which wages will not fall, welfare repeal opens up a giant sinkhole, pulling into it the rest of the working class.

It is worth noting here, and not simply as an anecdote, that the acceptability of forced labor through welfare repeal comes at a time when forced labor, as a category, is being rehabilitated generally, a case in point being prison labor. As a reflection of the influence of neoliberalism, the prison industry has become one of the fastest growing segments of the United States economy (as part of the large and ever expanding security industry sector). Rather than being publicly run and accountable institutions, prisons are now considered profit-making sites. As part of this, prison labor has been expanding from making license plates into other sectors of the economy, including areas that affect public sector workers. There have been various rationales for these moves, but one in particular is reminiscent of the arguments developed around welfare repeal: that society should demand that everyone earns his or her own; that is, no "handouts." This twentieth-century semi-Calvinism masks efforts to undercut free labor. How can decently paid, unionized public sector workers compete with prison labor, given comparative costs, especially in a time of declining budgets, tax freezes, and rollbacks? The same issue is at stake in the fallout from welfare repeal.

Welfare repeal and the prospects of greater numbers of TANF participants serving as forced co-workers of free workers presents the union movement with a dilemma similar to what it faced before and after the Civil War: inclusion versus exclusion. Should the union movement oppose the draconian intent and actuality of welfare repeal while reaching out to unite with and support the organizing of TANF participants? Do we simply say *no* to TANF participants and welfare repeal, and keep the TANF participants at arm's length? Or should we cut the best deal we can and hope that the use of TANF participants will not further affect incumbent workers?

In order for organized labor to answer these questions, it must first ask itself even more fundamental ones. Such questioning is brought on by the shift in the environment and the need to re-examine basic precepts. Specifically, who is or should be the constituency of the union movement? And, indeed, can the union movement transform itself into or be founded again as a labor movement?

Following David Brody and other labor historians, one can notice a transformation in what constitutes a labor movement over the course of the last 150 years. Besides the obvious differences — greater roles for women and workers of color — of particular interest is the entire understanding of the relative existence of a movement. By way of example, consider working-class organization and struggle in the nineteenth century, which existed on different levels. During the Jacksonian era and into the Reconstruction period, there were unions and also labor parties (some possessing a reactionary character, e.g., anti-immigrant), as well as secret societies, fraternal orders, and allied groupings. While labor parties decreased in number and size by the latter part of the nineteenth century, there were institutions through which the working class, in its various permutations, participated in real life. Many of them promoted a sense of being part of one labor movement. This was the case even when the working class was segmented by segregation (although with segregation and the AFL's capitulation to it, such an articulation became more problematic).

Well into the twentieth century, organized labor — in the form of trade unions — drew connections to other institutions as part of a larger labor movement, but following World War II this became less the case. With certain important exceptions, organized labor came to view its constituency as the already unionized workers. Particularly after the Cold War purges (by the CIO) in the late 1940s, the only qualifiers to the above were those few unions engaged in external organizing. Such unions may have expanded the conceptualization of their constituency to include the unorganized. Rarely since World War II has organized labor, in the form of the AFL, CIO, or the AFL-CIO, viewed the chronically unemployed and underemployed, the AFDC recipient or the day laborer, as part of its constituency. This stood in at least partial contrast to the 1930s, when sections of the CIO certainly exhibited an affinity for the militant unemployed councils. When economic hard times began to spread, with the recessions of 1973–74 and 1981–82, some unions began to work among the unemployed. Examples were the United Steel Workers of America in Western Pennsylvania (working to establish the Monongohela Committee of the Unemployed) and, in western Massachusetts, the United Electrical Workers. As positive as these efforts were, they remained narrow and primarily focused on former members who had been laid off. It can be said, then, that the union movement has, since World War II at least, not lived as a labor movement.

The obvious qualification here is that organized labor has been an important ally of other social movements on a variety of different initiatives, particularly in the matter of legislation. There is an important difference. Such efforts, as vital as they have been (as with the work of the AFL-CIO in support of civil rights legislation), have generally represented more an expression of solidarity than an identification with a constituency. This unfortunate course helped to lay the conditions that the political right was able to manipulate around welfare repeal. That is, given the extent to which sections of organized labor perceived the poor as "them" or the "other," to the extent to which sections of organized labor perceived community-based organizations doing workers' rights and economic justice work as interlopers or disruptive, it should come as no surprise that our own house was divided in its approach to these mean-spirited initiatives.

Unfortunately, the union movement articulated, explicitly and implicitly, that if one works in a unionized workplace and carries a union card, one is part of the labor movement. If one has been laid off for a prolonged period or has been struggling to get by and is part of the marginal — or marginalized — sections of the working class, one is not perceived as being part of the labor movement or as having any place in it.

The crisis brought on by welfare repeal, a crisis to which the union movement is awakening, challenges the terms of the discussion. No matter what one thought of welfare recipients, it is fast becoming clear that the corporate agenda aims to displace existing workers with workfare participants, to lower living and working standards, and to erode any bargaining power organized workers currently have. The threat from forced labor is compelling organized labor to address the tactical question: What should be done in the immediate future? It has the potential to pose the strategic question: Do we have a larger constituency than already unionized workers? If so, what is our obligation to them? The political right and the corporations are advancing the notion that nothing can or should be done by organized labor with regard to the growing presence of forced labor. In other words, that organized labor should accept forced labor as a reality. If labor does this, it does so at its own peril.

Can anything be done? The answer does have both tactical and strategic levels. At the tactical level, workfare participants must be organized into unions! This can be done by or with the support of community-based organizations, it can be done by organized labor, it can be done by both. In any case, workfare participants must not be allowed to work side by side with free labor at lower pay, fewer benefits, and poorer conditions. For organized labor, there is no room for passivity. It must take an aggressive role in organizing these workers.

Second, if the objective is to put people to work, then jobs must be created for them to fill. There are certainly enough infrastructure projects that need work — building and rebuilding bridges, tunnels — all of which are necessary for the economy. Such jobs are real jobs and should pay the prevailing wage. Minimum- or subminimum-wage workers should not be filling them.

Third, there must be renewed opposition to welfare repeal and its progeny, TANF. With TANF comes a variety of sins, including the cessation of any guarantees of cash assistance (therefore, a state can demand work and not offer cash for those unable to work), cuts in food stamps, Medicaid, and Supplemental Security Income, as well as block grants and so-called devolution, a nice word for states' rights and the deconstruction of the federal sector. The job of building opposition is all the more complicated, given the balance of forces in Congress (as of November 1996), but there are several fights that must be waged at both the state and federal levels over the coming years — fights that will determine whether a new and real social safety net is built.

At the strategic level, there is and will remain the question of constituency. In the spring of 1996, AFL-CIO president John Sweeney advanced the notion that "America needs a raise." This was co-opted by some in the Democratic Party as an exclusive focus on the minimum-wage debate. When the minimum wage was increased — an important victory — several Democratic Party luminaries proclaimed that America had gained a raise! This was not the case.

America's need for a raise goes far beyond the minimum-wage debate. It speaks to the issue of constituency. Not just unionized workers need a raise; so do nonunion workers.

Unemployed workers need a raise, not only in benefits but in opportunities to raise themselves out of unemployment and gain real employment. Congress, under pressure from organized labor and its allies, passed a minimum-wage increase only to have the rug pulled out under the unemployed by welfare repeal. What they gave with one hand, the proponents of welfare repeal took back with the other.

Young people need a raise, not just in wages, but in the chance to find employment now and after they leave school.

As labor addresses the dilemma that has haunted it since the slavery debate, it must attune itself to the sections of the working class that have not had the benefit of unionization. This means a fight for workers' rights and economic justice, not solely a fight for an improved collective-bargaining agreement.

This type of change in strategic orientation will necessitate a reformation of trade unionism in the United States. Forms of organization will need to be created, partly financed and supported by organized labor, even though their immediate objective may not be a collective-bargaining agreement. Such forms of organization might be councils of the unemployed and underemployed; they might be labor-led efforts at economic development, such as cooperatives; or they might be sports' leagues or associations.

Such efforts involve more than a laundry list of demands aimed at appeasing various groups. They call for an active outreach to different groupings in order to develop a common agenda. Organized labor cannot assume that nothing is happening among workers who are not members of unions. That is far from the case. Organized labor, can, however, become the overarching voice for that larger community of workers who are seeking economic and social justice.

The crisis brought on by welfare repeal can be the spark that ignites a reconsideration of labor's constituency and its reason for being. While organized labor must immediately address and organize workfare participants in order to safeguard their immediate future, it can reform itself in such a way as to lead a larger workers' movement into the twenty-first century.

Notes

1. This essay represents an elaboration on the themes raised at the Columbia University teach-in October 4, 1996, in the workshop entitled "Work, Welfare and the Labor Movement."
2. This author has been reluctant to use the official term "welfare reform" to describe the initiative that led to the cessation of AFDC and its replacement with Temporary Assistance to Needy Families (TANF). It is sophistry to call it anything but "welfare deform" or "welfare repeal." The entire essence of the system was gutted and replaced with something, the results of which are unpredictable, that has an entirely different philosophical basis.
3. South Carolina Senator John C. Calhoun was one of the visionaries on the side of the Southern slavocracy who conceptualized the possibility of an *alliance* between the pro-slavery South and the burgeoning union movement in the North. Calhoun repeatedly attempted to convince Southern plantation owners to make common cause with the union movement of the North against the industrial capitalists. Calhoun's

efforts, however, bore little fruit, as the Southern plantation owners were reluctant to consider the proposal seriously.

4. Under the leadership of Samuel Gompers, the AFL initially welcomed African-American workers into their ranks, but was unwilling — from its inception — to challenge Jim Crow segregation, which was gaining strength at the time. This exclusion was, over time, justified on the grounds that black workers were unorganizable, prone to scabbing, etc. Such justifications were also used with other workers of color.

5. History often overlooks the fact that independent black unions formed precisely because of the AFL's capitulation to white supremacy. Equally interesting was the rise of independent union movements in the West among Mexicans and Chicanos, as well as among Asians. These unions represented a very different vision of trade unionism from that represented by the AFL.

6. Contrary to the notion that welfare recipients were a horde of non-working people, the Institute for Women's Policy Research found that welfare mothers had an average of four years of work experience, and only 9 percent of those studied were not working, looking for work, caring for children, or disabled. Thus, it is not for lack of intent to work that people have found themselves on the welfare rolls.

7. Much as the British were successful in using the "orange card" in the north of Ireland to play off the Protestant-loyalist community against the Catholic-nationalist community.

12

Down by Law?

*History and Prophecy about
Organizing in Hard Times
and a Hostile Legal Order*

William E. Forbath

L ABOR'S FLAG is deepest red, as Richard Rorty reminds us in
this volume, and nowhere redder than in the United States,
where state violence against strikes and union organizing in the
nineteenth and early twentieth centuries was greater than anywhere
in Europe. The nation's courts were the architects of this labor policy, locking trade unions in a state of semi-outlawry, suppressing
peaceful boycotts and strikes, and voiding statutory reforms as unconstitutional.

The legal climate is harsh once more. In law, as in Faulkner nov-
els, the past is never dead. Even the liberal Warren Court never
looked kindly on organized labor and workers' collective action. But
today the right to organize is practically extinct, as old nineteenth-
century doctrines and values enjoy renewed vigor in the hands of
conservative judges and employers' attorneys.

Yet organizing the unorganized is the hope of the labor movement, now as in the past. Above all, the labor movement has its
sights on the millions of low-wage, largely new immigrant workers
in cities like my hometown, Los Angeles, where AFL-CIO helms-
man John Sweeney's Service Employees International Union, with its

Justice for Janitors Campaign, has scored great victories and become a model of sorts for organized labor's renewal. Those victories revealed the restiveness and organizing prowess of these workers. But they also revealed the extraordinary hurdles that the nation's legal order puts in the way of union organizers. Organizing along conventional legal lines means an endlessly protracted, procrastinating National Labor Relations Board bargaining-unit determination and supervised union-election process. Any determined employer can stymie the process, and pro-union workers have no real protection from reprisals. Faced with this reality, the SEIU turned to bold industry-wide, community-based strategies outside the framework created by the National Labor-Management Relations Act.

They re-invented the kind of organizing campaigns forged by unions of unskilled new immigrant workers at the end of the last century who also confronted a hostile, sometimes savage legal order. This earlier generation of immigrant workers often defied the law; their whole strategies were hedged with illegalities, and they confronted this situation in canny, imaginative ways that bear revisiting. Drawing on these experiences as well as the experiences of current campaigns like Justice for Janitors, I'll discuss some of the legal, political, and moral challenges ahead, in light of precedents we may have forgotten. I will address myself here, as I often do in L.A., especially to those who are thinking about a career in union organizing or union lawyering.

The Old Order

We're accustomed to thinking about the nineteenth-century legal world as one of laissez-faire. Harking back to the framers' vision of constitutional courts protecting the rights of property and contract against turbulent legislative majorities and ill-considered reforms, the *Lochner*-era judiciary invalidated such labor reforms as hours laws. The courts enshrined the laissez-faire ideal of liberty of contract, and from a worker's perspective this meant the right to sell one's labor or starve. Otherwise, the law left the employment relationship austerely alone.

This laissez-faire picture is a misleading one, however. The law of employment was one of hierarchy and subordination, of status as much as free contract. While the United States developed into a burgeoning industrial nation, employment law remained lodged in the master's household, in treatises on "domestic relations." Courts mingled free-contract principles with the much older doctrines of master and servant. The common law of employment, courts conceded, bore the "marks of social caste." The master's relation to his servant, like his relation to the other members of his household, was one of governance, discipline, and control.

In judges' minds, the felt necessity of governing the industrial workplace, of disciplining an unruly workforce, often recently immigrated from rural settings overseas, and of subduing a trade-union movement intent on challenging employers' authority and setting work rules of its own — all made the old common law of master and servant resonate with modern times. So courts continued to recognize an employer's property interests in his employees' or servants' labor, his right to their loyalty and obedience, his right to enjoin and unleash state violence against their organizing efforts, and his virtually unbounded sway over their wages, hours, and conditions.

Hundreds of constitutional cases like *Lochner* saw the courts striking down maximum hours, minimum wages, and other reforms, and thousands of less visible cases saw them issuing antistrike decrees forbidding workers and "whomsoever" from doing "whatsoever" to carry out a strike or boycott that the court had condemned. The decrees were like tailormade criminal codes outlawing not only quitting "in concert" and picketing, but also holding meetings, singing union songs, supplying funds or food or other support to striking workers, and publishing the names of "unfair" employers.

When unemployed, workers continued to feel the sting of caste. The tens of thousands of wandering unemployed turned loose from the factories by the nation's first industrial depression, in 1877, brought forth one of the country's first campaigns for uniform state laws — the "tramp acts." By the 1890s, forty-four states had enacted such measures, which recast the crime of vagrancy from an emphasis on begging to one on wandering without work. "In just principle," the era's leading criminal-law treatise declared, "there is nothing which a government has more clearly the right to do than to compel the lazy to work; and there is nothing more absolutely beyond its jurisdiction than to fix the price of labor."

Thus, this separate political world of employment seemed to be as the legal commentators described it: devoid of citizenship. This rule of the courts over the core social relations of work and livelihood, invested with the permanence of fundamental law, and constitutionally walled off from the changeability of democracy, was a caste-ridden regime. And this gave the labor movement the aspect of a civil rights movement. It meant that organized labor had a certain vision and vocabulary of reform in common with blacks' and women's movements: a vision of autonomy and respect, of relations of mutuality, cooperation, and exchange based on equality with erstwhile masters; a rights rhetoric aimed against caste and legalized subordination; a right of access to decent work and decent livelihoods and to a measure of independence and shared authority in employment and economic life.

Indeed, by the 1880s, the predominantly old-stock, white-male labor movement had evolved a broadly inclusive vision of unionism, one that — ambivalently and haltingly — embraced women, the unskilled and new immigrants, and, in Southern cities like Richmond, the black working class. When labor organizations strove to advance this vital but fragile vision of economic citizenship through reform legislation, the courts struck down broad, class-based reforms again and again. When they strove to advance class-based unionism through broad strikes and boycotts, they were greeted by "government by [judicial] injunction," as courts ordered the suppression of such concerted activities. By outlawing labor's most potent economic weapons, courts helped deprive labor of the economic clout that could have underwritten a broader and less exclusive unionism. Limiting, demeaning, and demoralizing workers' capacities for broad social and political action, the legal order helped give the upper hand to those labor leaders, like Sam Gompers, who championed a more cautious, "pure and simple" craft-based unionism.

What joined Gompers to the most diehard labor radical, however, was the conviction that the judge-made industrial order was
illegitimate. Unionists of all stripes contributed to an alternate constitutional outlook, which held that the First, Thirteenth, and Four-
teenth Amendments condemned "government by injunction" and
the common law's sharp constraints on collective action. Not only
did this outlook transform defiance into dignified civil disobedience, but, not uncommonly, labor's exiled constitutional arguments
found favor among elected officials. In this way and others, unions
made headway within and around a hostile, archaic framework, and
canny lawyers helped open strategic space for organizing and helped
craft more democratic legal orders for the workplace in its interstices. These experiences, in turn, have provided precedents to which I
often turn in talking with organizers, law students, and graduate
students involved in the seemingly unprecedented kind of organizing
in the works in Los Angeles.

Organizing the Unorganized Today*

Measured by numbers of workers, Los Angeles is now the nation's
largest manufacturing city; it also is home to the largest single concentration of unorganized workers. Some 350,000 of them, mostly
Latino immigrants, form the low-wage base for the hundreds of
light-manufacturing firms in the city's Alameda Corridor, the
twenty-two-mile industrial stretch that runs from downtown to the
Long Beach Harbor. Wildcat strikes have brought thousands of
these workers under union contract, and now organizing the hundreds of thousands of manufacturing workers in the Alameda Corridor is the ambition of a nine-union effort known as LA MAP — for
the Los Angeles Manufacturing Action Plan. LA MAP enjoys the
support of some of labor's biggest names: the United Auto Workers,

*This section draws on the journalism of my friend Jon Sawyer, chief of the Wash-
ington, D.C., bureau of the *St. Louis Post-Dispatch* and a great chronicler of American life.

the Teamsters, the Food and Commercial Workers, the Machinists, the Oil, Chemical, and Atomic Workers, the Steelworkers, and UNITE, the new combined union of textile workers. Indeed, many in the labor movement view LA MAP as the testing ground for John Sweeney's formula for the renewal of organized labor.

After all, LA MAP takes its inspiration largely from Local 399 of Sweeney's SEIU. That union's Justice for Janitors campaign, with its community-based, industry-wide organizing and in-your-face tactics, won contracts for thousands of Los Angeles' mostly Latino office-cleaning janitors. Joel Ochoa Perez, LA MAP's lead organizer, is a long-time union activist who left Mexico in the 1970s and became a U.S. citizen last year. For him, the Justice for Janitors campaign confirmed the central importance of "organizing beyond the workplace, reaching workers in their community associations and churches, their soccer leagues and country-of-origin clubs." Equally important was Justice for Janitors' strategy of organizing the entire industry and fighting for an industry-wide contract, instead of following the usual model of seeking union recognition through shop- or firm-based elections certified by the National Labor Relations Board. "If you organize shop by shop," Ochoa Perez explains, "you pull workers into a vacuum, where there are plenty of other workers out there who can replace them. Organizing shop by shop also means that the employer always will feel he can't afford a union wage because his competitors aren't paying one."

In effect, then, LA MAP will be applying, on the manufacturing side, much of the Service Employees' model for broad-based organizing among low-paid, largely immigrant workers. Friendly skeptics point out that it's easier to picket a posh downtown office building than a no-name sweatshop in south L.A. It's also a lot easier to move the sweatshop than to transplant the office building. Many of the industries populating the Alameda Corridor are intensely competitive ones. True, many of the employers are pursuing low-wage strategies that lock them into destructive kinds of competition with one another. But how can a union movement dislodge employers from these low-wage tracks without driving the firms and jobs away entirely to other shores, where wages are lower still? How can the unions deal all at once with global competition, a polyglot, often suspicious workforce — along with a hostile legal system?

Some Precedents

These questions are not new. Several times over the last century, comparable conditions confronted upstart unions aiming to organize immigrant workers in industrial districts like those of Los Angeles. In the early decades of this century, as now, there were many who insisted that the forces of market and international competition doomed the idea of creating unions in industrial districts like L.A.'s. *Don't talk union. The company will close up shop. Besides, these are immigrants. They're thinking about going home, buying land. They're not interested in unions. And they'll be at one another's throats.* But the history of these undertakings suggests that the oracles of ethnic and market determinism were wrong. There were shattering failures, but there were enduring successes. And what made the difference often was not the intensity of regional competition or the composition of the labor market. These operated as constraints, but looser than one might think. Other supposedly "softer" variables often spelled the difference between failure and success: the creativity of local leaders and local rank-and-file; the dynamics of particular immigrant communities; the character of local and state politics; and the forging of fruitful alliances with middle-class reformers, politicians, shrewd employers, and employers' associations; and — yes — canny lawyering.

Los Angeles' food-processing industry — the canneries, commercial bakeries, and tortilla factories — is one that LA MAP has set its sights on. In the 1930s this same industry saw thousands of Mexican and Mexican-American women workers band together with other immigrant women to create a network of effective, democratic unions. Not only did they forge effective bargaining relations; their unions also managed to negotiate maternity leaves and paid vacations, day care and a health insurance plan. How did they manage this?

Vicki Ruiz has reconstructed the story; her *Cannery Women* suggests that these unions succeeded largely because the immigrant women played a role at every level of union leadership, from shop steward to international vice president. The reasons were strategic. The women leaders could tap the strengths of the canneries' workplace cultures. They included their fellow workers in union decision-making, and they held the union brass to its commitment to entrust Chicana and other immigrant shop floor leaders with large responsibilities.

When the cannery workers' union, the UCPAW, set about organizing L.A.'s cannery workers, it campaigned across the whole industry, much as Justice for Janitors has done and LA MAP envisions doing. Thus, when UCPAW struck, it struck for recognition and a contract covering every cannery employer. During the long strike, the shop floor organizer Carmen Bernal Escobar was head of the food committee, wheedling generous contributions of food for strikers from the grocers of East Los Angeles. This was good advertising from the grocers' perspective. The cannery workers had kin throughout the community. The food drive's success spurred Escobar's committee on to new strategies. She and her fellow workers began to approach grocery managers all around L.A. and East L.A., urging them to refuse to sell the products of plants that did not recognize the union. Many agreed. Those which didn't would find a small band of women picketing their stores during business hours. The food committee became the boycott committee and scored well, enlisting the cooperation of countless grocers.

In general, wherever you find ethnic communities and nearby industries producing goods that the communities consume, you have fertile fields for boycotting. But union-led boycotts are sharply hedged by legal restraints today, as they were half a century ago. If union members picket shops, restaurants, or supermarkets that insist on carrying the products of a struck employer, the union can become liable for damages and the picketers subject to injunctions, arrests and fines, or jail. UCPAW avoided damage suits, but LA MAP, with its fuller coffers, may not be so lucky.

Union-led boycotts are hemmed in, but boycotts led by community supporters are not. Community organizations are not subject to the nation's labor laws, and recently the Supreme Court ruled that the First Amendment stanchly protects the boycotting activities of such organizations. Thus, LA MAP's Ochoa Perez may find new reasons for appreciating the strategic value of East L.A.'s soccer associations and country-of-origin clubs.

Of course, most of the industries LA MAP hopes to organize aren't vulnerable to traditional local consumer boycotts; they produce for a national market. That doesn't mean the boycott must be abandoned, as labor-community boycotts and "corporate campaigns" against national firms like GM, Coors Brewing, Farah Pants, J. P. Stevens, International Paper, and Hormel have shown; but it calls for more complex and aggressive tactics. Making such campaigns effective involves boycotting (and embarrassing publicity) aimed at banks, suppliers, retailers, advertisement carriers, and other firms connected in some way to the target employer.

Here again a legal thicket looms, and, again, building a labor-community coalition may prove the key, for legal as well as practical, political reasons. Practically, boycotts against large corporations rarely inflict serious economic injury; when the companies submit, they do so to control PR damage. And PR damage is greatest today when the workers' grievances are not represented solely as "labor" concerns but are linked to other movements. Thus, the UFW's grape boycott was not solely about unionization; it was about the human rights of Chicano migrants and immigrants. The Coors boycott embraced not only union recognition but also the demands of other groups on issues of discrimination, gay rights, and Coors's contributions to the Nicaragua contras. In 1986, the United Food and Commercial Workers, known more for hard-nosed pragmatism than social idealism, allied with the NAACP and African-American clergy and won the biggest organizing victory of the year at a Mississippi catfish-processing plant; the union president William Wynn summed up the strategy: organize "the community first and the plant second." Likewise, the GM/Van Nuys boycott, which succeeded in keeping open that company's last California plant, was framed around preserving decent jobs for the area's Latino, black, and women workers (who constituted over 70 percent of the work-force). Again, the boycott was led largely by clergy and community leaders, and because community organizations enjoy far greater legal freedom and First Amendment protection than do unions, their efforts were less vulnerable, while, at the same time, they had more political clout than a conventional "labor" boycott.

Organizing the Garment Trades in Early Twentieth-century New York — and Twenty-first-century Los Angeles

Ask any veteran organizer in the Los Angeles garment trades to name the main obstacles confronting LA MAP in that industry. She'll tell you: ethnic rivalries among workers and cut-throat competition among employers. Had you asked the leaders of New York City's Amalgamated Clothing Workers the same question seventy-five years ago, you'd have got the same reply. And the solutions they fashioned, brilliantly retrieved and recounted by Steven Fraser, remain notable. Italians and East European Jews were the industry's two major ethnic groups in early twentieth-century New York. Like L.A.'s Asian and Latino garment workers today, they had sharply different cultures as well as different places in the skill hierarchies of the trades.

Jewish men tended to be skilled craftsmen, like cutters, and to work in smaller shops; they often nursed the ambition of becoming petty manufacturers in their own right. Men from Southern Italy, by contrast, worked as semiskilled operatives in the larger factories in the centralized, capital-intensive sector of the industry; often believing their stay in America would be temporary, they had fewer entrepreneurial dreams than Jewish workers — or so the predominantly Jewish union leadership believed. While Italian men populated this modern branch of the industry, Italian women could be found toiling in the "medieval gloom" of the tenement workshop apartments that made up the industry's thriving premodern sector.

As with the industry's Asian and Latino workers in today's L.A., the existence of distinct ethnic niches created a daunting task for organizers. Given the cheap entry cost for petty entrepreneurs in this intensely competitive business — a few sewing machines and a rented loft — the contest focused on the costs and conditions of labor. Thus, smaller garment makers forever sought to underbid the bigger shops by reducing labor costs, and this led the large manufacturers to respond by farming out less-skilled work to homeworkers. As a result, Fraser points out, Italians and Jews could be pitted against one another, often unintentionally, because of their separate locations in the industry's structure. For the Amalgamated this meant that, as long as one group remained unorganized, unionism everywhere was imperiled.

But the impediments to organizing were many. Jews earned conspicuously more than Italians concentrated in semiskilled factory jobs and impoverished homework. Wisely, even before the Amalgamated was firmly established in the city's labor market, its Jewish organizers sold Jewish cutters and other skilled Jewish workers on the policy of demanding larger wage increases for the union's lowest-paid members, thus closing a gap that had aggravated ethnic tensions. LA MAP's organizers may do the same as they strive to create bonds between the city's Latino and Asian garment workers.

But like Latinos or Asians today, early twentieth-century New York's Italian workers also were divided among themselves. Back in Southern Italy, peasants from one village, who often viewed those from a neighboring town with intense suspicion, sometimes proved willing to scab on them in the brave new world of New York. To overcome such insularity, the Amalgamated worked with community organizers to engender a national identity among fellow immigrants — much as LA MAP works closely today with Guatemalan, Salvadoran, and other country-of-origin clubs. To foster such broader loyalties, the Amalgamated created "nationality locals." It combined this creation of broader ethnic ties with a left-wing version of Americanization, through newspapers and night classes that taught immigrants a new vocabulary of democratic participation and citizenship rights in industry and society. The union's educational program was no mere frill, but a serious effort that enlisted scores of New York's progressive intellectuals and academics to help

equip immigrant garment workers for self-rule and democratic culture at the workplace and beyond.

Here too LA MAP has a parallel vision. Ochoa Perez points with
relish to the vast numbers of Central American immigrants working
in the Alameda Corridor who have applied for citizenship under the
1986 amnesty program and soon will be full-fledged voters. Law
professors and law students have been active in teaching new immigrants to be their own advocates in the context of amnesty and citizenship applications. Living in small proletarian cities like Bell, these
citizens-to-be will constitute electoral majorities, or nearly so. With
hopes and desires educated by a common union culture, they could
hold sway in those cities and begin to reshape the L.A. area's politics.

Of course, New York's Amalgamated would not have survived
long if all it offered was night school. The union's success was en-
sured by what it offered employers as well as workers: a greater
measure of order and stability in a chaotic industry than employers
could attain by or for themselves. As in today's L.A., substandard
employers were a bane for other, particularly larger, firms, as well as
for their own employees. They cut corners on quality and safety,
drove workers beyond endurance, and gouged their wages. And
these practices, in turn, produced cycles of ruinous competition that
made the costs of production unpredictable and threatened quality
control throughout branches of the industry. Larger firms sought to
discipline such shoddy competitors on their own and failed. Only
the Amalgamated's industry-wide contract and its power to sanction
violations put competition on a healthy plane. Not only substandard
firms but testy workers' traditional forms of protest, the slow-down
and the "quickie strike," felt the union's new discipline. But, in
return, the union delivered a vastly better pay scale and a decent
grievance system.

Like their New York ancestor, after a few hard-fought battles, LA
MAP and UNITE may find a handful of firms far-sighted enough to
cooperate with the union in organizing the rest of the industry. This
also has been a key element of Justice for Janitors' success: seeking
control over all the key players in a local labor market and taking

labor costs out of competition. The slogan you'll find on Justice for Janitors' leaflets could have belonged to the Amalgamated: "One industry, one union, one contract."

To the employers in L.A.'s chaotic garment trades, LA MAP and UNITE hope to offer a deal similar to Amalgamated's. The firms get order and stability; the workers get better wages and a kind of "industrial self-government" in which they are citizens, not ciphers.

Of course, raising the possibility of such ambitious organizing recalls the warning that any union challenge will prompt the shops to pull up stakes and find cheaper labor beyond the borders and overseas. Goetz Wolf is director of UCLA's Center for Labor Research, where LA MAP is trying to find out hard facts about L.A.'s possible industrial future and whether such grim prophecies are sound. Graduate students working under Wolf and Gilda Hass, director of UCLA's Community Scholars program, spent the past year compiling a six-hundred-page dossier for LA MAP on the industrial sectors of the Alameda Corridor. Those familiar with the dossier call it a roadmap for industrial organizing: the industries and firms where profits are highest, those which depend on local suppliers or customers, those least likely to pull up stakes in the face of union challenge.

Several students focused on the garment trades; they found that in some sectors an organizing drive probably would produce an exodus of marginal firms. But in several thriving branches of L.A. garment making — women's sportswear and bathing suits, for example — quality control and the need to keep design, market, and "just in time" production in the closest possible proximity to one another have convinced manufacturers that pulling up stakes in search of cheaper labor "would be a disaster; they're staying put."

Even employers who are staying put are sure to resist unionization. The advantages of an industry-wide contract that puts competition on a plane that is better for them as well as their employees are advantages that most employers will have to be *forced* to appreciate.

Thus, industry-wide organizing will involve blistering publicity campaigns that employers will greet with libel suits and restraining orders; and hard-fought strikes, picketing, and militant protests that will be met by injunctions and mass arrests. Organizing, striking, and publicizing grievances outside the National Labor-Management Relations framework is still so unconventional that the borderlands of legality are barely lit. The law remains unfriendly, and the area is almost as hedged with illegalities as it was seventy-five years ago.

The Challenges of Democratic Advocacy

This will produce the kind of challenges lawyers everywhere prize, as well as challenges unique to lawyering for a democratic movement-in-the-making. Some seasoned advocates think this may be the context in which the federal courts finally resurrect the short-lived constitutional right to picket over a labor grievance — a right they recognized briefly in the 1940s but interred in the 1950s. The scanty First Amendment protection enjoyed by labor, as compared with community boycotts, rests on two shopworn notions. First, labor boycotts simply involve one self-interested economic actor seeking to inflict economic injury on another, whereas community boycotts involve matters of common public political concern like civil rights. Second, labor boycotts and labor picketing appeal to unthinking class feelings on the part of working-class consumers; they trigger a reflex, not a reasoned choice. Always laden with class prejudice, these notions seem especially vulnerable in the face of today's "corporate campaigns." As we've seen, this kind of organizing and boycotting has spawned labor-community alliances that dramatize the artificiality of the opposition of "economic" versus "political" or labor versus community protest. Thus, as the labor-law scholar Jim Pope has argued, campaigns like LA MAP may enable progressive attorneys to revive the courts' short-lived understanding of the public, political nature of labor grievances and weave the strands of First Amendment protection enjoyed by community-based pickets and civil rights protesters back into labor law.

Of course, in the context of ambitious campaigns like LA MAP and Justice for Janitors, pickets and protests are rarely the union's only weapon. Organizers often rely on litigation both as a shield to defend protesters and also, as one flinty union attorney I know put it, as a "brick" to hurl at recalcitrant employers. "We meet with workers and discuss their grievances," he explained. "Maybe they're forced to work twelve-hour days without overtime, or they're not being paid for all the time they have to be at work. Or maybe the company uses corrosive cleansers and other dangerous products without basic safety equipment. Almost always, a key grievance is also a clear violation of state or federal law. We discuss suing the employer. There is strength and visibility in numbers. If *everyone* sues, say, through a class action, 'the company cannot fire us all.'" And if it does, "we're already in court, and even conservative judges won't brook intimidation of parties in their courtroom."

The object is twofold. While the organizing drive is still under way, these suits or OSHA complaints show workers that the union will commit resources and bring results. At the same time, they "make the employer think about whether he'd rather be negotiating with the union, even a tough union, about these problems, instead of being hauled into court."

But what if the suit threatens to drive the employer out of business? "We'll know that," my friend explains. "We'll discuss it with the workers. Either it's a firm with a decent margin that can afford the remedy, or, if not, sometimes the workers will decide against suing. But often they'll end up reasoning as the union does: better to drive out marginal firms that super-exploit us. The buildings must still be cleaned, and the new contractor may be better heeled and, anyway, can't be worse than this one."

Sometimes the issues are knottier and the transformative possibilities surprising. I know an employment discrimination lawyer who has been working with employees involved in campaigns to organize California's fruit pickers. Pro-union workers asked him to prepare a sex-discrimination case against some of the most recalcitrant employers.

"All these growers rely on old-fashioned *padrone*-headed Latino family networks to supply their workers. The work is seasonal," the lawyer explains, "and they have an unbending custom of 'calling back' the men a good month or two ahead of the women. That's how the *padrones* want it, and the employers are glad to oblige. All seem to agree the men need the work most. The only problem is that the practice plainly violates Title VII." As with the safety and hours suits filed by Justice for Janitors, the union aims to show it's a force to reckon with, looking after workers' interests from every angle and forcing employers to rethink whether they wouldn't rather be negotiating and solving problems together instead of litigating.

But is that how the workers see it? Don't the Latino men have a stake in the system as it is? "Of course the *padrones* have a stake, but there are many cross-cutting forces. There are generational conflicts. The old extended family is disintegrating. Many Latinas are single mothers; the system only injures them. And like elsewhere, in the strawberry fields women are the biggest union supporters, and these suits have galvanized them. 'The union says the call-backs are illegal!'

"The idea isn't simply to dismantle the *padrone* system; it's putting something better in its place." The lawyer pauses. "I had a client in a suit like this a few years ago, a single mom, a Latina. We prevailed. 'Thanks,' she said. 'Now, I can go out and break my back for shit wages just like the men.'"

"She was just reminding me that my noble civil rights' lawyering looked a lot like simply rationalizing the harsh capitalist labor market. I was picking up the pieces of a disintegrating culture and plugging them, like little atomistic units, into the system. This may be different. The plaintiffs, dozens of them, are union activists; they think there's a shot at making a new culture, a new social organization where they'll belong."

Litigation like this is heady, forging new law, putting one's clients and the union on TV news. Other aspects of union lawyering can be less splashy but no less challenging. During organizing campaigns or in the context of an active rank-and-file, union lawyers constantly field questions about whether some contemplated protest or job action is legal. What will happen if we go on a quickie strike here, or throw up a picket line there? Nothing is more common in some old-guard unions than union counsel concluding that a particular tactic presents too great a risk of liability; the tactic is nixed by the union chiefs, and the organizer who proposed it feels the judgment call was usurped by the honchos, though the risks belong to the whole union. Whose counsel are you — the union's or the union leadership's? What happens when rank-and-file activists and shop-floor leaders want to know about the legality of a particular action? The tactical judgments of union officials may diverge from these others. But isn't the rank-and-file also entitled to your knowledge and counsel? In a corporation the same kind of question may not arise so sharply, because the premise is hierarchical. The boss is in charge; he gets your counsel. But the union's premise is democratic, and that creates unique challenges.

Of course, in many unions today officials are only too aware that bold organizing strategies, combined with an energizing internal democracy, offer the only path away from extinction. They don't need to be convinced that cautious, hierarchical "contracts are us" unionism is doomed. But being a lawyer for one of today's new model unions won't insulate you from dilemmas. You surely will face a fiery young organizer eager to throw up a picket line around a "secondary," and your job will be to offer a hard-headed assessment of possible consequences. Much as it did a century ago, the legal net can close with punishing swiftness around a few ill-placed pickets, and if the union has previously violated rules against "secondary picketing," that net can drag in the entire union treasury and its freedom to operate at all in a given city. Thus, if the old-guard union lawyer must remember that the risks he cautions against are not his risks, the new-model union organizer needs to remember that the risks aren't hers either. The challenge is one of enabling and prodding the union to act with well-informed imagination that avoids needless legal risk (using attention-grabbing costumes and pamphlets instead of picket signs, for example), and a decision-making process that ensures that risks are worth taking and are both well- and democratically reflected upon.

Democratic challenges will continue in other phases of this work. Once unions gain recognition and a first contract, fashioning grievance procedures will become part of the order of the day. As the technicians of process, lawyers will play a critical role here. But as every lawyer knows, process is never only technical. The shape of the process determines what counts as an injury or a claim, how it gets framed, and who gets heard. Unlike their predecessors in the 1910s, those who craft grievance procedures for the unions of the 1990s and 2000s will have decades of experience to draw upon. Their challenge will be to learn from this rich history something about the ways that grievance procedures can bureaucratize unions and undermine democracy, sapping unions' energies and severing the links between officials and constituents — and how they can empower workers and their representatives and enable workplaces to become fairer, more deliberative, and cooperative. As democratic technicians, the lawyers will be called on to connect the plumbing of process to the cosmos of unionism's highest values.

Of course, if creating such local institutions of workplace democracy, like engaging in broad-gauged organizing without legal protection and in the teeth of many potential prohibitions, are real possibilities today, they could be made vastly easier by labor-law reforms. Organizing the unorganized should not entail enormous costs for unions or for unorganized workers themselves; it shouldn't put livelihoods at risk or require elaborate lawyering and publicity campaigns.

Organizing is so costly because our labor laws supply no real protection for the shrinking proportion of the nation's workers whose organizing rights they ostensibly protect, yet they enable any determined employer to kill an organization that tries to follow the legally prescribed path toward union election and representation. But our labor laws could be changed to embrace those currently excluded, like the growing ranks of domestic workers in today's increasingly unequal society, like the casualized and contingent workers whose numbers are also burgeoning with the explosion of contracting-out and the disappearance of internal labor markets and promotion paths, and like those currently dubbed "independent contractors" or "supervisors," including college teachers and many others in need of a collective voice today. And our labor laws readily could be reformed to make the organizing campaign and the collective choice of a union much less costly and fraught with risks.

For example, the present union election system requires organizers to sign up a substantial number of employees before they can petition the labor board for a certification election; even if the union can produce cards signed by an overwhelming majority of workers, the employer isn't required to recognize and deal with the union on the basis of that informal showing. Rather, the showing merely alerts the employer that an organizing effort is under way and invites it to mount a protracted and threatening countercampaign. We could eliminate these countercampaigns.

Most Canadian jurisdictions rely simply on the union's authorization cards for certification. The labor board just checks to see whether a majority of employees was signed up as of the date the union applied. Two Canadian provinces have a somewhat more elaborate procedure, one that many United States reform advocates favor. These provinces use the quickie election; that is, if the union has more than a bare majority ready to sign up and pay a minimum fee as a token of seriousness, then the board conducts an immediate election. That way, employees still get an opportunity to have second thoughts and can express their final views in the secrecy of the voting booth, but there is no extended campaign during which management can pressure employees. The choice, after all, is properly theirs.

Similarly, reform advocates point to current Canadian proposals for "sectoral bargaining." Aimed especially at traditionally low-wage, underrepresented sectors, which often combine highly dispersed work sites with highly uniform work conditions, these proposals would enable a union demonstrating support among workers at different sites to bargain jointly with all the employers. In subsequent organizing during the term of the resulting contract, union certification at additional sites would automatically add the employers at these sites to the group covered by the contract, and the employers would join in the multi-employer bargaining in the next round. This reform would enable unions to bring the benefits of wage stability and the "leveling up" of competition to industries like office cleaning, without the needlessly arduous, costly, and conflict-ridden organizing required of Justice for Janitors today.

But just as the Civil Rights Act of 1964 and the Voting Rights Act of 1965 were not passed until the civil rights movement had mobilized support and mounted protests throughout the country, so it is likely that labor law reform will happen only when and if the labor movement once more takes on the aspect of a civil rights movement. That will require many more costly campaigns like Justice for Janitors and LA MAP; it will need hundreds of democratic technicians and imaginative organizers. And it will also demand that thousands of academics and intellectuals enlist again, ready to hand out pamphlets, to picket and get arrested, to publicize local union struggles, and to build a new national movement.

13

Beyond Identity Politics
A Modest Precedent

Todd Gitlin

L ABOR'S REVIVAL is good news not only for unorganized
workers but for most of the identity-based interest groups that
have flourished over the last quarter-century. For all their
achievements, surely minority interests have bumped up against distinct limits. Self-evidently, a common cause is desirable, yet in recent
years it has been hard to imagine the means. To call for a common
politics is one thing; to envision how the disparate elements come
together is another. But surely, if there is to be a powerful confluence,
it cannot do without labor.

Over the past quarter-century, the politics of group interest has
worked to the benefit of many women, African Americans, Latino
Americans, and Asian Americans, gays and lesbians, and the disabled. Their access to skilled jobs and higher education has generally
improved, especially among the educated middle classes. Members
of these groups are more visible and more legitimate; they play a
larger part in the "imagined community" that constitutes the nation.
Rank prejudice and social discrimination exist, but in weakened
form. Members of these groups have been recognized by the wider
society, and in particular by its powerful institutions — corporations, government agencies, universities, and other cultural gate-
keepers. Although these gains are commonly attributed to the assertions of interest groups, they both rest on the broader foundations

laid by the civil rights movement — demands for the universal achievement of individual rights and the inalienable rights of all Americans.

In the 1980s, the term *identity politics* came into use as a rubric for the common thrust of all these assertions and recognitions. The common denominator is the assumption that political positions and energies follow, and ought to follow, from membership in the groups to which people feel they belong. The term actually has a spectrum of meanings. In its loosest sense, it applies to the assumption that members of the group should band together to pursue their common interest. In its strictest sense, the assumption is that the group's identity is the only, or the overwhelming, motivating force for political action. In what follows, I use the term in the stricter sense, and ask how the limits of this sort of identity politics can be overcome.

Since the good of the whole society is in part a function of the well-being of the members of historically discriminated-against populations, the politics of group interest may be said to have been a considerable success. It has delivered a lot of goods — from university admissions to employment in police and fire departments, from bilingual signs to reforms in the development of AIDS drugs and facilities for the handicapped. But the cost of the emphasis on narrowly defined group differences — identity politics in its strict form — has been steep, and barely acknowledged by uncritical partisans. Partly because identity politics has been relatively successful, and partly because conditions have been inhospitable to a more common politics, there is an imbalance between the politics of group assertion and the politics of commonality. Political campaigns that require successful alliances — majoritarian alliances — have overall *not* developed. The poor, whose resources for successful interest-group politics are fewer, tend to get short shrift. Identity politics has improved the coloration and sex distribution of the wealth pyramid but left its shape untouched. Inequality is the issue that barely dares whisper its name. The suburbs are happy to walk away from the cities, the voters from the nonvoters, the winners from the losers. The social state withers; let the devil take those with the bad taste to be born poor, whether they work or not. The catastrophic defeat of health care and the dismantling of meager welfare guarantees underscore the progressive pathos.

Granted, the last two decades would have been a difficult time for a left politics of commonality in any case. Social reforms like school, health, and housing improvements usually require spending as a necessary though not sufficient condition, but Americans, wrongly convinced that they pay the highest taxes in the industrial world (in fact, we are among the least taxed), and often recoiling against minorities, have been in a revolting mood toward taxes since California voters passed Proposition 13 in 1978. Yet surely, if some of the energy devoted to cultivating difference had been devoted over recent years to attempting to bring together center-left majorities — if we had seen a Million Patient March for health care or a Million Parent March for school aid — we would not find ourselves reduced to shoring up a fragile welfare state against depredations still worse than the last season's, or protecting a status quo program, Social Security, against privatization.

Again, it would be foolish to pretend either that a politics of equality is bound to succeed or that it is easily undertaken. Identity politics carries its satisfactions. It cannot be lightly discarded for transient reasons. Inevitably, people turn to politics partly for the emotional solidarities they find there, and identity politics invokes solidarities and capitalizes on those which already exist. It plays upon a community of the similar. It starts with a sense of anchorage. It traces roots to the past. It points to a history of victimization — white supremacy, male supremacy, hatred of gays. Whether the principle of community is ethnicity, religion, sex, or sexuality, people find warmth and lineage in a world composed of those who resemble themselves. Having been stigmatized because of skin color, physical size and dependency, sexual preference, and so on, they naturally want to defend themselves by trying to turn the stigma into a point of advantage. In a world in which everyone seems to have been assigned an identity card at birth, who doesn't want to sign up for her own card? So the political weakness of the sum of identity groups is offset by day-to-day satisfactions. There are political successes and well-rewarded posts: the material and symbolic rewards of traditional interest-group politics.

In other words, actually existing identity politics delivers some goods. All the more reason why, after a full generation, identity politics has become a sort of tradition, institutionalized and built, in turn, on a historically weak national identity and a pluralism reared on immigration — language groups, ethnic-based machines, cultural diversity in the American grain.[1] University politics enshrines this tradition. A full generation of activists takes it for granted. Especially in university settings, where there are few penalties for militancy, it is relatively safe — and remarkably successful. Meanwhile, the politics of the common interest feels, to most people, abstract. It may sound like a good idea but it doesn't feel like much, because people tend not to live it. The payoffs for a politics of commonality remain largely hypothetical.

Still, the central effort for a progressive left-of-center must be a move against avoidable poverty and stupendous inequality of wealth and income. Hence our present dilemma. How can people organized around their differences from others coalesce with those others toward common ends? For so they must if they are to focus their resources — whether on material matters like paying for health care or raising living standards, or, for that matter, on matters of social discrimination. It is almost certainly most effective to argue against antigay legislation (like the Colorado initiative, later ruled unconstitutional by the Supreme Court, that would have prevented cities from banning discrimination against gays) by claiming the American value of tolerance and by labeling discrimination un-American. To win profoundly, identity politics must partake of a built-in paradox: based on minority identities, it must make claims on people regardless of *their* identities. Having come into being for defense of the group, it must resist the temptations of group self-absorption.

The moral core of the situation is clear. Each identity deserves a certain recognition. Under the dispensation of the much-maligned

Enlightenment, it is a modern right of individuals to be taken as they wish to be taken.[2] This is also a modern fact from which even universalist movements are not exempt. As Craig Calhoun has argued, workers traditionally demanded rights on the ground of what they felt to be an identity: *workers*.[3] Moreover, workers have often organized strongly when they shared religious or ethnic identities.[4] It is not to trivialize either the moral or the factual point to insist, at the same time, that identity politics has its limits. It may be necessary for workers to affirm a distinct ethnic or sex identity — but it is not sufficient. Such affirmations may, in fact, prove divisive. (In the extreme case, the use of African Americans as strikebreakers is depressingly traditional.) To say that identity politics ought to be transcended is not to say that it has no place, or that its place is unimportant. But its place is not every place. Difference is best expressed in a setting where commonality is also secured. An extremely diverse polity demands not only communities where people may, if they choose, express their cultural distinctness, but also a political community in which citizens cross boundaries, and where the essential means to a decent life are available to all.

Of all the prerequisites for overcoming the limits of identity politics, the most important is a revival of labor. The centrifugal tendencies of identity politics batten on the weakness of organized labor, and have a tendency to set group against group and weaken organized labor further. The good news is that labor, which ought to be the single most ecumenical institution for bringing diverse people together, wants to revive and is serious about reviving. The new leadership of the AFL-CIO asks for help. What higher priority can there be for intellectuals? A revival of union strength ought to be the single greatest priority for the progressive liberal left. Labor-law reform ought to be a priority, for unions' chances to sign up new members have been crippled by a generation of union-busters in power. There is not going to be any serious approach to shorter work weeks, work-sharing, democratic controls over corporate policies, health care, worker protection, or a reversal of the thrust toward inequality unless labor is rebuilt as a countervailing force. For the foreseeable future, labor is going to be the most important testing ground for a mobilization against greed.

Toward this end — reviving labor — working women and racial minorities will be crucial constituencies. Precisely because the population — not least the working class — is diverse, no large bloc is expendable. But this point applies to white males, too, who number roughly 37 percent of the population. The African-American population numbers about 12 percent. Blacks and whites, when surveyed about their opinion of the country's demographic makeup, systematically double the percentage — blacks, I would guess, out of their experience in a segregated world; whites, I think, more out of fear.[5] The fact remains that African Americans constitute a minority, and no wishful thinking or census projection changes this fact. Hispanics add up to another 10 percent (the public, regardless of ethnicity, overestimates this by 50 percent), and Asian Americans to another 3 percent (tripled or quadrupled by popular estimate). Not only are the numbers smaller than most people think, but the differences within these groups are themselves immense. South Florida Cubans and South Texas Chicanos do not constitute an automatic bloc, certainly not on class issues. Adding up abstract minorities does not automatically produce a victory for general justice.

These irrefutable but discomfiting facts produce a political problem. Oppressed and disadvantaged minorities are minorities. They win policies that work to their benefit when they persuade majorities. American history is replete with instances of minorities submerging their particular claims, only to be forgotten, and this is always a risk. But it is much too easy to lose sight of the opposite risk, that of narrowness, and of the gains that have accrued to minorities when broad-based movements — in particular, labor — have been strongest. The question is how to knit majorities into alliances where people understand that they need one another in crucial respects — although they are different, even at times somewhat antagonistic, and will continue to differ on many grounds. Not to try creating the ground for progressive policies is to be doomed to marginality. But is there any reason to think that this ground may exist? Under what circumstances?

There is no magic bullet. But surely common ground on class issues can be found across race lines — or, better, common ground can be *made,* for it is not lying around in a state of nature, to be stumbled upon like nuggets fallen from a rainbow. It has to be created by organizers who are self-conscious about the urgency of forging cross-identity links, committed to the difficult work of overcoming group rancor and forming alliances, flexible in their methods, mutually supportive, and willing to learn from mistakes. There are precedents. Perhaps I can best approach the question of how to transcend the divisiveness of identity politics with a slice of recollection about some modest successes of the past. The story may offer a clue — not a formula for surmounting present-day dilemmas, but a way to think about how to proceed.

In 1966, I was writing and working as a community organizer in the Uptown area of Chicago, an impoverished neighborhood on the North Side where unemployment and crime were high, housing was decrepit, and many people depended on welfare. The majority of the residents were white, many of them recent arrivals from the Appalachian South, some from elsewhere in the South. Many were overtly racist and were not shy about saying so. It was common to hear, in communities of this sort, that the civil rights movement had "gone too far" in seeking, for example, to integrate housing. The community organization JOIN had been started by Students for a Democratic Society as part of the Economic Research and Action Project, a national attempt to organize what we immodestly hoped might turn out to be "an interracial movement of the poor." There were about a dozen more or less full-time organizers in Uptown, in loose association with another dozen each in both white and black neighborhoods in Cleveland, Newark, Baltimore, Boston, and, at various times, smaller numbers in Philadelphia and Chester in Pennsylvania, Hoboken in New Jersey, Cairo in Illinois, Louisville and Hazard in Kentucky, and Oakland in California.

ERAP sprang from a perception of the black movement's dilemma. By 1963, it was clear to much of the civil rights leadership that the movement was in the process of winning its original demand to abolish legalized segregation. And then what? The movement was going to suffer from success. From then on, the central social problems affecting African Americans would be economic. In the motto of the time, what good was the right to sit at a lunch counter if you couldn't afford the price of the hamburger? (This was before environmentalist consciousness, and hardly anyone questioned whether hamburgers were the best food either for eaters or the planet.) The great August 28, 1963, March on Washington was, after all, called the March on Washington *for Jobs and Freedom,* the word *jobs* coming first.

One of the first, if not the first, to come up with the idea of organizing the white poor into alliance with the black poor was Stokely Carmichael, a rising star in the Student Nonviolent Coordinating Committee (SNCC), at a meeting that same month with the recent SDS president Tom Hayden. The formula was "Whites should organize whites" — which begged the difficult question: organize around what? Implicitly, the answer was: common needs. In the meantime, before the enunciation of Black Power (also by Stokely Carmichael) in 1966, it was still possible for white organizers to live and organize in black communities; Hayden and others went on to do just that in the heart of the Newark ghetto.

The governing assumption was that the needs of blacks required radical changes in the economy, but the question had to be raised: where was the political support for such changes to come from? There were, of course, liberals who (so we thought) could be counted on — in the churches, unions, and liberal city and state Democratic organizations. But the engine of the necessary coalition would have to be the poor themselves — and since a majority of the poor were (and remain) white, the white poor would have to be mobilized into an alliance with the black poor around concerns they shared.

In SDS, we were not naïve about the racism of poor whites. The struggle against the Klan-ridden, fire-bombing, cross-burning, murderous white South was formative to our sense of ourselves. Many of us had done civil rights work in the heart of the South and had organized support campaigns for the courageous SNCC workers. We knew that the Populist alliances of the 1890s had been wrecked because push came to shove; the whites, once defeated, had turned on the blacks. C. Vann Woodward's *Tom Watson, Agrarian Rebel* told that story all too poignantly. We knew something of the history of Bourbon Southern elites tossing poor whites a subordinate caste to despise — "You've got more than the blacks; don't complain," in the words of Bob Dylan, who caught this mentality in his perfectly named and duly noted song "Only a Pawn in Their Game."

From the beginning of the ERAP projects, in other words, we were aware that poor whites were a volatile population who could go either way. We tried to look on the bright side. We hoped that the Abolitionist history of the Appalachians might rub off. We looked for signs of flexibility. The organizers, most of whom had had experience in the civil rights movement, frequently wondered what to do about it. There were two strategies, (though even by calling them strategies I am making them sound more deliberate than they were).

One was to counteract racism by bringing Uptown whites and blacks from outside the neighborhood into contact at early stages of organizing so that the notion of a common struggle would have a palpable form. At the inception of JOIN in 1964, when the thought was to organize the unemployed and demand "Jobs or Income Now," comparable to Chicago's JOIN on the (largely white) North Side, there was to be a unit on the (largely black) South Side funded by the United Packinghouse Workers, with a black union staffer. That office, however, got nowhere. Twice we brought together white and black community people from the various projects at national meetings so that they could get accustomed to common discussions across race lines; these were inspiring, though occasional. The JOIN organizers had frequent contact with Southern Christian Leadership Conference staff members who had been sent to Chicago as an advance party, preparatory to Martin Luther King, Jr.'s open housing campaign. Some of the more committed Uptown community people, along with organizers from black community organizations elsewhere in the city, came along to these gatherings. Race relations were reasonably cooperative. At this time, the SCLC leadership in Chicago was black (led by the Reverend James Orange), but there were also white organizers on staff.

During the summer of 1966, some of our staff, led by Rennie Davis and Bob Lawson, were trying to organize young white men. They were pretty tough, these "young guys," as we called them — hard drinkers, few with regular jobs, the toughest of them (and the one with the biggest following, it seemed) in and out of jail. Since their most deeply felt grievance pertained to police brutality, that was the issue on which the organizers worked. Copying a tactic that had been used in Watts, we organized a community patrol, driving around behind police cars on weekend nights, with cameras and notepads at the ready. Eventually, we decided to organize a march on the local police station, calling for an end to police brutality and demanding the punishment of one particularly menacing cop. At the same time, similar campaigns were being mounted in other parts of the city — by organizations that were almost exclusively African American. In the course of this campaign, the organizers took the Uptown street leaders to meetings with their black counterparts.

We discovered something simple. When the Uptown whites felt they had achieved forward motion, they stopped race-baiting black allies. They were suddenly willing to enter into coalitions. By the same token, when the campaign against police brutality produced no results, and it looked as though there would be no payoff for keeping the coalition together, race-baiting returned, along with other varieties of grumbling, all-around bitterness, and gloom.

The second move required racial integration from the start, in the heart of the organization. This dynamic developed with welfare organizing. Women in Uptown, like others around the city, began to organize for increased allotments (in 1966, Illinois allotted twenty-two cents per child per meal) and against punitive rules. In the JOIN welfare group, two of the most active and talented women were black. Their centrality to the welfare rights group threw white women into a quandary. If they were to insist on expressing bigoted attitudes, they would have to forgo working in the organization. If, on the other hand, they worked with these black women, they might see some results. It was too soon for them to see material rewards; that would take time. But by working in an active, sensible, productive interracial group, they felt momentum — the sense that they were on the move, that cooperation and the direct expression of solidarity had serious prospects. This coalition held together for years. So did similar groups in Cleveland, the site of ERAP's other main attempt at organizing poor whites.

In one case, cross-racial coalition from without; in the other, cross-racial coalition from within. The second lasted longer, though there was more than one reason for that: the welfare mothers were a steadier, more stable group than men in their teens and early twenties. In both cases, the concrete results were subject to all the limits of 1960s' organizing in general. But the point is that, in both cases, the whites who were organized into coalitions with blacks were not supposed to have been interested in or capable of doing that at all. A few steadfastly antiracist organizers countered conventional wisdom. On the issues of police brutality and welfare reform, the results were certainly no worse for cross-race coalitions than for all-black organizations. Arguably, they were better.

These were tiny experiments by a handful of organizers. What are the implications for today? What more might be possible with a coherent application of energy and care by a new generation of union and community organizers? If anything, the lessons of cross-racial organizing might apply better to labor today than in the 1960s. Workplaces today are racially more diverse than neighborhoods; this implies that multiracial, multiethnic, multisex organizing is more likely to succeed on the job than elsewhere. Even where a workforce (and therefore a union local) is relatively homogeneous, union representatives from various locals have to work out forms of cooperation in order to make progress beyond the local level. In this sense, labor is probably the most fruitful area in which to test the potential of a politics beyond segmented identity.

Meanwhile, invigorated labor should be pressed to support the just demands of identity groups, to put the spirit of movement back in the labor movement, to renew labor's claim to bearing in mind the people's whole interest. Campaigns to raise the minimum wage, and to require localities to pay living wages, set a good precedent; but labor needs to campaign for affordable housing, health care, and child care as well. Labor has the difficult but not impossible task of siding with the excluded while it also serves as the voice of the half-included. Asking this of labor is only just, but it is most effectively done from within the labor movement and not against it.

In truth, we know very little about what could be achieved by moving beyond the politics of identity. What we do know, after a generation of experience on the left, are the self-limitations of identity politics and the existence of largely untested possibilities. My appeal to those who have tilled the ground of identity as the core of their practical politics is twofold: first, to consider whether diminishing returns have set in, and second, to consider whether their achievements have (rhetoric aside) presupposed the existence of broad-gauged coalitions that are threatened and need to be tended. Can we try to find out what else might be possible? If not now, when?*

Notes

1. I have elaborated on this history in Chapter 2 of my *Twilight of Common Dreams: Why America Is Wracked by Culture Wars* (New York: Metropolitan–Henry Holt, 1995).

2. Charles Taylor, *Multiculturalism and "The Politics of Recognition"* (Princeton: Princeton University Press, 1992).

3. Craig Calhoun, "Social Theory and the Politics of Identity," in Calhoun, ed., *Social Theory and the Politics of Identity* (London, UK, and Cambridge, MA: Blackwell, 1994), p. 18.

4. For a recent example, see Roger Waldinger et al., "Justice for Janitors," *Dissent*, Winter 1997, pp. 37–44. In Los Angeles, the influx of Latinos into janitorial work increased the sense of workers' solidarity and boosted the union's prospects.

5. *Washington Post*, October 8, 1995, p. A1.

*The author thanks Steven Fraser, Michael Kazin, and Alan Sokal for their comments on an earlier draft of this essay.

14

The Labor of Whiteness, the Whiteness of Labor, and the Perils of Whitewashing

Michael Eric Dyson

BITTER CONFLICTS over the politics of identity are at the heart of contemporary debates about the labor movement, the political left, and the American academy. Such debates are often burdened by a truncated historical perspective that overlooks crucial features of the story of how identity politics, and the alleged special interests upon which such politics is said to rest, have come to dominate our intellectual and cultural landscape. This essay, then, has a modest ambition: to provide a small corrective to such stories by emphasizing how whiteness — which has reflexively, if unconsciously, been defined in universal terms — is composed of particular identities. These particular white identities have, until recently, been spared the sort of aggressive criticism that minority identities routinely receive. I will also argue that some critics of identity politics ignore these facts, and this ignorance smoothes the path for false accusations against blacks, women, and other minorities as the source of strife and disunity in the labor movement. Finally, I will suggest that, based on the uses of whiteness in the labor movement, the politics of identity was a problem long before the fuller participation of blacks and other minorities. Indeed, identity politics is most vicious when it is invisible, when it is simply part of the given, when it is what we take for granted.

One of the unforeseen, and certainly unintended, consequences of recent discussions of race is that we have come to question the identities, ideologies, and institutional expressions of whiteness.[1] For most of our national history, the term *race* has meant *black*. The collapse of the meanings of blackness into the term *race* has led to a myriad of intellectual blind spots, not only in the narrow conceptualization of black identity, but in the severe lack of attention paid to how whiteness serves as a source of racial identity. The result of this is a cruel irony: whiteness, the most dominant and visible of American racial identities, has been rendered intellectually invisible, an ideological black hole that negates its self-identification as one among many other racial identities. In the absence of viewing themselves as having a race, many whites latched onto citizenship as a vital means of self-definition. Whites were individuals and Americans; blacks, Latinos, Native Americans, and other minorities were collectively defined as members of racial and ethnic subgroups. Whiteness had a doubly negative effect: it denied its racial roots while denying racial minorities their American identities.

Prior to conceiving of whiteness as a social construct — as a historically mediated cultural value that challenges the biological basis of white identity — most blacks and whites viewed whiteness as a relatively fixed identity. For blacks, the meaning of whiteness was singularly oppressive. The varied expressions of whiteness were viewed as the elaboration of a single plot: to contain, control, and, at times, to destroy black identity. For whites, their racial identities were never as concretely evoked or sharply defined as when the meanings of blackness spilled beyond their assigned limitations to challenge white authority. In part, whiteness was called into existence by blackness; a particular variety of whiteness was marshaled as a defensive strategy against black transgression of sanctified racial borders. At the least, whiteness was tied to blackness, its hegemonic meanings symbolically linked to a culture it sought to dominate. As a result, blackness helped expose the dominant meanings of whiteness and helped reveal the meaning of whiteness as domination.

To be sure, whiteness as domination had many faces, though the body of belief they fronted shared profound similarities. White supremacist ideology united poor whites in the hoods of the Ku Klux Klan and sophisticated scholars in robes in the halls of academe. Still, if domination was the hub of the meaning of whiteness, there were many spokes radiating from its center. First, there was *whiteness as the positive universal versus blackness as the negative particular*. On this view, the invisibility of whiteness preserved both its epistemic and ethical value as the embodiment of norms against which blackness was measured. White styles of speech, behavior, belief, and the like were defined as universal standards of human achievement; their origins in particular ethnic communities were successfully masked. Through this meaning of whiteness, whites were able to criticize blacks for their failure to be human, not explicitly for their failure to be white, although in principle the two were indistinguishable.

Then there was *whiteness as ethnic cohesion and instrument of nation-making*. This meaning of whiteness consolidated the fragmented cultures of white European ethnics and gave social utility to the ethnic solidarity that the myth of whiteness provided. The genius of unarticulated, invisible whiteness is that it was able to impose its particularist perspective as normative. Thus, the resistance of blacks, Latinos, and Native Americans to absorption into the white mainstream was viewed by whites as viciously nationalistic, while white racial nationalism managed to remain virtuously opaque.

Next, there was *whiteness as proxy for an absent blackness it helped to limit and distort*. The accent in this mode of whiteness is on its power to represent the ideals, interests, and especially the images of a blackness it has frozen through stereotype, hearsay, and conspiracy. In important ways, this use of whiteness parallels Renato Rosaldo's description of imperialist nostalgia, where a colonial power destroys a culture, only to lament its demise with colonialism's victims.[2] In the present case, whiteness claims the authority to represent what it has ruined. The exemplars of this function of whiteness voice, instead of nostalgia, a presumptive right to speak for a minority it has silenced. Thus, there is a coercive representation by whiteness of the blackness it has contained. Needless to say, coercive representation often presents images that are feeble, distorted, or the idealizations of domesticated, colonized views of black life.

Finally, there was *whiteness as the false victim of black power*. This mode of whiteness is the ultimate strategy of preserving power by protesting its usurpation by the real victim. The process was driven as much by the psychic need of whites for unifying inclusion as it was by a need to find a force to combat the exaggerated threat of black power. Thus, whites were able to make themselves appear less powerful than they were by overstating the threat posed by blacks. D. W. Griffith's film *Birth of a Nation* exaggerated black male threats to white womanhood to justify the lynching of black men and to increase membership in white hate groups like the White Knights of Columbus. And in our own day, widely voiced complaints by "angry white males" about unfair minority access to social goods like education and employment often misrepresent the actual degree of minority success in these areas.

These strategies of dominant whiteness, as well as the orthodox views of race on which they are premised, held sway until the recent rise of constructivist views of race. One fallout from such constructivist views — challenging the racial stereotyping of minorities by dominant communities, as well as criticizing the romantic representations of minorities within their own communities — has been the wide denunciation of identity politics. It is not, I believe, coincidental that identity politics, and its alleged ideological cousins, political correctness and multiculturalism, has come under attack precisely at the moment that racial, sexual, and gender minorities have gained more prominence in our culture.

Although I favor forceful criticism of vicious varieties of identity politics — the sort where one's particular social identity is made a fetish, where one's group identification becomes an emblem of fascist insularity — the rush to indiscriminately renounce group solidarity without fully investigating the historical contexts, ideological justifications, and intellectual reasons for identity politics is irresponsible and destructive. If the labor movement, the left, the academy, and communities of color are to enjoy a renewed alliance, such investigations are crucial.

Still, taking history into account is no guarantee that the outcome will be just, or that it will profit the sort of balanced perspective for which I have called. Many critics have launched sharp attacks on identity politics as, among other things, the source of sin and suffering within the academy, the left, and the labor movement.[3] Many critics argue that the left — including civil rights groups, feminists, gays and lesbians, and elements of the labor movement — has, through its self destructive identity politics, undermined the possibility of progressive consensus and community. The Hobbesian war of all against all, pitting minority groups against the majority — blacks against whites, gays against straights, and the handicapped against the able-bodied — results in each group talking (or, more likely, hollering) past the other, leading to a destructive politics of purity. Many critics suggest that the energy squandered on identity politics is nothing less than an American tragedy, because it negates a history of left universalism even as it supports a bitter battle over select identities. On this view, the larger tragedy is that right, long identified with privileged interests, increases its appeal by claiming to defend the common good.

Like these critics, I am certainly worried about the plague of the politics of identity when it is unleashed without concern for the common good.[4] I, too, lament the petty infighting and shameless competition for victim status among various groups. Still, such analyses inadequately explain how we got into the mess of identity politics to begin with. Such critics of identity politics fail to grapple with the historic meanings and functions of whiteness, especially the harsh stigma that whiteness brings to those identities and social ideals which fall outside its realm. Moreover, they do not account for the narrow definition of universality and commonality on which such a project of left solidarity often hinges. To paraphrase Alasdair MacIntyre, "Whose universality and which commonality?"

But if such critics' efforts at explicating our national malaise fall short, Michael Tomasky's similar story falls far shorter.[5] In trying to figure out where the left has gone wrong, Tomasky is even more unrelenting in assailing the left's "identity politics, and how those [intellectual] underpinnings fit and don't fit with notions about a civil society that most Americans can support." According to Tomasky, "the left has completely lost touch with the regular needs of regular Americans." He contends that the left "is best described as tribal, and we're engaged in what essentially has been reduced to a battle of interest-group tribalism." Further, Tomasky claims that "solidarity based on race or ethnicity or any other such category always produces war, factionalism, fundamentalism." He concludes that "[p]articularist, interest-group politics — politics where we don't show potential allies how they benefit from being on our side — is a sure loser." Tomasky warns that "will never do the left any good, for example, to remonstrate against angry white men." Tomasky says that this "is not to say angry white men don't exist. But what's the use in carrying on about them?"

Tomasky is certainly right to criticize the left for its failure to show possible fellow travelers how they might be helped by tossing in with our project. And he's within reason to decry the destructive tribalism of the left. But he fails to comprehend that creating a civil society that has the support of most Americans cannot be the goal of any plausible left in America. The role of a marginalized but morally energized American left is to occupy an ethical register that counters injustice, especially when such injustice passes for common sense. The welfare debate is only the most recent example of how the left should gird its loins to defend those who are unjustly stigmatized against the advocates of universal values and common sense. But nowhere is Tomasky's fatal lack of balanced historical judgment seen more clearly than in his dismissal of the political and social effect of "angry white men." Tomasky fails to understand that such anger often grows from the historical amnesia encouraged by the ideology of white supremacy and by the politics of neoliberal race avoidance as well.

Tomasky, and other critics of his ilk, are, to varying degrees, victims of what I term *whitewishing*. In my theory, whitewishing is the interpretation of social history through an explanatory framework in which truth functions as an ideological projection of whiteness in the form of a universal identity. Whitewishing draws equally from Freud and Feuerbach: it is the fulfillment of a fantasy of whiteness as neutral and objective, the projection of a faith in whiteness as its own warrant against the error of anti-universalism because it denies its own particularity. Whitewishing is bathed, paradoxically enough, in a nostalgia for the future: too sophisticated simply to lament a past now gone (and in some ways never was), it chides the present from an eschatological whiteness, the safest vantage point from which to preserve and promote its own "identityless" identity.

Tomasky's and other critics' whitewishing permits them to play down and, at times, erase three crucial facts when it comes to the labor movement. First, identity politics has always been at the heart of the labor movement, both to deny black workers, for instance, their rightful place in unions and as wage earners in the workplace, and to consolidate the class, racial, and gender interests of working elites against the masses of workers. The identity politics now allegedly ripping apart the labor movement — as well as balkanizing the academy and the left in general — is a response to a predecessor politics of identity that was played out without being identified as such because of its power to rebuff challenges brought by racial, ethnic, and gender minorities. Even white proletarians enjoyed their second-hand brands of universalism. This shows how the move to decry "special interests" — that is, blacks, Latinos, Asian Americans — within the labor movement denies a fundamental fact: all interests are special if they're yours.

Second, as the work of David Roediger has shown, race and class were integrally related in shaping the (white) working class in America.[6] The class interests of white workers were based on their developing a sense of whiteness to help alleviate their inferior social status: they derived benefits from *not* being black. This simple fact is a reminder that, from the very beginning in the labor movement and in working-class organizations, race played a significant role in determining the distribution of social and economic goods. Such a fact flies in the face of arguments that the labor movement must reclaim its identity by retreating from identity politics to focus once again on class.

Finally, many debates about labor and identity politics are ahistorical in another way: they presume a functional equivalency between the experiences of all workers who are presently making claims about the weight certain features of identity should carry in a consideration of getting work, keeping work, and job advancement. The real history of racial and gender discrimination in the labor movement, and in the job sector, means that the affirmative action claims of blacks, Latinos, Asian Americans, Native Americans, and women are not special-interest pleadings, but a recognition of their just due in arenas that were segregated by race and gender. To think and behave as if these differences are equal to the forms of disadvantage that white workers face is to engage in another form of whitewishing.

The only way beyond vicious identity politics is to go through it. As with race, we can get beyond the nefarious meanings of racism only by taking race into account. We cannot pretend in the labor movement that significant barriers have not been erected to prevent coalition and cooperation between minorities and the mainstream. Many of those barriers remain. Only when we engage in honest conversation, accompanied by constructive changes in our social practices, will we be able to forge connections between labor, the left, the academy, and communities of color that have the ability to empower and transform each partner in the struggle.

Notes

1. There is a growing literature on the socially constructed meanings of whiteness. For some of the best of this literature, see David Roediger, *The Wages of Whiteness: Race and the Making of the American Working Class* (New York: Verso Press, 1991); David Roediger, *Towards the Abolition of Whiteness: Essays on Race, Politics, and Working Class History* (New York: Verso Press, 1994); Theodore W. Allen, *The Invention of the White Race: Volume One: Racial Oppression and Social Control* (New York: Verso Press, 1994); Fred Pfeil, *White Guys: Studies in Postmodern Domination and Difference* (New York: Verso, 1995); Jessie Daniels, *White Lies: Race, Class, Gender, and Sexuality in White Supremacist Discourse* (New York: Routledge, 1997); Matt Wray and Annalee Newitz, eds., *White Trash: Race and Class in America* (New York: Routledge, 1997); Michelle Fine, Lois Weis, Linda C. Powell, and L. Mun Wong, eds., *Off White: Readings on Race, Power, and Society* (New York: Routledge, 1997).

2. Renato Rosaldo, *Culture & Truth: The Remaking of Social Analysis* (Beacon Press, 1989, 1993), pp. 68–87.

3. For a small sample of such criticism, see: Todd Gitlin, *The Twilight of Common Dreams: Why America is Wracked by Culture Wars* (New York: Metropolitan Books, 1995); Michael Tomasky, *Left For Dead: The Life, Death and Possible Resurrection of Progressive Politics in America* (New York: The Free Press, 1996); Arthur Schlesinger, Jr., *The Disuniting of America* (Whittle Direct Books, 1991); and Richard Bernstein, *The Dictatorship of Virtue: Multiculturalism and the Battle for America's Future* (New York: Knopf, 1994).

4. See Michael Eric Dyson, *Reflecting Black: African-American Cultural Criticism* (Minneapolis: University of Minnesota Press, 1993); *Making Malcolm: The Myth and Meaning of Malcolm X* (New York: Oxford University Press, 1994); *Between God and Gangsta Rap: Bearing Witness to Black Culture* (New York: Oxford University Press, 1996); and *Race Rules: Navigating the Color Line* (New York: Addison-Wesley, 1996).

5. Tomasky, *Left For Dead,* pp. 10, 15, 16, 17.

6. Roediger, *The Wages of Whiteness* and *Towards the Abolition of Whiteness.*

15

Who Is an American Worker?

Asian Immigrants, Race, and the National Boundaries of Class

Mae M. Ngai

T HE CHORAL GROUP of Local 23–25 UNITE (Union of
Needletrades, Industrial, and Textile Employees) in New York
City is one of the union's many social projects. Comprising
several dozen garment workers, all Chinese immigrants and mostly
women, the chorus performs at labor meetings and rallies throughout the city. They are an impressive display of solidarity as they sing
union songs in both Chinese and English. Their repertoire includes
the union-label song — the one with the familiar refrain "Look for
the union label . . . it says we're able . . . to make it in the U.S.A.!"

The presentation of the union-label song by Chinese immigrant
garment workers has always struck me as ironic. The union label is
one of the labor movement's most cherished symbols, but I confess
to having ambivalent feelings about it. The label is, of course, a
message to consumers that the product it adorns is made by union
labor, by workers who bargain collectively and earn a decent wage.
Moreover, it is an emblem of labor's dignity, of the pride workers
have in their work and their unions. But if the union label's message
is one of solidarity, that message has at times been a mixed one,
compromised by boundaries drawn along lines of race and nationality. Solidarity among whom — and against whom? Asian immigrant
workers have not always been included within the union label's

borders of solidarity. Historically and today, Asian immigrants have carried the twin burdens of race and foreign birth, both barriers to being considered "American workers" in the fullest meaning of that concept.

The new leadership of the AFL-CIO has made a commitment to "inclusion" — that is, to bringing greater numbers of workers of color and women into both the ranks and the leadership of the labor movement. Such changes are obviously needed and are welcomed by all concerned with rebuilding a vigorous and socially progressive labor movement. At one level, the issue concerns the need to make the ethnic and gender makeup of the leadership of unions more representative of the workforce. That is a big challenge, because the preponderance of white men in the upper ranks of organized labor is institutionally entrenched. But inclusion is about more than identity group politics within the AFL-CIO. At a more fundamental level it is about labor's definition of itself and its purpose. One of the most profound paradoxes of the American labor movement has been its exclusion of some workers from such universal precepts as "an injury to one is an injury to all." It is a particular legacy of craft unionism in the AFL-CIO — the conservative defense of relative positions of privilege — but it also derives from the contradiction between race and democracy in American society.

The origins of the union label lie in the anti-Chinese movement in the American West during the late nineteenth century. Its direct antecedent was the so-called white label, a creation of craft workers and guilds in San Francisco in the late 1860s. White shoemakers and cigar makers used the label to urge consumers to boycott products made by firms employing Chinese workers. For example, the white label pasted onto cigar boxes read: *The cigars herein contained are made by white men. This label is issued by the authority of the Cigar Makers Association of the Pacific Coast.*

By the early 1880s the anti-Chinese and trade-union movements in California, which overlapped almost entirely, had achieved important political success with the passage of the first Chinese Exclusion Act, in 1882 — labor's first national legislative victory. That same year the San Francisco Trades Assembly adopted the white label, in effect using race to promote unionism. In 1884 the Cigar Makers International Union organized a local in San Francisco. The CMIU's label was also an icon of white labor, but the union's strategy went beyond the boycott: it demanded the wholesale expulsion of Chinese workers from the industry. The CMIU successfully pressured cigar firms to sign pledges to discharge all Chinese employees by guaranteeing white replacement workers at the same wages. During the next few years the union recruited (and advanced railway fares for) over four hundred unemployed cigar makers from the East Coast. Chinese, who had made up at least 75 percent of the industry in the early 1880s, virtually disappeared from the trade and were soon driven out of other manufacturing sectors as well.

In many ways the experience of Chinese laborers was similar to that of other immigrants during the late nineteenth century. Chinese, like Eastern and Southern Europeans, came from capitalism's rural peripheries to fill the ranks of unskilled labor in America's burgeoning urban industrial economy. Like other new arrivals, Chinese were used by employers to undermine the wages and organizing efforts of more established workers. Chinese and European unskilled workers both faced resentment from native-born craft workers anxious over the deskilling of their labor. And, like European immigrants, Chinese workers also demonstrated their capacity for class-conscious behavior. In 1867 over three thousand Chinese railroad workers struck the Central Pacific, demanding the same wages as white workers; in 1884 Chinese cigar makers in San Francisco waged one successful strike for higher wages and lost a second strike for a union shop. During the 1870s a few manufacturers in the eastern United States experimented briefly with Chinese labor, hoping to use it as a wedge against militant Irish workers. They soon abandoned the strategy, at least in part because the Chinese workers staged strikes of their own.[1]

Yet, while successive generations of European immigrants fought for and ultimately won their places in the house of labor, Chinese remained stigmatized as cheap and docile labor, signs of their supposed racial unassimilability, excluded by statute from citizenship and by charter from union membership. Chinese exclusion was the result of much more than ethnic job competition; it grew out of two of the nineteenth century's most important political and ideological currents: free labor and manifest destiny. Northerners commonly believed that free labor (by which they meant the labor of small producers, although skilled wage workers also used the term to describe freedom of contract — the right to quit, as it were) was the central requirement of liberty and independence. The antithesis of slavery, free labor was synonymous with white labor. Tellingly, anti-Chinese labor leaders in California often invoked the "irrepressible conflict between slave and white labor" to justify their cause. They branded Chinese workers "coolies" to give them a slavelike status, thereby further inscribing them with race dependency and inferiority. Manifest destiny — the brash claim that providence intended the West for white people — was one outgrowth of free-labor ideology. In the republican ideal, the West was a land of economic independence, free not only of slavery, but of all black people. Moreover, manifest destiny would clear Indians out of the way and annex half of Mexico. In 1858 the popular Northern democrat Walt Whitman articulated manifest destiny's melding of race, nationalism, and free labor:

> We shouldn't wonder if [the] total prohibition of colored persons became quite a common thing in [the West]. If so, the whole matter of slavery agitation will assume another phase . . . It will be a conflict between the totality of White Labor, on the one side, and, on the other, the interference and competition of Black Labor, or of bringing in colored persons on *any* terms. Who believes that Whites and Blacks can ever amalgamate in America? Or who wishes it to happen? . . . Besides, is not America for the Whites? And is it not better so? (emphasis in original)[2]

Notwithstanding the rapid degradation of free labor in the West by landed and manufacturing monopolies and a consolidating national economy, the AFL championed Asiatic exclusion well into the twentieth century. In this context Chinese and other Asians were racialized as unalterably foreign and denied membership in the legitimate working class.

Continued economic marginalization and social isolation reproduced the taint of unassimilability over the years, although by the mid-twentieth century organized labor treated Asian workers more with benign neglect than with overt hostility. But race and nativism were never too far beneath the surface. During the 1970s, when the domestic auto industry lost a substantial share of the market to Japanese manufacturers, "buy American" became the clarion call of organized labor. Unions promoted the slogan along with the American flag on union labels as well as bumper stickers, buttons, T-shirts, placards. By railing against "foreign imports," labor not only sidestepped the real issue — the failure of American automakers to meet consumers' demands for fuel-efficient cars — but encouraged dangerous racial impulses. Buying "union" became the same as buying "American," an act of patriotism against a new yellow peril. The sentiment against Japanese imports stirred racial antipathies associated with World War II and with the United States' recent loss of the Vietnam War. The appeal to national chauvinism led to the ritualistic smashing of Toyotas (never Volkswagens) at union rallies and, ultimately, to the murder of a young Chinese American, Vincent Chin, in 1982. Ronald Ebens and Michael Nitz, former employees of General Motors, beat Chin to death in the parking lot of a Detroit tavern. They called Chin a "Jap" and accused him of taking their jobs. Ebens and Nitz were actually not union members — they were foremen — but their behavior was of the same culture. The United Auto Workers opposed the killing and stated that race should not be an issue in the campaign against imports. But the union's hands were soiled, because organized labor's emphasis on buying American was the central source of the obfuscation of class, nationality, and race.[3]

Over the last ten years perceptions of race and nationality in the labor movement slowly changed. Protectionism proved to be a failed strategy for saving American jobs as more "imports" were products made by American companies abroad. The concept of buying

American lost practical meaning as American-owned companies produced more and more goods overseas, weakening the link between American workers and American products. And, as U.S. multinational corporations exported capital and jobs, corporate raiders made millions in profits through mergers and leveraged buyouts and the attendant elimination of whole companies, factories, and workforces.

Moreover, the division of the world into an advanced industrial sector in the West and a backward Third World sector, while not eliminated, has become less starkly dichotomous. Advanced technological sectors *and* low-wage, low-skill sectors coexist in both Western and Third World countries. In the United States work is becoming concentrated at these two ends and is unstable at each. The "good union jobs" — the jobs that didn't require a college education, paid a living wage, and promised long-term security — have been disappearing. It is as though the global restructuring of capital has destabilized the categories of class, nation, and race on which labor had imagined itself and constructed its program.

The grittier realities of the global economy, combined with an increasingly conservative domestic political climate, led some union leaders to rethink their strategies. Labor focused more on corporate greed and irresponsibility to communities than on foreign imports. Faced with the power of transnational capital, unions rediscovered the importance of international labor solidarity. Moreover, some unions found success in organizing low-wage workers, often minorities, immigrants, and women; and often in areas traditionally considered the most difficult to organize, such as the service sector and the South.

In this context, the AFL-CIO became more receptive to the needs of Asian-American and Asian immigrant workers. In 1992, with the support of unions that have large concentrations of Asian members — the garment workers, hotel and restaurant workers, and service employees unions — the AFL-CIO formed the Asian Pacific American Labor Alliance (APALA). A constituency group modeled after the Coalition of Black Trade Unionists and the Coalition of Labor Union Women, APALA seeks to be a voice within the AFL-CIO for the estimated 300,000 Asian-American union members in the United States. The organization promotes and assists with organizing the unorganized, advocates for civil rights, encourages the development of Asian-American trade-union leaders, and builds bridges between the labor movement and the Asian-American communities.

Formal recognition and institutional support from the AFL-CIO are obviously important, but Asian workers are not merely objects whom the labor movement either includes or excludes; they are subjects who have always made their own history. APALA was formed on the strength of work that Asian Americans have been doing in unions and communities for the past twenty years. These labor activists organized ethnic clubs and caucuses in locals of the teachers, garment workers, electricians, and other unions. They formed community-based Asian labor organizations like the Asian American Federation of Union Members in San Francisco and the Asian Labor Committee in New York. They participated in such historic organizing campaigns as the San Francisco Jung Sai garment strike in 1974 and the unionization of New York Chinese restaurants in 1979. They organized the "uprising of the 20,000" — the 1982 New York Chinatown garment workers' strike, which shook the industry, the community, and even the union, and produced another generation of activists from the union rank-and-file.

Asian-American labor activists built bridges of international solidarity with unions in South Korea and the Philippines; two Filipino-American leaders of the longshoremen's union in Seattle, Silme Domingo and Gene Viernes, paid for solidarity with their lives. In 1982 agents of the Marcos regime murdered the two men, who were outspoken opponents of Marcos and supporters of the banned KMU (the May 1st Movement) labor federation. Although largely invisible in the labor movement, Asian-American trade unionists have "paid their dues," as both union staff and elected representatives, in the hard and sometimes thankless day-to-day work of building their locals: organizing drives, grievance representation, contract negotiations, membership mobilizations and education, and so on.[4]

Moreover, their experience in community-based labor organizing suggests both practical and strategic lessons for the union movement. Consider, for example, UNITE's work in Sunset Park, a recently settled Chinese community in Brooklyn, New York. The area has 150 Chinese-owned, nonunion garment contract shops that employ five thousand Chinese garment workers, including undocumented immigrants. Many factories are sweatshops, operating in violation of health, safety, wage, and hour regulations. UNITE has organized in Sunset Park since 1990. Recognizing the impossibility of unionizing the industry on a shop-by-shop basis, the union decided instead to organize the community. It offered free English classes to garment workers, out of which grew the Garment Workers Justice Center. The center now has nine hundred members, of whom a third are UNITE members working in union shops in Manhattan's Chinatown and living in Sunset Park. The center is a model of grassroots education, organizing, and empowerment. English-language classes are combined with workshops on basic workers' rights, immigrant rights, welfare reform, and domestic violence. A workers' committee, an elected leadership body, mobilizes volunteers for phone banking and door-to-door campaigning, organizes community events, and leads workshops. The center sponsored a mass march in the community to protest sweatshops and sent volunteers to other cities to participate in union-organizing blitzes. In 1996 the center helped workers collect $400,000 in back-wage claims. And all this was done by a handful of staff organizers who worked out of the trunk of a car.

By fighting for workers' rights, the union established a mass base in the community. That in turn pushed the problem of sweatshops into the foreground of the community's consciousness. Working with local authorities, the union has made it harder for sweatshops to function; the fire department and district attorney's office have shut down shops guilty of flagrant safety violations; and the Department of Labor's policy of seizing "hot goods" (apparel made by contractors in violation of labor laws) has helped shift pressure upward, onto the manufacturers. But UNITE's community organizers say that simply shutting down the sweatshops is not enough. Thus, they have joined with community organizations, the contractors' trade association, and local elected officials to promote the establishment of a *legitimate* garment-industry center in an industrial zone adjacent to the community. They hope to obtain state economic-development funds to offset rents and assist contractors to invest in new technologies. A legitimate industry, they argue, affords stability for both contractors and workers.

Asian labor organizing in Sunset Park challenges a number of assumptions about immigrant workers and union organizing in general. First is the widespread belief that immigrant workers cannot be organized. The conventional wisdom holds that immigrants from impoverished Third World nations who come seeking the American dream are willing to work for low wages and endure nearly any abuse, especially if they are undocumented. Those who work for co-ethnics are said to be unable to make class distinctions (an odd claim, given the strength of race and nationalism among white American workers). But Chinese workers in Sunset Park are not only organizable; they are militant and democratic. Fundamentally, organizing immigrants is like organizing all workers — it can be done with resources, respect, creativity, and hard work. As in the past, the difficulty in organizing immigrant workers has more to do with the labor movement's priorities and prejudices than with the presumed deficiencies of immigrants.

The Sunset Park project also raises the issue of organizing in low-wage manufacturing sectors where the pressure of "global competition" is fierce, such as the garment industry. Employers, of course, routinely threaten to relocate offshore if workers demand too much. But, curiously, union leaders often invoke the same rationale to support their conclusion that organizing in these strata is not strategic or, worse, is futile. This is not to say that the changes wrought by transnational capital over the last twenty years have not been profound. But are we to simply give up because companies threaten to close and move? Clearly, just saying no is not enough; unions need to be creative. In some respects, UNITE's work in Sunset Park is familiar as militant grassroots organizing. At another level, it breaks with traditional union approaches. The union organizes and represents all garment workers in the community, not just those in shops with collective-bargaining agreements. It has established a base of considerable mass support and its organizers have become respected leaders in the community as a result of many years of work; such entrenchment cannot be attained through organizing "blitzes," in which unions send organizers into a town for a few months to organize a shop. Moreover, the union joined forces with employers to promote community-based economic development. That alone will probably not save the garment industry. But sweatshop jobs can be replaced with decent union jobs, and labor can be a progressive force for social and economic justice in the community. That's not a bad start.

Finally, the labor movement must come to terms with immigration at the level of policy. Race and nativism have acquired new force in the nation's discourse, their programmatic articulation — welfare reform and immigration restriction — now supported by both political parties. The 1996 welfare reform bill eliminated needs-based entitlements like food stamps and Supplemental Security Income to nearly all noncitizens and TANF (Transitional Aid to Needy Families — formerly AFDC), Medicaid, and a host of other benefits to new legal immigrants for the first five years, on the dubious theory that making life in the United States unattractive will discourage future immigration. The immigration bill, passed shortly after the welfare act, provided for an enlarged Border Patrol, imposed stiff income requirements on family reunification, and weakened sanctions against employers who discriminate against immigrants in employment.

Stripping legally resident immigrants of the right to public services violates their constitutional right to equal protection under the law. It suggests a major shift in the nature of American immigration policy by treating immigrants not as prospective citizens but as guest workers. The AFL-CIO rightly opposed the attacks on legal immigrants. It also opposed proposals for measures that treat undocumented immigrants inhumanely, such as denying them emergency medical care and throwing their children out of public school, the subject of Proposition 187 in California. But the AFL-CIO generally opposes illegal immigration, especially in employment. At one level, it seems commonsensical to oppose illegal immigration, if only because it is unfair that some people wait for years to immigrate legally while others enter unlawfully. Moreover, illegal immigration creates a marginalized stratum of labor that exacerbates racial inequality and social division.

But focusing on illegal immigrants as the problem puts us on a slippery slope. Practically, it undermines unions' own efforts to organize and represent all immigrant workers, because in many workplaces legal and undocumented immigrants work side by side. Indeed, they are often members of the same family. A union with an ambiguous policy cannot win the trust of the workers and unite them against the employer. Imposing sanctions against employers who hire illegal workers has done little to stop illegal immigration, yet it has led to employment discrimination against legal immigrants and Latinos and Asians generally. Moreover, opposing the employment of undocumented immigrants could lead to a national identification system, something Americans have always considered offensive to their sense of civil society. Short of militarizing large areas of the country, including cities, illegal immigration is difficult to stop; the border is porous, and, more important, many businesses profit from the cheap labor of undocumented workers. The real solutions to workers' economic problems lie elsewhere, in union representation, in living wages, in the enforcement of labor and environmental regulations, in higher workplace standards, and in the retention of jobs in the United States. Instead of policing immigrants (and, ultimately, all of us), we might consider government control of the export of capital as a more effective remedy for the loss of union jobs.

All immigrants — legal and illegal — are part of the American working class. Our understanding of "American" is so freighted with the ideologies of race and empire that few native-born white people can identify with nonwhite immigrants from poor Third World countries as fellow Americans, even as prospective Americans. But immigrants are not birds of passage or guest workers.

They reside within the borders of the American nation-state, raise families, pay taxes, and contribute to local economies; they labor in workplaces putatively under the jurisdiction of American labor laws; they work side by side with workers born in the United States. If unions proceed from these realities, they will understand that all workers in America are, in effect, members of the American working class that the union movement seeks to represent, morally and organizationally.

Workers once considered marginal in organized labor's constructed image of the American working class — Asian and Latino immigrants, African Americans in the South, women workers — are moving into the mainstream of a newly invigorated labor movement. Their struggles challenge the ideological and organizational arrangements that place white male craft workers and Northern industrial production workers at the center of the labor movement (or at its head). They invert the positions of the marginal and the mainstream, potentially redefining the strategic program that is based on that mapping.

Perhaps most important, struggles among immigrants and workers of color in the lower strata of the workforce bring the labor movement into close association with the struggles of those communities for racial justice. Out of such associations grow possibilities for building a progressive movement for social change.

The new leadership of the AFL-CIO feels this push of history, but it is not yet clear whether it fully understands or accepts its strategic implications. It is unlikely, however, that the labor movement will be transformed from the top down. There is an inherent tension in the federation's commitment to inclusion, because, while that commitment is undoubtedly sincere, it challenges its own vested interests. Inclusion must go beyond a pluralist recognition of "the changing face of labor"; it must be more than a celebration of our multiethnic diversity. The danger is that organized labor will merely incorporate those on the margins into the existing paradigm without fundamentally changing its top leadership and strategic orientation. Immigrants and other workers of color don't want to trade exclusion for paternalism. The transformative impulse to realize the full meaning of solidarity will continue to come from below.*

Notes

1. Alexander Saxton, *The Indispensable Enemy* (Berkeley, 1971), pp. 74, 214–218 on union label and generally on anti-coolieism in the labor movement. On Chinese labor see Sucheng Chan, *Asian Americans, An Interpretive History* (Boston, 1991), pp. 45–51, 82–83; Ronald Takaki, *Iron Cages* (New York, 1979), pp. 233–235; Renqui Yu, *To Save China, To Save Ourselves* (Philadelphia, 1994), p. 8.
2. Brooklyn *Eagle,* May 6, 1858, cited in Alexander Saxton, *The Rise and Fall of the White Republic* (London and New York, 1990), p. 154.
3. Ronald Takaki, *Strangers from a Different Shore* (New York, 1989), pp. 481–484; *Solidarity* (Detroit), April 1982 and August 1983.
4. For more on Asian-American labor activism, see "Asian Pacific American Workers: Contemporary Issues in the Labor Movement," special issue of *Amerasia Journal,* vol. 18, no. 1 (1992).

*The author would like to thank Matthew Finucane, Danyun Feng, and Andrew Hsaio for their assistance.

16

Women

The Future of Labor

Karen Nussbaum

O VER THE CENTURIES, around the world, women have been a slight majority of the population and essential producers — whether paid for their labor or not. As the Chinese proverb puts it, "Women hold up half the sky." As it turns out, it may actually be slightly better than half.

But how women are seen, whether they are paid, and what power they have — as workers, as citizens, and as wives and mothers — has varied greatly. Changes today, from the global economy to the family, converge to make women powerful new actors, central to the future of the labor movement both here and abroad.

The More Things Change . . .

Women's work has always been essential. Unpaid work, on family farms, in kitchens, nurseries, and sickrooms, has changed into paid work, for the most part, although most women still work at least two jobs — one paid, and the other an unpaid shift at home. Women are nearly half the paid workforce in the United States today (47 percent), up from 24.4 percent in 1940. Their participation rate nearly doubled since the time their grandmothers worked — in the unlikely event, for white women, that their grandmothers had jobs.

Despite the explosion of women joining the workforce in the last generation, unions have been slow to pick up on the transition. In my own experience of organizing working women for more than twenty-five years, I've heard a wide range of reasons that we should *not* pay attention to women workers as women, from the labor leader in the early 1970s who explained that you couldn't organize working women because they "think with their c — ts, not their brains," to the progressive organizer I talked to recently who said, "Organize women? Everyone knows you can organize women — it's *men* we need to worry about!"

There's a similar pattern in politics. A generation ago, women were considered the reliable second vote of their husbands. A growing gender gap in the voting patterns of men and women has done little to discourage common assumptions about how women will act. While men still think their wives will vote as they do, the wives know better. In the last election, 75 percent of men thought that their spouses would vote the same way they did, but only 39 percent of women anticipated voting the same way. And although 1996 was the year the gender gap hit its peak and women attained an unprecedented level of attention in politics, the Women's Campaign School at Yale University, which prepares women to run for political office, had this advice for students as they prepared for the serious work of politics: "Cross your ankles, not your knees . . . Eye makeup is the most important makeup . . . Control your emotions . . . [and] keep smiling and smiling and smiling and smiling."

Indeed, it does seem that the more things change, the more they stay the same. But the role of women as workers is changing the direction of politics, and if the union movement takes advantage of this opportunity, women will change the face of labor.

In the last generation, people are just beginning to understand that things have changed, and now it is our job to make organizing a credible solution. The role of women is central to this new opportunity.

Changed Conditions

What has changed for American working families?

When I grew up, economic growth meant that everybody advanced. Between 1950 and 1978, in a period of economic growth, family income grew at all levels of the income scale. Whether you were at the bottom or the top or anywhere in between, family income doubled, more or less. But that has changed. Since 1979, we have been growing apart, and only those at the top have seen their incomes rise. Incomes rose 17 percent for the top 20 percent. The lowest fifth saw their incomes fall 18 percent. And the middle is just barely hanging on or falling behind. There is a greater gap in income in this country at this time than in living memory, and there is a greater gap here than in any other industrialized country.

Women are working in record numbers. Though African-American women have always worked for pay in large numbers since slavery, overall there's been a big increase in women joining the workforce in the last generation, up from 17 million in 1948 to 61 million in 1995. And women are the majority of workers in the growing service sector.

Finally, 99 percent of women in the United States will work for pay at some point in their lives. The argument that there is a deep division between the woman who works for pay and the one who works in the home doesn't hold true. If she isn't working today, then she worked yesterday or will work tomorrow. Nearly every woman has a stake in what goes on in the workplace. And even more important, she will tell you that. As a woman in Richmond, Virginia, said, "This is the 1990s; there are a lot of single mothers; there are a lot of single women. I need money just like my husband does."

Changed Consciousness

And that leads to my second point. Ideas — that is, consciousness — have changed. When I first started organizing, in the early 1970s, white women often thought of themselves as in the workforce only until they achieved some short-term goal. The office where I was a file clerk was typical. One secretary was saving money to get married. Another was saving money for her children to go to college. A third intended to return to school. Regardless of how long women stayed in the workforce — and the average woman at that time worked for thirty-four years — they took solace in the notion that their passage through the low-paid, low-prestige jobs that were, and still are, the province of women was only temporary. One woman captured the conflicts in the image and reality for working women when she wrote to our fledgling organization, 9 to 5, "It's time we took responsibility for what goes on at work, or we'll be called 'girls' till the day we retire without pension."

Now these ideas seem as old-fashioned as the term "pin money." We saw the seeds of dramatic economic and demographic changes twenty-five years ago, trends that were interdependent: the globalization of the economy; the shift from a manufacturing to service-based economy; the rise of new technology; the flood of women into the workforce; the budding income inequality. The seeds are in full flower now. The changes beginning to take place in the 1970s created discontent as women looked on their work lives with denial and growing disappointment, blaming the problems on their own inadequacies.

But there is a historical lag — a gap between a change in conditions and a change in consciousness. Consciousness — women's views of themselves as workers and citizens — is catching up with conditions. Women see themselves very differently now from the way they did twenty-five years ago.

Women see themselves as permanent, not temporary, members of the workforce. In fact, if anything, they fear they will never stop working. A nurse in Atlanta told me that she provides for her growing children and her aging mother and expects to work until she drops. An airline reservationist in her fifties who shares an apartment with other adult women envisions herself working at 7-Eleven when she is seventy-five. Public opinion research shows retirement income as the sleeper issue for women of all ages. And why not? Less than half of all working women in the private sector receive pensions, and what they get averages only about half of men's pension income. With family income down, less money is being saved privately, and personal debt is up. Nearly one out of five workers expects to be providing care for an aging relative in the next five years. In the twenty-first century more employees are expected to be caring for elderly relatives than for children.

Women believe they contribute half or more of their family's income. Until recently, women saw themselves as secondary wage earners. Now surveys show women asserting they are essential and, increasingly, primary sources of family income. In 1992, one out of six women were heads of household. In several recent studies a majority of married women in two-income households described themselves as contributing half or more of their family's income.

It is unlikely, however, that women do contribute that much. Women still earn only 75 percent of what men do on a weekly basis, earn less than men in virtually every job category, and are more likely to work fewer hours a year than men do. The statistical studies required to prove differentials in family income do not exist. What is important here is the *perception*.

Women know they are not treated fairly. While this may sound obvious, it hasn't always been so. When we started organizing 9 to 5, the Organization of Women Office Workers, in Boston in the early 1970s, our first task was to convince women that the problems they faced on the job stemmed from an unfair system of employment rather than from their personal failings. The word *discrimination* was as foreign as *organizing* among these traditional women workers, and 9 to 5 staff and leaders didn't use either word for some time for fear it wouldn't be understood or believed.

Women now assume that discrimination is part of the job. In "Working Women Count!," an unprecedented survey conducted by the U.S. Department of Labor Women's Bureau in 1994, women described discrimination as one of their top concerns, and felt that they had little or no opportunity for advancement. And the issue reverberates among women throughout the workforce — from the grocery store clerk who told me, "I love my job, I love everything about my job. I love stacking the shelves, I love working the deli counter, I love checking out the customers. But I've been here thirty-two years and I know I'll never make manager because I'm a woman"; to the construction worker who said, "My head aches from bumping up against the glass ceiling"; to the business executive who confided to me, "We participate in a conspiracy of silence." Women assume they will experience discrimination in their careers if not in the jobs they hold right now.

Surprisingly, men acknowledge that discrimination is a problem for women. In a study by the AFL-CIO to measure the attitudes of Americans toward the economy, a majority of women said that enforcing equal-pay laws was one of the best ways to improve people's economic situation. Men echoed their point of view, with nearly half (49 percent) agreeing that stronger equal-pay laws would help.

So the realities of work — lower pay and fewer opportunities — have become part of women's assumptions, and consciousness of being workers has become part of women's identity. "Working woman — that's just who I am," said a white woman in Baltimore. An African-American woman reflected, "I look at working women as women who need money. I look at myself." A Latina described herself and others like her as "strong women . . . because we are willing to do anything. We work."

But it is also true that women's roles in their families and communities influence them as workers and citizens.

Women are more likely to identify with the problems of others. "My job is secure," the medical office secretary said, "but my heart breaks when I see the people come through here who can't pay their bills. We should do something about that." "I don't have young children anymore," the woman in her fifties wrote in, "but I still think child care is the most important problem we have." The pivotal issues of the 1996 elections — Medicare, Medicaid, education, and the environment — were signals to the government to act on behalf of those who need it most. This was a women's agenda.

Women tend to be concerned with practical problems. While Republican politicians were ranting about the budget deficit as our biggest problem and a balanced budget as our nation's greatest need in the early 1990s, women were focused on their family budgets. "Kitchen table economics," as the Democratic pollster Celinda Lake put it, was what women really cared about — the issues that women fretted over when sitting around the kitchen table after the dishes were done. Can you afford new shoes for the kids? How are you going to pay the dentist? How can you save for a college education and pay the electric bill at the same time? "It's not macro-economics," Senator Barbara Mikulski explained; "it's macaroni and cheese."

Women are more likely to feel a community of interest. Women are more likely to volunteer in their communities, schools, and churches and to see their sphere of concern as being broader than their immediate families. Women believe that people caring about one another is the first step to solving society's problems. Seventy percent of women in the New Providers study reported that they worry a great deal about people not caring about others; they give a higher rating to that obligation than to any other societal concern. And in other polls, women are overwhelmingly in favor of joining together to get ahead rather than each looking out for herself.

These are the reasons we have the widely celebrated gender gap in politics, which reached epic proportions in the elections of 1996. If 1992 was "the year of the woman" in the number of women elected, then 1996 was the "year of the woman voter." Most candidates in 1996 had polling data that told them to court women voters. From the extraordinary Women's Night at the Republican convention to the endless references to the Family and Medical Leave Act by the Clinton campaign, the rhetoric was way up. And the proof was in the voting patterns. Women voted on the issues of education, crime, and Social Security; men were more oriented toward taxes and the deficit. The result? An extraordinary seventeen-point gender gap, with women voting for Clinton over Dole, and an even more pronounced gap, of twenty-one points, among *working* women.

But this new consciousness — women bringing their roles as providers into the voting booth — is also changing women's view of themselves in the workplace. And that brings me to my third point — a growing gender gap in *organizing*.

Years ago, common wisdom had it that women workers just wouldn't organize. They were too close to the boss, didn't identify enough as workers, were too reluctant to take action — they were just weak, weak, weak. It was true that women were less likely to be union members than were men. In 1974, women made up only 21 percent of union membership, though their workforce participation rate was 39 percent.

Many argue that this low union participation rate was due less to the weakness of women than to their lack of opportunity to join — women were being disproportionately employed in the unorganized service sector. That seemed to be confirmed in research done by the AFL-CIO for its 1985 study "The Changing Situation of Workers and Their Unions." In response to a public opinion poll asking, "If you could vote to join a union tomorrow," more women responded positively than did men. This was a fact so surprising that it was immediately forgotten — it just didn't fit into the assumptions of union leadership.

But women were voting with their feet. In the last twelve years, more women than men organized into unions. As a result, women's participation rate in unions increased from 34 percent of all members in 1984 to 39 percent in 1995. Women as a proportion of union members nearly doubled in twenty years.

Recent polling by the AFL-CIO confirms the gender gap in attitudes. Nonunion, nonmanagerial women consistently display a more positive response to organizing than do a similar group of men. Forty-nine percent of the women say they would vote for a union if an election were held tomorrow, compared with 41 percent of men. When asked whether people need to join together in groups to improve their work situation, 56 percent of women say yes, compared with 44 percent of men.

The statistics are confirmed by a gaze around the organizing landscape. Who is organizing? Hotels and casinos, textiles and light manufacturing, health care and nursing homes, food service and public sector — all industries populated by women workers.

And all this at a time when the National Labor Relations Act effectively bars a majority of women from access to collective bargaining, according to a study done by the labor expert Dorothy Sue Cobble. The current labor-law system was designed for a mass-production industrial workplace with a full-time male workforce. Now our economy is service-dominated, computer-based, and global, and employees have an ever more tangential relation to their employer. Witness the growth of part-time, temporary, leased, and contracted-out work. Cobble estimates that 39 percent of women — domestic workers, agricultural workers, supervisors, and others — are explicitly exempted from the National Labor Relations Act and the NLRB process effectively bars many more women who do temporary or part-time work from exercising their rights. Add the fact that a worker is fired every hour for trying to organize a union — ten thousand a year — making it the most costly right to exercise in this country — and it's a miracle that any women organize at all.

Global Trends

More women are working. Their paid work is changing their identity, and their character as women is changing their view of their workplace. And it's not happening only here. Similar changes in the role of women are taking place worldwide. A report for the Population Council, called "Families in Focus," looked at demographic and economic data around the world and the ways that families are changing in form and function. The report identified such global trends as more women working for pay in every region of the world, families and households becoming smaller, women marrying later and getting divorced at a higher rate.

While divorce is not a platform plank of the new AFL-CIO Working Women's Department, it is part of a global trend that can be described as follows. *A shifting global economy drives women into the paid workforce, increasing their economic independence and thereby making them stronger economic and social actors.* Women workers of the world, unite! And this is a good thing. The anthropologist Judith Bruce, one of the authors of "Families in Focus," formulated this simple equation: "Women in groups, good. Men in groups, bad."

Of course, the policy of the AFL-CIO is that both women and men should be in groups so that they can bargain collectively. But we would do well to pay more attention to building on this new strength, the growing numbers of women who seek to take more control over their lives. It would not be wrong to look to women, recruited from the kitchens and nurseries of their homes to work for pay in factories, stores, offices, fields, and restaurants — and in other people's kitchens and nurseries — whether in Indianapolis or Indonesia, Tacoma or Thailand, Birmingham or Brazil, Santa Fe or South Africa — as agents of change. Perhaps not the first generation of new workers, still reeling from the shock of entering the paid workforce and living a new life in which their wages sustain their families, but the next generation, for whom conditions have had a chance to create a new reality, and whose consciousness has caught up. These women appear ready for a fight.

The signs of organizing are everywhere. Women are organizing in the Self-Employed Women's Association in India, a combination trade union and cooperative of two hundred thousand artisans and homeworkers, and into informal organizations and formal unions in free-trade zones in the Far East and Latin America. Public Services International (PSI), the international trade union secretariat representing public sector workers around the world, went to the union women in Uganda when it sought to increase membership involvement. Now the women provide its leadership and have doubled its membership. Women unionists also won a major victory in Brazil two years ago, when the CUT, the biggest labor federation, passed a resolution requiring that a minimum of 30 percent of all executive board members be women, and, in an act of transcendent optimism, established a ceiling of 70 percent females.

It is, of course, not only a fight for women. Men in this country also suffer from the growing wage gap, watch their incomes and security plummet, and are disenfranchised when it comes to the right to organize. But women have an important, perhaps deciding, role to play. We seek to restore balance in our world — between the rich and the rest, between work and family, between men and women — in which women are economically independent and families are stable. Are women ready to change the rules?

Organizing for Change

Working women in this country have become eloquent about the problems they face. They articulate a clear agenda for change and use a common language to express it. In the "Working Women Count!" survey, over 250,000 women sounded the same themes over and over — pay and benefits, work and family, respect and opportunity. In more recent survey research, diverse groups of women came up with the same lists of issues and priorities: health care and child care, equal pay and pensions, more control over their hours.

While there's little mystery about the agenda, most working women are lost when it comes to implementing it. When asked, "Who do you turn to when you have a problem on the job?," women are far more likely to reply "My mother" than to mention a union, a women's or civil rights organization, or a government agency. But they are open. They are waiting for us — the union movement — to be what they need.

Today, with more than 5.5 million women members, the AFL-CIO is the largest working women's organization in the country. Yet few people think of us that way. We need to become credible to working women through what we do, who we are, who speaks for us, and what they say. We need to change, change a lot, and change fast. Here are some starting points:

- Reach out to working women — those in unions and those who are unrepresented — and involve them in setting the agenda. Women want to have a say and know they are part of a responsive organization.
- Work on issues working women tell us they care about. The Coalition of Labor Union Women (CLUW) has pioneered for years on women's concerns, and many unions have bargained

successfully for what are thought of as "women's issues." But the AFL-CIO needs to put its full weight behind such matters as child and elder care, equal pay and pay equity, and paid family leave.

- Women leaders should be seen, heard, and promoted. Working women are doubtful that organizations with only men in leadership positions can really understand their needs — or welcome their suggestions.
- Change the culture of organizing. As the labor movement retools to make organizing its top priority, the lack of experienced organizers is a chief obstacle. But as long as organizing requires consistent twelve-hour days and constant travel, few women *or* men — especially those with children, but even those who just want a life — will still be at it ten or fifteen years later, just when their experience really becomes valuable. The labor movement needs to have so much organizing going on around the country and so many trained staff that organizers can work where they live, and have a family life, too.
- Build life in the union movement at every level. We need to move away from a staff-intensive model that relies on paid staff to handle everything from grievances to the phone bank to banquet dinners. We need to change our priorities — replace some of those banquet dinners with house calls to prospective members — and restructure our activities so members are the lifeblood in organizing, politics and servicing, whether its an hour a month, a day a week, or lost time to run a campaign.

The principles behind these recommendations — that leaders should reflect their base and that strength grows out of an active, engaged membership — apply not only to women but to all the diverse groups that make up the current and potential membership of unions.

Today we have an opportunity to reach out to working women that we didn't have twenty years ago, and may not have twenty years from now. An office worker in New York was unusually clear when she answered a question about what she needed in order to make changes in her job: "I've got plenty of information; it's power I don't have." We have the power that working women need — we need to be the organization that working women want.

The irony is that employers drove women into the workforce because they were cheap and compliant. Our success as a labor movement may well lie with burying the notion of woman as kitten and unleashing the lioness. Our job is to feed her red meat.

17

Black Leadership and the Labor Movement

Manning Marable

FOR WELL OVER A CENTURY, the African-American community has been conducting an internal debate over what strategy would best promote group economic advancement and greater income equality with white Americans. The personalities advocating specific programs and organizational affiliations have shifted dramatically over the decades, but the general ideological conflict over what strategic vision is appropriate for black economic development has remained remarkably consistent. In its most basic terms, the debate concerns the complex relationships among race, class, and economic power. How does a minority group, with limited resources of capital and credit, devise a strategy to lift incomes and to promote group economic development?

The starting point of one approach to this problem is the concept of *race*. The argument is simple: race is the most important factor in determining the availability of jobs, career advancement, access to credit and capital. Race must therefore be the framework for coordinating black producers and consumers to achieve empowerment within the capitalist system. The opposite approach begins with the concept of *class*. Black Americans overwhelmingly are working people, who share common class interests with workers of different racial and ethnic backgrounds. By building solidarity between African-American leadership and the labor union movement, and by expanding black union membership and participation, the black com-

munity's political and economic clout will be increased. The en-
hanced power of African-American movements and labor movements will place greater pressure on the federal government to support more of the progressive social policies — like affirmative action
and job programs — that disproportionately aid racial minorities.
This will increase the incomes and standard of living of the entire
working population. Combined with liberal government policies
aimed at reducing poverty and joblessness, the result will be dramatic improvements in the economic condition of the black community.

While it is certainly true that these two arguments are not mutually exclusive — labor unions and capitalism have coexisted for
many years — the division between these two schools of thought has
fostered very different perspectives among African-American leadership.

The first architect of the blueprint for black capitalist development was Booker T. Washington, founder of Tuskegee Institute in
1881 and the National Negro Business League in 1900. Washington
aggressively opposed labor unions and urged African Americans to
seek employment as scabs to undercut racist white workers. By
building black-owned businesses to provide goods and services to a
mostly segregated market, African Americans would create jobs for
themselves. This strategy of economic self-reliance was later accompanied by an explicit rejection of government as an effective tool for
addressing income inequality.

In the generations of black leadership since Washington, the
strategy of capitalist development has been embraced by advocates
of both racial integration and black nationalism. Marcus Garvey,
the Jamaican black nationalist and leader of the Universal Negro
Improvement League in the 1920s, was a staunch proponent of
Washington's economic strategy. In the 1980s, black conservatives
aligned with the Reagan administration, including the economists
Thomas Sowell, Glenn Loury, and Walter Williams, preached racial
self-help, black private entrepreneurship, and an easing of government regulations and restrictions on the market.

Today, many of the same economic ideas are being championed

by two seemingly very different black leaders: Colin Powell and Louis Farrakhan. Both men would favor blacks becoming "less reliant" on governmental programs. Both support black entrepreneurship, and both probably believe that the black middle class has the unique responsibility to uplift the rest of the black community. One leader is the darling of moderate Republicanism and white suburbia, and the other has become a spokesperson for the alienation and rage in black inner cities. However, this does not alter the fact that their economic arguments are similar. As Peter Drier has noted: "According to Farrakhan, the road to black success is through entrepreneurship: by blacks owning businesses and keeping economic resources in the African-American community. This goal resonates with the American Dream, but it is a far cry from economic reality." What was "tragically absent" from Farrakhan's address at the Million Man March of 1995, notes Drier, was any mention of "the institution that has played perhaps the largest role in improving the economic condition of black Americans: unions."[1]

The practical experiences of most black working people also undercut the strategy of petty entrepreneurship. More than two thirds of all black-owned "businesses" do not have a single paid employee. Four out of five African-American businesses close or go bankrupt within three years of starting. The difficulties involved in developing a successful small business are challenging for any entrepreneur, but are far greater for African Americans. As many black Americans know, banks and financial institutions are extremely reluctant to lend investment capital to start-up enterprises. Insurance companies routinely charge significantly higher rates for coverage in minority urban areas. Small-scale businesses in the retail trade are also at a competitive disadvantage in marketing and pricing goods and services, compared with larger corporations. In short, the typical mom-and-pop restaurant in Harlem or South Central Los Angeles is usually unable to compete with McDonalds and Kentucky Fried Chicken. "Black capitalism" in the era of globalization is a road that leads nowhere.

The case against the economic strategy of black-labor solidarity partly rests on the long history of racial discrimination within the white working class. The historian William H. Harris has eloquently characterized the racial exclusion as a central theme for the entire history of American labor:

> The importance and centrality of race in America comes forth in so much that has been part of the American labor movement, and raises without question the most important issue with which organized labor must contend if labor will continue to have a major place in American society. History is replete with examples of why this is so. For instance, railway engineers were not solely responsible for the failure of Eugene V. Debs' Pullman strike. The decision of numerous black workers to refuse to join the American Railway Union, and thus, in effect, become strikebreakers, contributed to Debs' failure as well. Yet the very reason that black workers did not make common cause with the American Railway Union, namely, because white railway unionists would not permit blacks to join the unions or to take certain railroad jobs such as engineers, brakemen, and conductors, requires historians to question whether the term scab really fits their actions. Is one a scab or strikebreaker when one takes a job during a strike when the striking workers, all of whom are white, have themselves gone on strike to keep black workers out? During the late 19th and 20th centuries, white workers initiated more than 100 strikes in order to keep black workers from gaining access to certain jobs.[2]

The pattern of racial exclusion was deeply entrenched in the American Federation of Labor and was only partly broken when the Congress of Industrial Organizations organized workers of both races. Racial progress was particularly slow in many craft trade unions. In 1960, for example, only 1.5 percent of all employed electricians were nonwhite. It was only when the Department of Labor under President Lyndon Johnson decided to pressure the skilled trade unions to desegregate that this rigid pattern of exclusion began to soften. In 1969, the Nixon administration started to implement the Philadelphia Plan, which was specifically designed to increase the number of African Americans and other racial minorities in the skilled trades. The Department of Labor directly funded several minority apprenticeship programs, such as the National Urban League's Labor Education and Advancement Program, which trained African Americans for skilled jobs as carpenters, ironworkers, heavy-equipment operators, and electricians. By 1980, nearly 5 percent of all employed electricians were African Americans. By 1995, approximately 15 percent of the one million jobs in the skilled trade unions belonged to black workers.

But black workers have learned that access to apprenticeship programs does not necessarily mean regular full-time employment. Under the Philadelphia Plan, contractors who bid for government-financed construction projects were required to meet goals for minority employment established by affirmative action guidelines. The contractors shifted the burden of achieving these goals to the union locals that supplied the workers. And it is at the local level that racial bias is perpetuated. In Philadelphia, Local 542, for example, once maintained mandatory hiring halls, where all job assignments were placed. But as competition for jobs increased in the late 1980s, the white-dominated locals allowed contractors to hire union members without going through the hiring halls. In effect, this permitted white foremen to select their relatives and friends for positions and to discriminate against minorities. One study of Local 542 indicated that, while 30 percent of all workers sent out for jobs were minorities, they worked only 16 percent of all hours worked by local members.[3]

The retreat from equality represented by the Philadelphia Plan is also symbolic of the distinct differences between the workplace experiences of African Americans as compared with those of whites — regardless of whether they are members of unions. The critics of African-American solidarity with the labor movement make the argument that race rather than class is the more profound factor in determining what happens on the job and in determining the availability of employment. There is considerable evidence to support this thesis.

First, social scientists for decades have observed a wage gap between whites and African Americans that is profoundly structural:

regardless of education, vocational training, and so forth, nearly all blacks at all levels still earn less than whites. During the civil rights and black power movements, and especially with the implementation of affirmative action and equal employment opportunity measures, the income gap between blacks and whites narrowed dramatically. In 1967, black men earned 45 percent less than white men. By 1977, the wage gap had narrowed to 29 percent. After that, the racial wage gap stagnated and to some extent grew wider again. The economist James P. Smith illustrates the racial stratification of wages by isolating the work experiences of college-educated African-American men since the 1960s. He observes: "Among new college graduates, black men earned 83 percent as much as comparable white men in 1967–1968; by 1971–1972 there was complete wage parity. After 1971–1972, wage gains of young black workers steadily eroded. For college graduates, this erosion marked both decades until we had come roughly full circle with a wage differential in 1990 little different than that with which we started." What was even more striking was the widening of the wage gap between races within the same age groups. For example, Smith notes that "among college graduates who entered the job market in 1971, wages of blacks exceeded those of comparable whites by 2 percent. Within this cohort, black males' wages were only 75 percent as much as those of their white counterparts 18 years into their careers in 1989."[4]

The racial wage gap also persists among union members. In 1987, African-American union workers earned an average of $387 per week, compared with $458 per week for white union members. By 1994, white unionists received $514 a week on average, compared with $405 for black union members. The African-American unionists' average wage was only a small amount above the average weekly wage of $385 for all unionized and nonunionized, nonsupervisory workers.[5]

The racial stratification of the work experience even extends to the rates of joblessness and re-employment. In periods of economic hardship, whites are far more likely than blacks to gain re-employment. For example, in the period 1979–83, 77.9 percent of white men were re-employed, compared with only 63.1 percent of black men. For women workers, the difference was 62.9 percent for whites, 53.8 percent for blacks. The racial division of displaced workers who found re-employment was particularly sharp for workers who had less than three years of tenure on their last job. In 1984–86, a period of relative economic growth, of displaced workers who had been employed on their previous job for less than one year, 81.7 percent of all white men were re-employed, compared with only 66.6 percent of the African-American men. For displaced women workers in this category, white women again had higher rates of re-employment over black women: 61.2 percent versus 52.4 percent. Only in the managerial, administrative, and professional occupations, sectors where there are still relatively small numbers of minorities, are African-American displaced workers as competitive as their white peers in obtaining new jobs.[6]

Once out of work, it takes most African Americans a much longer time to be re-employed in the same occupation or industry than it does whites. Citing data from a 1988 Department of Labor survey, the economist Lori G. Kletzer observes:

> In the 1984–86 period, 15.5 percent of white men and 11.4 percent of white women reported experiencing no joblessness following displacement; among blacks, the percentages were much smaller, 5.4 percent of men and 6.6 percent of women. At the other end of the joblessness distribution, long-term joblessness — that exceeding twenty-six weeks — was more prevalent for sampled blacks than for sampled whites. For the 1984–86 period, 37.8 percent of black men and 29.5 percent of black women reported at least twenty-six weeks without work, compared with 18.8 percent of white men and 22.4 percent of white women.[7]

For displaced workers who had been unemployed for more than one full year, the racial stratification of experience remained: for men, the jobless rates were 5.0 percent for whites, 9.5 percent for blacks; for women, 6.6 percent for whites, 14.8 percent for African Americans.

As a consequence of the racialized patterns of discrimination in career advancement, wages, job displacement, and re-employment, most black workers have been losing ground economically over the past two decades. Only a minority of African-American workers — those who have high levels of skills and education and those located in professional, technical, and administrative positions — have done comparatively well. Lou Ferleger and Jay R. Mandle note that "while the proportion of black families with incomes of more than $50,000 (adjusted for inflation) increased from 4.7 percent in 1970 to 8.8 percent in 1986, the percentage of poor black families — those with incomes of less than $10,000 — also increased, from 26.8 percent to 30.2 percent."[8] About a fourth of all black adults are no longer in the formal labor force, and in some urban communities like Harlem, the percentage exceeds 40 percent. The informal economy, both legal and illegal enterprises and markets, increasingly supports growing numbers of black working people. This has had a devastating impact, particularly on young African Americans, many of whom have no experience or expectation of obtaining a real job in their lifetimes.

There is no question that race remains a critically important factor in determining the life chances — employment, income mobility, housing, health care, education — of all African Americans, even a generation after the civil rights movement. But African Americans as a group have always understood that "race" does not and cannot explain everything. Much more frequently than white American voters, the black electorate makes its political choices based on ideology rather than on the race of the candidate. Similarly, from their practical experiences in the workplace, most blacks and other minorities have concluded that a strategy of class solidarity and unions, even with all of their problems and contradictions, is still the best hope for raising incomes and improving the economic life of their communities. The best evidence of this is provided by public-opinion polls. In one 1989 Associated Press–Media General national survey, more than eleven hundred adults were asked about their attitudes toward organized labor. When nonunion workers were asked, "Would you join a union at your place of work?" those responding *yes* included 56 percent of the African Americans, 46 percent of the Hispanics, and only 35 percent of non-Hispanic whites. When asked whether they had a generally "favorable" opinion of unions, 62 percent of both blacks and Hispanics responded positively, compared with only 43 percent of whites.[9]

This pro-union perspective is deeply rooted in the social consciousness and the political terrain of black history. Partly, this intimate connection to the labor movement is based on the activist leadership of black trade unionists like A. Philip Randolph, founder of the Brotherhood of Sleeping Car Porters in 1925. Randolph directly linked the struggles of the black working class for higher wages and better working conditions with the cause for desegregation and civil rights. In the 1950s and 1960s, despite all of its many contradictions, organized labor provided critical support for the mass desegregation campaigns across the South. It was labor, not the mainstream of the Democratic Party, that endorsed the 1963 March on Washington, D.C., which called for the adoption of the Civil Rights Act. During the black power movement in the late 1960s, the most significant radical tendency of African-American activism was arguably not the highly publicized Black Panther Party, but the League of Revolutionary Black Workers. From Montgomery to Memphis, black trade unionists and working-class people generally were central to the African-American struggle.

There is a common recognition among black workers that their earnings, fringe benefits, and general working conditions improve with unionization, relative to black nonunion labor. In 1987, for example, black union members earned an average of $387 per week, 51.8 percent more than black nonunion workers, who averaged $255 per week.[10] It is for these reasons that African Americans are assuming a more important role within the labor movement. While white male membership in unions has declined from 55.8 percent of the white male workers in 1986 to 49.7 percent in 1994, African-American representation has increased in these same years from 14 percent to 15.5 percent. Even more important is the race and gender profile of organized labor today. As of 1995, only 14.8 percent of all white workers aged sixteen and above were union members. Black men now have the highest union membership rate, 23.3 percent, followed by black women workers, at 18.1 percent.[11]

With their growing numbers, African Americans in recent years have become more directly involved in union politics. As late as 1984, African Americans were leaders of only two of the AFL-CIO's ninety-five affiliates: Henry Nicholas, head of the predominantly black National Union of Hospital and Health Care Employees, and Frederick O'Neal, president of the Associated Actors and Artists of America. By the late 1980s, a group of powerful black leaders had emerged: William Lucy, secretary-treasurer of the million-member American Federation of State, County, and Municipal Employees; Mary H. Futrell, president of the 1.6 million-member National Education Association; John N. Sturdivant, president of the 700,000-member American Federation of Government Employees, the largest union of federal workers; Marc Stepp, vice president of the United Automobile, Aerospace, and Agricultural Implement Workers of America; Leon Lynch, vice president of the United Steelworkers of America; Henry Nicholas, president of the National Union of Hospital and Health Care Employees; and Robert L. White, president of the National Alliance of Postal and Federal Employees.[12] With this new concentration of black leadership, the Coalition of Black Trade Unionists (CBTU), founded in 1972 as a pressure group for African Americans within the labor movement, has exerted greater political influence.

This new power became apparent during the 1995 contest, for the AFL-CIO's presidency, between John J. Sweeney, president of the Service Employees International Union, and AFL-CIO secretary-treasurer Thomas R. Donahue. Black union leaders were not consulted in the selection of the candidates, and the CBTU decided to pressure both candidates to accept fundamental changes in the federation. The CBTU's list of demands included: that more minorities and women be members of delegations sent to AFL-CIO conventions; that more minorities be added to an expanded AFL-CIO executive council; that more African Americans be hired for federation staff positions; and that black labor leaders be consulted in the future "in the drafting of strategies for organizing industries and plants that employ a higher percentage of minorities." Sweeney's October 1995 election as president pointed the federation toward a more progressive position on issues of race and gender. The AFL-CIO 1995 convention voted to increase the number of racial minorities and women on its executive council. With these changes, the number of minorities on the executive council went from four out of thirty-five (11 percent) to eleven out of fifty-four (20 percent).[13]

What are the prospects for African-American and other minority workers as they enter a new century? The globalization of capital and the information revolution have greatly transformed the system of production and even the character of work in the United States. Demographically, the racial, ethnic, and gender composition of the American working class is changing rapidly. For the period 1990–2005, the Bureau of Labor Statistics projects an increase of white males sixteen years and over in the civilian labor force of only 17.4 percent. For women and minorities, the projected percentages are significantly higher: women workers, 26.2 percent; African Americans, 31.7 percent; Asian and Pacific Island Americans, 74.4 percent; and Hispanic Americans, 75.3 percent from their 1990 numbers.[14]

The current national debate about competitiveness in the global economy, for example, must take into account the demographic transformation of the U.S. labor force. For many years, both organized labor and capital largely ignored the black worker. They can no longer afford to do so. As Lou Ferleger and Jay R. Mandle observe:

> More than at any time in the past, the interests of the black labor force coincide with those of the nation as a whole . . . If the United States is to compete effectively in the future, it will require a renewed attention to the productive competence of its labor force — including its sizable African-American component. If this is not done, not only will African-Americans suffer economically, but the country's businesses will continue to decline in world marketplaces.[15]

In the growing trend toward multiculturalism, at least at the present time, the corporations are in some respects ahead of both organized labor and such public and private institutions as universities. Globalization has forced multinational corporations to approach markets in entirely new ways. Both employees and consumers are increasingly multiethnic and transnational. Managers recognize that crosscultural awareness and fluency enhance efforts to enter and exploit new markets. Global corporations that traditionally were run exclusively by Europeans and white North Americans now frequently recruit managers from non-Western societies or from black, Asian, and Latino populations inside the United States. Large firms have initiated "cultural audits" or workshops on diversity training for their managers and sales personnel. In the United States, corporations now often fund multicultural events for employees during African-American History Month or Cinco de Mayo. "Corporate multiculturalism" is the coordinated attempt to manipulate diversity to maximize profits. Labor must surely be as "multicultural" as capital as it considers the demographic trends and social composition of the United States and global workforce.

The long-term question confronting organized labor, however, is whether it will merge the interests of the black freedom movement within its own agenda for social reform. "Race-based" politics cannot address the basic economic interests and problems within the African-American communities, and most black workers implicitly understand this. But organized labor will not make its case for solidarity to minority workers unless it develops the capacity to address class and racial issues simultaneously. The model I have in mind is best represented by Randolph's Negro March on Washington Movement of 1941, which pressured the Roosevelt administration to sign an executive order outlawing segregation in military industries. To Randolph, racial equality as a goal was always tied to economic parity, but the issue of race could not be simplistically reduced or subordinated to the category of class. The historian William H. Harris reminds us that "Randolph saw the Brotherhood of Sleeping Car Porters as an agency to be involved in fomenting social change across the fabric of America and, if he had his way, across the fabric of the world."[16] The twelve-year struggle to achieve a contract for the members of the Brotherhood with the Pullman Company was important but not enough. Labor had the moral and political obligation to fight for social justice and the dismantling of institutional racism.

The basic challenge ahead for black labor is the construction of an alternative political culture, one that can transcend the ideological boundaries and the political limitations of black liberal leadership in the Democratic Party and the civil rights community. "Organizing" is not just a means to articulate grievances or to demand higher wages. Its power lies in the transformation of its subjects. Ordinary people begin to see themselves in a different way. Workers acquire a new sense of power and possibility — that they can change the way things are, both in the workplace and where they live. The rhetoric of divisiveness and racial exclusivity offers no hope for black working people to challenge corporate capital or to reverse the conservative trends in public policy on issues of race. Most black people really understand this. The act of organizing requires people to make effective connections with others who speak different languages or who represent different cultural traditions, nationalities, ethnicities, and religions. There is no monochromatic model for democratic social change in a pluralistic society.

To restate the political query raised by Martin Luther King, Jr., in the aftermath of the triumph over legal segregation: "Where do we go from here?" Black labor will be able to lead only when it can incorporate critical elements of African-American popular culture into its approach to organizing and into its normal political discourse. The model I have in mind here is the civil rights movement. Oppressed people throughout the world for centuries had engaged in civil disobedience, the disruption of the normal activities of the state and civil society. But in the context of the desegregation struggles across the South, civil disobedience was articulated as the "sit-in movement." The creative site of popular protest moved from the courtroom into the streets, to the segregated lunch counters, to department stores. Black workers saw themselves as actors in their own history. The new protest terms, such as "sit-ins" and "freedom rides," established a way of talking about empowerment and resistance. That new language must come from the expressions of daily life and the reflections of struggle that black workers themselves feel and know as their reality.

Notes

1. Peter Drier, "What Farrakhan Left Out: Labor Solidarity or Racial Separatism?" *Commonweal* 122, December 15, 1995, pp. 10–11.
2. William H. Harris, "The Black Labor Movement and the Fight for Social Advance," *Monthly Labor Review* 110, August 1987, pp. 37–39.
3. Louis Uchitelle, "Union Goal of Equality Fails the Test of Time," *New York Times,* July 9, 1995.
4. James P. Smith, "Affirmative Action and the Racial Wage Gap," *American Economic Review* 83, May 1993, pp. 79–84.
5. Norman Hill, "Blacks and the Unions: Progress Made, Problems Ahead," *Dissent* 36, Fall 1989, pp. 496–500; Larry T. Adams, "Union Membership of Wage and Salary Employees in 1987," *Current Wage Developments* 40, February 1988, p. 8; and Uchitelle, "Union Goal of Equality Fails the Test of Time."
6. Lori G. Kletzer, "Job Displacement, 1979–86: How Blacks Fared Relative to Whites," *Monthly Labor Review* 114, July 1991, pp. 17–25.
7. *Ibid.,* pp. 23–24.
8. Lou Ferleger and Jay R. Mandle, "Whose Common Destiny? African Americans and the US Economy," *Socialist Review* 20, January–March 1990, pp. 151–157.
9. Gregory Defreitas, "Unionization among Racial and Ethnic Minorities," *Industrial and Labor Relations Review* 46, January 1993, pp. 284–301. Also see Opinion Research Service, *American Public Opinion Data* (Boston: Opinion Research Service, 1990); and Thomas A. Kochan, "How American Workers View Labor Unions," *Monthly Labor Review* 102, April 1979, pp. 23–31.
10. Hill, "Blacks and the Unions," p. 497.
11. Bureau of Labor Statistics, "Union Members in 1995," Internet Homepage, February 16, 1996.
12. Douglas C. Lyons, "The Growing Clout of Black Labor Leaders," *Ebony* 44, June 1989, pp. 40–46.
13. Drier, "What Farrakhan Left Out," p. 11.
14. Howard N. Fullerton Jr., "Labor Force Projections: The Baby Boom Moves on," *Monthly Labor Review* 114, November 1991, pp. 31–44.
15. Ferleger and Mandle, "Whose Common Destiny?" p. 156.
16. Harris, "The Black Labor Movement and the Fight for Social Advance," p. 38.

18

Labor and the Intellectuals

Paul Berman

I N THE FALL of 1996, Columbia University held its famous teach-in on the suddenly popular topic of relations between intellectuals and the labor movement, and, because my name figured on the advertised list of speakers, the National Writers Union called me up to express the hope that, somewhere in my talk, I might give the union a friendly mention. The National Writers Union? I was happy to comply. The teach-in got under way. My turn at the mike arrived. Instantly I proclaimed myself a member of the union in question. Better: a *charter* member. To be honest, I have never been an especially active or useful member of the National Writers Union, apart from paying my dues. I have even wondered about those dues, sometimes. The National Writers Union puts up a good fight, but it is not yet a very powerful force in the world of writing, and the benefits that come showering down upon its dues-paying rank-and-file are less than vast, relative to the dues, and when I tally up the short-term advantages in my membership — why not admit it? — I start to fidget.

But, then, I didn't join our meager, struggling writers' union looking merely to the short term. In my family, we have been joining unions for what will soon be a hundred years, which makes me a wizened expert on the long term. My grandfather the tailor joined the International Ladies Garment Workers Union in 1902, meaning that in his own union, so much larger and brawnier than mine, he too was a charter member, or very nearly one. Grandpa served as the union steward at his factory for several decades, until his retirement, and was always proud of his activities and of the grand old labor leaders he had known. He thought the world of David Dubinsky. My mother the art teacher served in turn as the delegate of the United Federation of Teachers in her junior high in the Bronx for a number of years. In my case, during my student days I joined the American Federation of Musicians, Local 802, due to my exploits on the trombone, and when the exploits proved less than lucrative, I made my way to a taxi garage and ended up with a membership in the New York taxi drivers' union.

A few years later I went to work at the *Village Voice* and joined the oddly titled District 65, Distributive Workers of America, who did a very good job of distributing some of the *Village Voice*'s profits to us employees. District 65 was a fiesty little union, and when you visited the headquarters you saw framed photographs of the union's long-time leader with his sober Jewish face standing in comradely solidarity next to Martin Luther King, Jr., and the effect was cheering. Then I moved along to the writers' union, which, in the fullness of time, chose to affiliate with the United Auto Workers, meaning that, in the end, I have become an auto worker, organizationally speaking. And from these many affiliations and a stream of dues payments that has gushed outward from my family into the treasuries of one union after another from 1902 to the present, what exactly have I received?

By my figuring, a lot — some of it owing to the specific services that unions provide their members, some of it owing to the wider role that unions play in American life. The unions have always campaigned for more government benefits, more public education, more opportunities for those in short supply; and I was the beneficiary of those many campaigns long before I was born. I grew up in a home with college-educated parents because (on my mother's side) the ILGWU had helped her father survive the Great Depression without sinking into poverty, and because New York City, as a good labor town, had somehow maintained a free public college for both my parents to attend (which, in our current reactionary age, has ceased to be free, needless to say). My own education, at a private university, was munificently subsidized down to the last penny by the kind of state program that the unions have always supported, thereby rendering the private public. My teeth are wealthy with gold and porcelain because of the wise generosity of a variety of union dental plans. And so it has been with me — and with any number of beneficiaries of the labor movement who have similarly used their opportunities to take up an intellectual occupation.

I know that, to many people, the idea of any connection at all between labor and the intellectuals seems faintly ridiculous. I am always astonished at how many of my bookish friends, not excluding the true-blue liberals among them, innocently picture the labor movement in grisly colors as a Mafia-led mob of horny-handed bookless know-nothings, pursuing their own petty advantage and nothing else. The preamble to the old IWW constitution famously thundered, "The working class and the employing class have nothing in common"; and these dear friends instinctively make the same thundering declaration about labor and the intellectuals. Nothing in common. Different spheres entirely. Yet there is quite a bit in common. Family histories like mine are a main thread in American society. It's just that, when Americans speak about upward mobility, they like to puff themselves up with the slippery old phrases about hard work and rugged individualism, and they forget that, for many millions of people, boot-strap self-advancement also comes in the highly efficient form of rugged collectivism.

There is another, more theoretical, link between the labor movement and the intellectuals — though to see the additional link you have to agree on a specific definition of an intellectual. In one sense, an intellectual is somebody — anybody at all — who takes a lively interest in abstract ideas and may even read books on the topic. In a stricter sociological and economic sense, an intellectual is somebody who makes a living by developing ideas or by communicating them to the world — certain kinds of writers, editors, teachers, scholars, scientists, and so forth. But there is also a third sense of the intellectual vocation, which is more of an ideal than a reality, easily embraced by people on the liberal-left side of political opinion, though not necessarily by everyone else — an ideal of intellectual life that stands midway between crusading liberalism and abstract reflection. An intellectual in this third sense is somebody who believes in truth and social justice, without squirming too much over words like *truth* and *social justice*; believes that, through rational analysis, truth and justice can be understood and advanced; believes that an intellectual's duty is precisely to achieve such understandings and advances. An intellectual, to put it another way, is someone, half activist and half savant, who recognizes a beloved and honored ancestor in Zola, the hero of the Dreyfus Affair — the Dreyfus Affair, during which people for the first time used the word *intellectual* in the liberal sense that I am discussing.

Now, from the vantage point of this kind of intellectual, the whole question of labor and its relation to the intellectuals is complicated by still another ideal or, better stated, a theory, older and more venerable even than the Dreyfusard notion of the activist-savant. It is a theory about the labor movement and its place in the world — a theory that labor is an interest group unlike all other interest groups; that labor fights on its own behalf, yet also on behalf of all society; that labor gazes upon the world with clearer eyes than do the other great social forces; that labor's goals are mankind's. The theory maintains that, like the liberal activist-intellectuals, labor, too, stands for truth and justice, except that labor takes its stand in muscular, practical-minded ways that may actually make a difference in how the world is run.

There were always good reasons to be a little wary of certain grandiose elements in that very old and exalted theory, and we ought to acknowledge that, in recent times, the good reasons have fattened into better ones. To suppose that any group of people at all, in the labor movement or anywhere else, are inherently, by definition, fighters for the good and the true always did require a leap of faith. And what can prevent the theory about labor's inherently progressive quality from metamorphosing into a systematic lie, cleverly deployed to shine a flattering light on the bullying actions of a few? Bakunin, in the course of his debates with Marx in the 1870s, was the first to notice the malign uses to which such a theory could be put. According to Bakunin, the people who talk about the working class and its destiny to redeem mankind tend to be theory-besotted intellectuals, and what those intellectuals really mean is this: the intellectuals will rule. Which, as everyone has to admit today, was a very astute observation on Bakunin's part. For what was communism in its early, revolutionary years, before the bureaucrats took over — the years when many a person with the best of intentions still pictured communism as pure and idealistic? It was a dictatorship of the intellectuals, hidden under its proletarian coat and cap.

So — let us avoid reviving the creaky old belief in the grandiose and universal virtues of labor. And yet the notion that labor is not exactly the same as all other interest groups, that labor stands for a larger cause and not just for a narrow set of benefits — this ancient notion still seems to me, in spite of everything, to contain, deep within it, a limited truth. I say a limited truth because I don't want to suggest that labor's virtues, such as they are, genetically derive from some unalterable and invisible trait. But — this is my speculative thought — maybe the labor movement does contain, here and there, a few lingering inheritances from certain generous and imaginative world-views of the past, which survive into the present the way old family customs sometimes survive half-consciously through the generations. There used to be, for instance, a craftsman's noble idea of work, according to which a diligent devotion to a useful trade conferred a special dignity and worth on the individual.

The labor movement in its early years considered itself the bearer of such a concept, meaning that, from the days of its founding era, the movement upheld principles about virtue and a good life that, at least in theory, applied to everyone, not just to the signed-up members of the labor guilds and organizations. In the case of our own American labor movement, it may be worth adding that, from Samuel Gompers on down to today, any number of people have come to their union work from a background in the socialist organizations — even though most of those people eventually shook off their sectarian affiliations and the more rigid socialist dogmas. Or perhaps the generous quality that I am ascribing to labor is owed to other factors, maybe a combination of them — a social-minded heritage from Roman Catholicism, for instance, or the moral precepts of social gospel Protestantism.

The American labor movement's record of standing for the interests of the larger society remains, in any case, quite impressive if you tally up the achievements. There is the example of labor's aggressive role in making possible the New Deal — not just the legislation that benefited unions directly but also the social measures that, by affirming government responsibility for society, benefited the unionists and the nonunionists and even the antiunionists. There is the example of labor's role in the civil rights revolution — a revolution in which many individual white trade unionists stood to lose their narrow privileges of caste but in which, even so, organized labor provided a large part of the institutional support. Or to cite another achievement, there is American labor's record in battling a frightening range of totalitarian movements of the left and the right, at home and around the world.

Whole epics of that particular story, American labor's war against totalitarianism, remain even now virtually unknown to the general public. The role of, for instance, the UAW — my own union! — in trying to undermine the Franco dictatorship in Spain through the distribution of handsome American subsidies to the underground persecuted Spanish anarcho-syndicalists — who knows anything about that? It hardly needs repeating that American labor's struggles against the totalitarianism of the left took a few wrong turns now and then. The American labor movement has never been immune to the zealotries and misconceptions that sweep across other parts of American life, and during the McCarthy era and again during the Vietnam War the labor movement, except for a few smaller unions, was not always the home of wisdom. Persecutions at home, complicity with all sorts of ghastly, pact-with-the-devil foreign-policy campaigns abroad — yes, those were real enough, and there's no point in failing to acknowledge it.

Yet we also ought to acknowledge that communism did pose a danger to civilization, and the American labor movement was right in wanting to oppose it. The labor movement was right to oppose the communists within its own ranks (where the Communist Party did, for a while back in the 1940s, control 20 percent of the CIO). And it was right to lend a fraternal hand to working people in other countries in their own battles against communism. The support that American labor gave to the democratic and libertarian unionists in Western Europe, in their competition against the communists, was high-minded, in my judgment, even if sneaky. To encourage the workers of France to support the noncommunist unions over the communist ones was a favor to France. As for the American labor movement's activities in encouraging the underground anticommunist unionists of the Eastern bloc, this epic, nearly unknown even today, has got to be one of the grandest of all.

Who in American society rallied around Polish Solidarity during the dismal years when communism seemed undefeatable? It wasn't the university activists, except for a very few. The AFL-CIO might well have looked on Eastern Europe's sufferings as a matter of no concern to America's unions — might even have worried that the workers of Eastern Europe, should communism ever be overthrown, might pose a competitive challenge to the workers of America. But, no: in regard to the oppressed proletariats of the Soviet empire, the American labor movement took the same enlightened view as it did in regard to the oppressed blacks of Jim Crow America. Labor interpreted its own interests in the context of society's, and figured that working people would prosper more surely in a democratic world, and American labor stood, as a result, for the universal cause — for the cause of freedom and justice everywhere, not just the cause of better pay and conditions for a small group of people in the short term. Right now we can see that same broad-visioned instinct at work in American labor's effort to support the trade unionists of Mexico and other countries in Latin America. Which is, by the way, yet another story that, even now, remains almost wholly unknown to the wider public.

Why the lack of knowledge about labor and its achievements? Why is it that, even among some of the intellectuals who take seriously the old ideals about truth and justice, labor's good name to-day remains submerged in a gray cloud of unexamined assumptions about bureaucratic selfishness, lack of imagination, me-first curmudgeonliness, mobster stupidity, and so forth? I agree with everyone who points to the Vietnam War. The painful slowness of the bigger unions and the AFL-CIO as a whole to wake up to the war's futility and human cost was an error on the most enormous scale. And among the many disasters that resulted was a pitiful downturn in relations between labor and the intellectuals.

A good many younger intellectuals during the Vietnam years and for a long while after, veering sharply to the left, went about reviving the old-time Marxist-Leninist interpretation of American labor, according to which America's labor organizations are a mainstay of capitalist imperialism — as explained by Lenin himself in his dolefully influential pamphlet *Imperialism: The Highest Stage of Capitalism*. The younger scholars ended up adopting a strangely split feeling about the labor movement: a heartfelt nostalgia for labor's glorious, early, militant days, combined with a sinister view of what (in the eyes of Lenin's readers, and the readers of his readers) labor had become, especially in its foreign policy. And the labor movement responded to this calamitous drop in its prestige by sinking into a morose silence.

George Meany was a scary character. Lane Kirkland spent a long reign at the AFL-CIO in the apparent belief that nothing labor might say would influence public opinion. It is said that Kirkland's heart lay in Eastern Europe, as if he were the president of the AFL-CIO's foreign affairs committee and not of the federation itself. No one in the upper reaches of the labor movement seems to have been tempted to follow the example of the American Federation of Teachers, which took the trouble to expound its views to the outside world by purchasing weekly advertisements in the general press under a grainy photo of Albert Shanker's haggard face. Most of the labor press, judging from what I've seen, has been moronic for a long time now (though there was a time when labor papers routinely published first-rate journalism and even literature). And so, during the last few decades, the intellectuals, especially the intellectuals of the left, who normally might have championed labor's cause, lost respect for the labor movement, and played no part in helping labor express itself — and sometimes even heaped abuse on it. And labor itself, like a sick and elderly person suffering a stroke, stared out at American society from its hospital bed with an anguished expression, utterly mute.

The idea behind the teach-ins of 1996 was to spark a new friendliness between labor and the intellectuals. The possible benefits that might accrue to certain kinds of writers and scholars from a warming of relations are easy to imagine. To mention a few: the writers and scholars may discover that, in American society, intellectuals don't have to be doomed to the lonely isolation that sometimes seems to be their fate. They may discover that there is life beyond the university. They may find themselves refreshed, stimulated, corrected — excited by new fields of inquiry and by new readerships.

On labor's side, the potential benefits come with a few dangers, too. Trade unionists should ask themselves what would happen if, as a result of improved relations, the university intellectuals and their most idealistic students come stampeding into the labor movement, and, like a herd of healthy-looking livestock, turn out to be infected with mad cow disease, in a university version. The labor movement has so far managed not to tear itself up in internal wars over identity politics (except in a few unhappy unions, such as the hospital workers of New York, several years ago, before they were rescued by new leaders). But a general disaster is entirely possible. Any country can become Yugoslavia. All you need is a few people with the sophisticated ability to coat the crudest of ethnic and gender resentments in a sheen of glamour and brilliance, and not enough people to put up a contrary argument.

Still, I hope the labor movement will go ahead with its new friendliness with intellectuals. Many a decade has come and gone since anyone looked to the American labor movement for much original thinking or clear expression. But there is no reason that labor shouldn't be a center for such things, for intelligent and open debate, and for serious journalism. The labor movement has amazing stories to tell about its achievements and about the conditions in which ordinary people find themselves today. There is no reason that it cannot learn to tell those stories more articulately than in the past. Establishing a new friendliness with the intellectuals and the universities is a good, modest way to begin. Everyone stands to benefit — not just the unionists and the friendly intellectuals but society as a whole.

19

Intellectuals and Unions
Retrospect and Prospect

Norman Birnbaum

THE RELATIONSHIP of trade unions to intellectuals in the United States has been marked by all the vicissitudes of the spirit in modern society. The attraction of intellectuals to movements of social transformation organized around the working class has not been less in our nation than elsewhere, but it has not been larger. In the frenzy of self-exculpatory writing by the Counter-Enlightenment's bastard descendants — with its persistent excoriation of other intellectuals as addicted to utopian illusions — it is sometimes forgotten that as many American intellectuals have attached themselves to the established institutions of culture and property as have thought of replacing them.

I will seek to draw from our past ideas for an alliance of intellectuals and trade unions in a new project of social transformation in the United States — a project that, for the moment, exists as a collage of hopes, lessons, and programs. A heterogenous coalition for modifying American capitalism lacks a common denominator, is uncertain of both strategy and tactics, and, above all, has no confidence in its ability to convince a fragmented and disoriented public of both the desirability and the possibility of the profound changes it seeks. In a society with a rising level of formal education, intellectuals may be thought uniquely situated to articulate discontents, explain discontinuities, and translate public aspirations into practical and sequential politics.

In our deformed public sphere, however, the intellectuals who set the agenda are hardly advocates of changes that would reallocate power and wealth — unless it be upward. The media distributing images of society and notions of historical possibility to our citizens are indeed responsive to ideas — as long as they legitimate the present institutions of American capitalism. The unashamed bias and rancid provincialism of much reporting on matters economic and social nicely complement the vacuous escapism of much of the culture fabricated for mass consumption.

The one Asian immigrant many of us find authentically repellent, Mr. Rupert Murdoch, has denounced the excessive "liberalism" of his competitors in press and television. Murdoch's unintended joke reminds us of the waking nightmare in which we are immersed. The agencies and persons responsible for our plight are many, but a great many intellectuals are surely prominent amongst them. David Riesman once observed that America's intellectuals were of more use to their country when they had less use for it. He spoke as our postwar social contract, a considerable achievement, was still in effect. Why, with the conditions that enabled it to function now altered, have so many intellectuals shown indecent enthusiasm for what their fathers (or their younger selves) thought they would never have accepted, a systematic attack on the theory and practice of social solidarity?

Unions often concern themselves primarily with conditions of work, hours, and wages rather than with larger economic and political issues. Even this ordinary unionism is a matter of large indifference to intellectuals whose abstract adherence to the idea of a nation of equals has given way after their integration into at least the middle, if not the upper middle, of our economic and social pyramid.

I term intellectuals those who, directly or indirectly, shape our ideas of the public sphere. That would encompass artists, cineasts and dramatists, musicians, scholars and writers, and natural scientists, too. Ideas do not exist in self-contained forms, and those who transmit ideas have no less claim to be considered intellectuals: editors and publishers, journalists and teachers, an entire industry of culture. Ideas change, for the better or worse, in use; those who employ ideas to interpret their circumstances are also intellectually active, and they too can be deemed intellectuals. I understand intellectuals in this larger sense — and where I restrict the argument to specific groups, I shall say so.

Intellectuals, in any usage of the term, have had and have three sorts of connection to trade unions. They may themselves unionize: think of teachers' unions or the Newspaper Guild. They may work for unions in an intellectual capacity, as advisers and researchers. Union leaders had and have decided intellectual profiles: John Sweeney's familiarity with, *inter alia*, Catholic social thought as well as secular political economic discussion is conspicuous in this respect, but not unusual. However, the most important relationship of intellectuals to unions is an open and unprogrammatic one. Since the advent of industrial capitalism, some have fashioned ideas of labor and its divisions, wealth and its limits, justice and its dimensions, that explain and legitimate unionism. That task has been part of a larger one: the interpretation of the historical movement of society and its implications for moral and political action. If American unionism is to reverse its recent decline, millions of our fellow citizens will have to be convinced that they should either join unions, or regard the work of unions with something other than their current mixture of privatized indifference and anxious hostility.

In educational institutions, the media, the cultural industry generally, intellectuals are potentially capable of altering the terms of national debate about the control of the economy, the division of income and wealth, the balance of private and public interest, market and state. They could also devise experiments in new forms of economic and social organization to meet the changes that now engulf us, indeed, immobilize us. If there is an item of American faith, it surely resides in our belief in progress — but for the moment that is more evident in rhetoric than anywhere else. One striking, even astonishing, aspect of the present situation is the systematic depiction of our intellectuals as dangerously subversive of the beliefs and practices of American capitalism. The criticism, set against the actual influence of critics of capitalism in the academy and of our intellectual life generally, seems utterly disproportionate. Perhaps it is a pre-emptive strike, an anticipatory compliment — if, for the moment, a largely unmerited one.

Movements of social reform in the United States invariably have drawn on the ideas and moral energies of intellectuals. That is especially true of the conflict between our idea of a republic of equals and the omnipotence of the market. American republicanism extended the idea of citizenship to the workplace, and the nascent union movement in the middle of the nineteenth century understood itself as struggling to achieve the ideals of the American Revolution. The prolabor intellectuals who insisted on continuity in our secular history were joined by others, no less fervent in their support of workers, who spoke in religious terms. A direct line of personal and spiritual descent connects the Protestant Abolitionists to the proponents of the Social Gospel. Catholics, priestly and lay, insisted on the primacy of community, on the dignity of the person. The conversion of Jewish messianism into a secular millennialism of social justice was, by the end of the century, yet another element of intellectual support for both the unions and social reform.

Successive groups of working-class immigrants frequently brought with them pronounced ideas of the dignity of labor, even of class struggle. American capitalism was terribly harsh, and ethnic solidarities were immensely important as great waves of immigration broke upon our shores after the Civil War. American democracy was invigorating, and the immigrants joined with Americans of older origins to reinvigorate our politics by giving it a radical social cast.

The nascent union movement had another consequence. It encouraged middle-class thinkers to turn to social reform. The relentless march of the Abolitionists through the institutions of society, to the point at which the question of slavery dominated national politics, was accompanied by discussions of a complex of questions: education, feminism, health, immigration. Gradually, the issue of labor came to preoccupy many of the educated. The world of the factory was new, quite different from the farm and workshop that had dominated the landscape in which the generation that came of age shortly before the Civil War grew up. The idea of free labor played a significant role in the debate on slavery. The taunts of George Fitzhugh, depicting slavery as benignly paternalistic and the Northern factory system as coldly exploitative, had an effect — if not quite the one he intended. A significant number of Abolitionist thinkers began to develop an extended idea of freedom for the newly emerging masses of factory workers. Their intellectual offspring were the Progressives.

Historians have depicted Progressivism as the work of men (and women) of the Word, lawyers, pastors, thinkers, writers, who found the brutality and selfishness of the new capitalism at the end of the nineteenth century repugnant. What they feared and hated, as well, was the rending of community. The violence of class conflict as the century neared its end confirmed their worst apprehensions: unless checked, wealth would become not merely the dominant power in the nation but the only one. They drew upon republican traditions and developed a contrasting vision, in which the rights of labor were conjoined to a conception of citizenship. Consider that Edward Bellamy's *Looking Backward*, a plea for a cooperative commonwealth, had editions of 500,000 copies. It stimulated the formation of hundreds of clubs organized to advance the idea of a new American commonwealth, clubs that were part of the effervescence that also generated the Populist movement — if with a different social composition and a far more Eastern and urban basis.

The Progressives were frequently paternalistic and patronizing — of the immigrants in the working class and the native-born rural migrants to industrial cities. Under Theodore Roosevelt, Progressivism was a part of an American social imperial doctrine and practice. Just as the British Fabians advocated a welfare state to strengthen the nation in competition with Germany, the first Roosevelt and the thinkers who were enthusiastic about his program anticipated what later was to be called the American Century. Progressivism, then, had a component of anxiety. The Progressives saw their version of a relatively harmonious nation as threatened by rampant capital. It was no less threatened by many of the enemies of capital: the farmers who in the Populist movement and with William Jennings Bryan rejected any and all of the Eastern elites, the immigrant socialists who had brought doctrines of revolution with them. The cultural repugnance of the Progressive intellectuals for both Catholicism and urban immigrant culture was evident in the campaigns against the corruption of the urban machines and for health and temperance.

By 1900, the Progressives were hardly the only socially conscious intellectuals in the nation. The union movement did include leaders and militants who read and thought for themselves. The sources of their thought were as varied as the cultural and ideological roots of early American unionism itself. We can begin with social interpretations of Catholicism and Protestantism, the former insisting on community and the latter on justice, but each concerned with the dignity of labor. The secularization of Judaism in the nineteenth century rendered the Jewish immigrants susceptible to socialism. Marxism was familiar in the United States, not least among German immigrants (but also English ones influenced by the First International Workingmen's Association) well before the Russian Revolution of 1905. A number of variants of socialism found expression in movements from the Knights of Labor to the Industrial Workers of the World. Books, newspapers and pamphlets, conferences, meetings and informal gatherings, served to propagate these ideas. The intellectuals in the labor movement were by no means confined to editorial or propagandistic tasks — and we can certainly think of Gompers and Debs as intellectuals themselves.

At the turn of the century, the question of labor was central to theological discussion and so brought religious ideas into a national debate. Catholics were, mainly, immigrants, and often the clergy took the side of their working-class parishioners in conflicts with capital. The bishops, however, were decidedly cautious and, at times, even quietistic. Opposed conceptions of Catholic adaptation to the United States were at issue. The conservatives favored the encapsulation of Catholics; the modernists, integration in the society. Most bishops remained skeptical of the redistributionist positions of the Catholic Welfare Conference, but the social Catholic Party insisted that it was acting in the spirit of the Papal Encyclical of 1891, *Rerum novarum*. Many Catholic laymen, in any event, saw no contradiction between their faith and a profound engagement in unionism. A subsequent generation of bishops and theologians were to support the New Deal, in a belated but convincing triumph for the early social party.

In the several spiritual worlds of American Protestantism, the Social Gospel induced many in the educated middle class to sympathize with unionism at the turn of the century. A prophetic reading of the two Testaments provided a millennial, which is to say critical, interpretation of capitalism. Congregationalism affirmed the rights of communities to self-governance, and this was transposed into rejection of the economic power of the distant centers of capitalism. Finally, the cultivation of conscience demanded exemplary opposition to exploitation. From Washington Gladden to the young Reinhold Niebuhr, Protestant pastors who were by no means from working-class families took up the cause of labor. We may recall that when Jefferson died, in 1826, he regarded the commercialized nation with melancholy distance. Unlike Catholic priests or Jewish intellectuals, the Protestant clergy had familial memories of an eradicated and idealized American past. The past gone, they interpreted a distressing present in the light of a splendid future. Nostalgia gave rise to a progressivist eschatology that inclined many Protestants to seek very radical reform.

Jews are not the only people with a book — but it is hard to imagine Jews without one. The literate (and obsessively quarrelsome) Jews who came to the United States from Central and Eastern Europe were predominantly proletarians, but proletarians of a specific sort. They were already accustomed, unlike some other immigrant groups, to living in the interstices of capitalism. Having endured anti-Semitic persecution and economic discrimination under czarism, contested rights in the Austro-Hungarian and German empires, they had every reason to interpret the new country, with its enormous freedoms, as a promised land.

The transformation of religious energies into secular doctrines of salvation was an experience of conversion: Jews cast off tradition to become Americans, social reformers, and socialists. The burdens of proletarian existence in the new land stimulated unionization — of a highly self-conscious sort, accompanied by an outpouring — no, a torrent — of theoretic argument and justification.

The close connection between a social setting, a cultural tradition (even a tradition in conflict, as most traditions usually are), and intellectual activity characterized American intellectual life up to the Progressive epoch. Attachment to the union movement, or sympathy for it, was a by-product of the intellectuals' integration in their milieux. The epoch, however, marked a break in historical continuity. Progressivism, for all of its ties to the disappearing or lost republican past, was the work of a new type of intellectual, whose origins were less important than the occupation of newer social functions. The new intellectuals were not found in law offices, pulpits, or in the solitude of their remote studies. Neither did they work directly for social movements or parties. They were employed, instead, in the expanding industry of culture, in the new research universities, and in government itself.

One of the consequences of capitalism, of the spread of large-scale ownership, was what Alan Trachtenberg termed "the incorporation of America." Local industry gave way to production for a national market. A new culture of consumption was made possible by gradually rising living standards, even within the fluctuations of the business cycle. A national intellectual market emerged, in which entertainment and instruction, high and low culture, were often inextricably mixed.

The ethnic communities kept their own languages. The churches continued to rule large segments of the American spirit. Regional distinctiveness was prominent. Still, a process of assimilation and even secularization was begun on a national scale. Book and magazine and newspaper publishers demanded copy: an ascendant generation of writers was ready to provide it. These intellectuals lived by their wits. Their social anchorage was not fixed in what had been relatively traditional patterns. They were by no means all disinterested servants of the truth, but they were of professional necessity attuned to what was new, conflictual, in society. Some chose to side with labor, by depicting exploitation and injustice. Others accepted market (which is to say, employer) restraints, by no means always

tacit, on what they could write. We can say that for these intellectuals, rather unbound to milieux, the cultural market was decisive.
Many manipulated it for private ends. Others, fewer, sought employment and patronage from the unions and the radical social
movements around them. All had an increasing awareness of dependence on the owners of the means of cultural production. If their
working situation was in critical respects analogous to that of other
workers, most preferred to see it that way only as metaphor.

The emergence of American universities as centers of systematic
research around the turn of the century gave us another set of Progressive intellectuals. Many of the scholars of the founding generation went to Germany to study and encountered a very different
variant of capitalism. Germany had a combative and self-conscious
working class, a socialist party — and a system of social protection
instituted by elites to prevent the rupture of the nation. That im-
pressed the younger Americans, who developed, in economic, political, and social studies (and in the law, a previously impregnable
fortress of capitalist ideology), a body of doctrine for American
social reform. They were not without antagonists in the universities
(especially on their lay governing bodies and among their administrative servants, for neither of whom academic freedom was a primary value). A substantial body of the new social science had a
distinctly reformist cast. Many in the academy responded with gen-
teel shock, others fought it ferociously, and very few sided directly
with labor or the socialist movements. Still, it was this academy
which gave us John Dewey and Felix Frankfurter. More important,
perhaps, it widened the scope of public discussion — and began that
long process in which the ideas of the New Deal were conceived.

The increased participation of the educated in politics was yet
another change in intellectual life in the Progressive era. The movements for reform in education, health, women's rights, were obviously broader than campaigns for good government — and distinct
from the class militancy of the unions. Still, they mobilized much
intellectual energy to redefine and enlarge the public sphere in ways
that were explicitly critical of unregulated capitalism. Finally, as
the competence of government was extended, the intellectual com-

position of the public service was altered. As advisers and officials, economists, political scientists, lawyers (and natural scientists) joined federal and state governments. The "Brandeis Brief," with its introduction of economic and social argument in place of legal formalism, dates from 1908. The law had been politicized from the beginning of the Republic; now lawyers could no longer deny that they were anything but neutral.

With the changes of the Progressive epoch, American intellectual life was cast in an institutional framework that was to last almost to our period. The relationship of intellectuals to unionism has to be read in this historical setting. A severely, but not impossibly, condensed version of the process might read as follows.

The social choices of intellectuals had been determined by their milieux: church, class, ethnic group, family, race, region. That is, intellectuals up to the beginning of our century worked with the traditions they were born into. Of course, there were exceptions: we can think of Henry Thoreau and Walt Whitman as achieving a rare view of the nation as a whole. More typical was the patrician George Bancroft, the apologist for slavery George Fitzhugh, even the utopian Edward Bellamy: in his utopia everyone could be a Bostonian. In this setting, a spokesman for the exploited like Eugene Debs was bound to come from, and address, a working-class milieu, just as the supreme American intellectual William Du Bois was torturedly confined to blackness, and William Jennings Bryan expressed agrarian rage.

With the nationalization of the economy and the rationalization of capitalism, culture too was nationalized and rationalized. Paradoxically, it was organized in milieux of its own. The academy, the arts and literature, the cultural industry as a whole (expanded to include the vastly important realm of film), the sciences, became separate domains. Their autonomy was limited, but not entirely spurious, and the limits were frequently uncertain and unfixed — if less so in the sectors producing directly for a mass cultural market. Careers were now made in these new cultural milieux by persons detaching themselves from their cultural and social origins. The process was gradual, any number of persons were implanted in two places at once (a source of creativity and personal tragedy, too), but in the end we had, by Wilson's presidency, a national intelligentsia.

The union movement in the changed cultural circumstances of the nation increasingly needed the academic knowledge, ideological legitimation, and intellectual skills that the educated could provide. Catholic and Jewish daughters and sons of the working class, the first generation of their families to graduate from universities, were available for these tasks. Alternatively, they entered public service as officials eager and ready to develop an American welfare state when the occasion presented itself. The New Deal drew upon this reserve army of reform when it recruited from the states that had experimented with economic regulation and social welfare before 1933.

The new forms of intellectual organization did not mean that the intellectuals were sovereign, but they did entail new relationships to power. The national intelligentsia developed enormous sensitivity to political possibilities just over the historical horizon — a secularization of the prophetic mission of the American clergy. The intelligentsia also sought channels and gateways to influence, sometimes by addressing an enlarged national public — or by direct service to elites in an advisory capacity, discrete or otherwise. The situation, in all of its complexity, sometimes narrowed and sometimes widened choice — and, occasionally, left space for the invention of new choices. The intellectuals could not escape the burdens of choice — but their servitude was and is, in a society in which relatively few had and have the luxury of any choice at all, a form of freedom.

That freedom was from time to time exercised on behalf of working people. The intellectuals' relationships to unions have fluctuated with their militancy and strength. When the unions were actually or potentially ascendant, important or even decisive actors in a continuing historical drama, they interested intellectuals greatly. Intellectuals were drawn to unions if they themselves had not only hopes for social transformation, but a historical and social vision of how it could be achieved. The pathetic history of the Commission on Industrial Relations created by Wilson, which began as a national forum for altering labor relations and ended in impotent strife, is instructive. The academic experts who sympathized with labor were systematically undermined by the intellectual and political manipulation of pseudoreformists in the service of capital.

In the great wave of union organization and strikes that immediately followed the First World War, intellectuals already connected to labor were solidly and sometimes (in the academy and journalism, where they were often hard pressed themselves) active and vocal on the unions' behalf. That was especially true of those excited by the early promise of the Soviet Revolution, although those less enthralled by it were often no less appalled by the repression (frequently of the most brutal and primitive sort) inflicted upon the unions — which followed the savagery of the assault on those who had opposed American participation in the war. That repression at local and state levels coincided with an offensive against the unions (and economic and social regulation, generally) in the courts. It coincided as well with the systematic and quite unconstitutional program of persecution of the left initiated by Attorney General Palmer. The unions' militancy subsided, and on the historical balance sheet defeat outweighed victory. Some intellectuals maintained their commitments — by working in the unions, or propagating the ideas of the nascent American Communist Party or the revived Socialist Party, by joining the Farmer-Labor campaign of La Follette. Others in the universities persisted in the critique of American capitalism.

As a new generation of writers came to maturity, its cultivation of a distinct version of American modernism, the beginnings of an ethnically and racially mixed society in New York, were not explicitly political. Yet the depiction of American society in *The Great Gatsby* and *Main Street,* Hemingway's exploration of the lostness of the lost generation, were preconditions for the sort of cultural-political criticism that exploded in Dos Passos's *USA.*

Women obtained the right to vote, and their labor force participation increased, reinforcing the determination of a small but growing cadre of women intellectuals and professionals to pursue women's issues with implications for family, state, and workplace. Finally, the cities continued to grow — with New York consolidating its position as a world capital of culture and commerce, and

Chicago functioning as a secondary capital for much of the nation. Some of the states — among them Massachusetts, Minnesota, New York, Wisconsin — extended government's reach in matters economic and social. As the educational level generally increased and higher education expanded, the offspring of working-class immigrants with union experience acquired degrees. They provided an enlarged public for socially critical ideas, sometimes worked for unions.

What had been a patrician Protestant notion — that the nation had to be retaken from those whose most visible social characteristic was wealth — was also congenial to the rural and small-town younger Americans who came from the state universities. The ambiance of Chicago and New York also socialized the geographically and socially mobile among the educated in ways that made them actually or potentially sympathetic to unions. Think of the young people from Muncie, Indiana (the Lynds' *Middletown*): they entered, in the cities, another world. It would be absurd to ignore the college and university graduates who saw no reason to reject the dogma they had heard from their conservative professors — if, indeed, they had bothered to stay awake in class. John J. McCloy, the later chairman of the American establishment, came to New York from a modest background in Ohio after sharpening his ambitions at Amherst College: there is no evidence that he attended socialist discussion clubs. There were, however, the younger Edmund Wilson and, a bit later, Dwight Macdonald.

The unions were hardly in a period of latency in the twenties, even if the postwar wave of militancy subsided. The debates within and between communist and socialist formations on an industrial and labor strategy were often scholastic and tortuous, but they did give to the unions cadres who thought in larger terms. With the Depression, followed by Franklin Roosevelt's administration, came an entire generation of intellectuals ready to do battle. Some were in the unions already, others in the cultural industry (where, as in Hollywood, they propagated images of society consonant with New Deal ends), others in the universities. Perhaps the most important were those who were new recruits to the federal government —

from state governments or the academy or the professions. They provided the bureaucratic support, the legal skills, for the political decisions of the New Deal — not least the decision to use the powers of the federal government to support labor.

No doubt, the unions had to help themselves, and did so in the remarkable organizing drive conducted by the CIO and the occupation of the GM plants. Had it not been for the prolabor civil servants in the government, had public opinion not been convinced by a very considerable campaign that labor's claims were just, the drive might well have been less effective. We do well to recall, too, that many of the organizers of the CIO's drive were college educated — recruited directly by the unions, often from the Communist Party or the various socialist formations. However wracked the American left was by the torment caused by Stalinism and its crimes, all of its factions agreed that the *via regis* to American socialism led through a strong labor movement.

The New Deal ended, however, in 1938. It was the war that brought full employment and that enabled the unions to begin negotiating the social contract of the period, which lasted through the Nixon and even Ford and Carter presidencies — if in increasingly attenuated form. The period (including the war, despite the truce agreed to by many of the unions for its duration) was hardly free of strife. We can cite the strikes of 1946, the counteroffensives of American capital in the 1946–48 Republican Congress, and the return of an only slightly enlightened Republicanism in 1952. It was a period in which the unions functioned as a powerful interest group in a limited recrudescence of American pluralism. In his statement immediately after Truman's re-election in 1948, the chairman of the Democratic National Committee declared that the triumph owed most to labor. Under Kennedy and Johnson, labor was treated as an estate of the realm — although of a realm that was, shortly, to disintegrate.

What were the consequences for the relationship of labor to the intellectuals? One of the preconditions of the postwar contract and the ideology and practice of consensus was the elimination and marginalization of thinkers and groups that sought a more profound transformation of the relationship of market and society. Elimination was accomplished with unashamed brutality by the organized persecution of the Communist Party and those who could, with extremely varying degrees of plausibility, be accused of any degree or type of association with it. To some considerable extent, that process entailed an uncivil war between segments of the American intelligentsia. The examples are plentiful, but surely two instances of consummate lack of nobility may be found in Professor Daniel Boorstin's testimony to the Congress and Irving Kristol's praise for Senator McCarthy in *Commentary*.

Entire segments of experience (and of history) disappeared from the consciousness of American intellectuals. Hannah Arendt's *Origins of Totalitarianism* was an account of the extreme fragility of capitalist society; it was systematically misinterpreted as a defense of liberalism. There were, of course, honorable exceptions. Dwight Macdonald's *Politics* hardly ignored the problems of work, and it was Macdonald in *The New Yorker* who brought Michael Harrington's *The Other America* to the attention of a broad public (and John Kennedy). Lewis Coser and Irving Howe led the group that founded the one journal that kept a connection to the labor movement, *Dissent*. Harrington, Howe, Macdonald *et al.* were, however, marginalized, if with respect, as "social critics." Their insistence that postwar America was not quite utopia achieved relieved the conscience of their readers, who took the very utterance of criticism as proof that the system was benign. It can be argued that John Kenneth Galbraith, in *The Affluent Society,* did raise serious questions and that he was a senior Democrat. True, but he was sent to New Delhi as ambassador and not appointed secretary of the treasury. His *American Capitalism: Countervailing Power* actually provided the theory of the social contract but did not anticipate its demise. C. Wright Mills, in *White Collar* and *The Power Elite*, questioned both the durability and the extent of the contract; he was both widely read and widely patronized as an early twentieth-century radical lost in the century's middle.

Who read these thinkers and participated in the debates they engendered? The first thing to be said is that debate was limited.

More intellectual energy was spent on celebrating and rationalizing the postwar consensus (as in the book by Louis Hartz, *The Liberal Tradition in America*) than in questioning it. (Daniel Ernst objects that Hartz could be read as very critical of a nation without political alternatives. Perhaps — but for his initial readers, the notion of an absence of alternatives confirmed their own tepidity.)

The postwar labor movement was five times the size of its ancestor in 1930. Large numbers of activists and militants found work in the movement, and joined graduates of an expanding higher educational system in its ranks — often in education and research or editorial and legal tasks. Others sympathetic to labor (including, again, large numbers of younger people of working-class origin who went to college and university after 1945) found employment in federal, state, and local government. Both groups were involved in the routine administration of the social contract, rather than in a strenuous effort to rewrite its terms. A limited amount of attention was given, before the civil rights movement, to the situation of black workers, and the record of some industrial unions (the United Auto Workers, for instance) was entirely credible — in contrast with that of craft unions. The failure of the postwar organizing drive in the American South, however, meant that a large section of the nation was devoid of the contract.

The older intellectuals attached to the labor movement, and some of the newer generation, worked with the unions. What about the majority of the newly educated? In an expanding labor market for managers and professionals, scientists and technologists, organizational and sales specialists of every sort, they streamed into the tertiary sector. In two occupations influencing opinion formation, education and journalism, they even encountered unionism. The National Education Association had begun its own long march from submissive gentility to militant unionism; the American Federation of Teachers needed no persuasion. Recruits to journalism often found that their employers had settled with the Newspaper Guild. The NEA and the AFT campaigned, regularly, for more funding for education but were hardly vanguard organizations on the model of the French Fédération de l'Éducation Nationale (which led the opposition to the Algerian war). As for the Newspaper Guild, its members enjoyed advantageous contracts — but on no account challenged either the corporate ownership of the media or the view that journalism was "neutral." Their reporting reinforced the most philistine of social philosophies, that the world is as it seems. There have been only isolated instances of disputes between owners and journalists on the contents of the latter's work in any of the media.

In colleges and universities, especially public institutions, there was some collective bargaining — but most of the research and teaching institutions at the apex of the academic pyramid were completely untouched by unionism. When, in opposition to the Vietnam War and to provoke a discussion of the political and social uses of science, faculty at MIT called a one-day "research strike," it was for many participants a break with their complete integration into that curious fusion of extreme corporatism and extreme privatization that marked most American university faculties. Of course, there were institutes of industrial and labor relations at any number of universities, and some had close ties to the labor movement — but they were far outnumbered by business schools and economic research centers totally integrated with capital. The intellectual legacies of John Commons and Selig Perlman were, to be sure, very much alive — and incarnated in newer forms by academic economists who, like John Dunlap and George Schulz, each became a secretary of labor. Their attitudes were perfectly matched to the business unionism of the late stages of the social contract. Ray Marshall and Robert Reich in the same position were closer to the unions — without having major influence on policy.

Clerical and technical employees of some universities did unionize, sometimes engaging in bitter struggles with the wealthiest institutions. Yale disgraced itself thoroughly by resisting unions in a way that would certainly have delighted one alumnus, Chief Justice William Howard Taft. As for Harvard, under the presidency of the labor lawyer Derek Bok — who had often written of the positive functions of unionism — it acted as if union busting were a cherished New England cultural trait. In government, *per contra*, the postwar expansion led eventually to large-scale unionization at lower and intermediate levels. In the health services industry, the same sort of unionization (at lower and intermediate levels) occurred, especially in larger cities with union traditions. Physicians remained adamantly outside unionism, if given to their own forms of corporatism; nurses were far more likely to organize. In the private sector outside universities, most professional, scientific, and technical employees did not envisage unionism (or any form of militant organization) as a possibility. Indeed, private sector white-collar unionism at any level is sparse, although it is interesting that the unionization of industrial workers in a firm or industry has a positive effect on the readiness of others in the same settings to confront their dependency.

If we turn to the intellectual situation as the social contract neared its apogee in the Kennedy years, the striking fact is how little attention was given to unions, work, and workers. Daniel Bell published *The End of Ideology* in 1960, with his excellent essay, "Work and Its Discontents" — but what was discussed was his view of the terminal condition of larger ideas.

Hannah Arendt's *The Human Condition* of 1958 contained a serious discussion of work, was treated with respect, and not considered further. Herbert Marcuse had published *Eros and Civilization* in 1951 and continued the argument with *One Dimensional Man* in 1964, but his assertion that work had changed in nature and social consequence from Freud's period was considered an interesting idea of no immediate political relevance. The statement by a group of American thinkers, *The Triple Revolution*, 1964, dealt seriously with work but was received as an academic exercise. Interestingly, it was published by Students for a Democratic Society.

Unions, ordinary work, and the people who did it had receded over the horizon. They were not so much ignored as taken for granted. Many American intellectuals sympathized with unions, but they took their positive role in the moral economy of the nation as a given. With the civil rights movement, the question of race became acute. Harrington's book had brought poverty into public discussion. Vietnam was to provoke a national conflict of enormous intensity. The class structure, as such, was hardly evoked.

I come to the problem of the American New Left. The European

New Left saw its task as the rejuvenation of routinized parties and unions. The American New Left most certainly acted as if it believed that there was little to rejuvenate. Yet its familial, ideological, and organizational descent from an older left closely tied to unions is uncontestable. The themes developed by the New Left, not always with historical and intellectual sophistication, were surely not impossibly remote from the concerns of the labor movement. The question of personal autonomy and dignity, the distortion of resource allocation, poverty in this country and in the Third World, racial justice, women's rights, all connect with the long-term interests of labor. That the New Left's mode of addressing the public showed neither skill nor tact is clear.

The New Left's antagonism was directed, precisely, at the liberal-labor elite, at the party that had conceived and managed the American social contract. It was that contract, after all, which had expanded higher education and made possible the bureaucratic and professional careers the New Leftists so obviously disdained. Those in the elite were indignant that their own *bona fides* (and, of course, their power) were challenged. The organized working class interpreted much of the revolt as middle-class self-indulgence — or as the colossal ingratitude of the working-class students who joined the new movements by the hundreds of thousands.

Having left the education of the working class, largely, to the mass media, the unions were helpless in the face of the upsurge in their ranks of unreflective chauvinism, outraged philistinism, and fearful racism. Some union leaders, of course, thought of these responses as a laudable defense of family, community, and nation.

The New Left, the debate over the Vietnam War, and the rapidly fragmented civil rights movement divided the intellectuals themselves. It is useful to recall that Norman Podhoretz can claim to have been a founder of the New Left, with his critical editorials in *Commentary* after his assumption of the editorship in 1960, and the space he gave to Paul Goodman, Staughton Lynd, and David Riesman. Podhoretz by the end of the decade had joined other serious intellectuals (Nathan Glazer, Jeane Kirkpatrick, and Daniel Patrick Moynihan) in a fraction of the Democratic Party organized by the

AFL-CIO, the Coalition for a Democratic Majority. Their project insisted on an aggressive American foreign policy but attached equal weight to the continuation of the social contract.

Michael Harrington and Irving Howe sought other terrain — supported in their turn by the leadership of the United Auto Workers and of the American Federation of State, County, and Municipal Employees. The black and feminine components of their membership predisposed it to skepticism of the Coalition for a Democratic Majority's not-quite-implicit claim that the United States embodied an achieved revolution.

The revolution of the New Left, at any rate, was totally unachieved. Its long-term cultural and political effects are of course a matter of debate — but the retroactive demonization (frequently not merely absurd but grotesque) of the New Left surely attests to its importance. At one point I termed it "an anticipatory strike by the labor force of tomorrow." Those who participated in the New Left are now indeed in the labor force — reason enough for them to be glad, presumably, that they struck at least once.

The New Left never developed an intellectual synthesis. It was far more articulate and convincing about what in our society should be changed than about the means to effect that change, or about the alternative institutions it wished to develop. Its intellectual legacy is utterly fragmented. A significant set of its veterans, however, turned to the labor movement (just as others pursued careers in those segments of the professions which offered scope for care and conscience). A smaller group has a significant achievement to its credit, the enlargement as well as the revivification of the writing of American labor history.

There have been two general conditions under which intellectuals were induced to ally themselves, in one or another way, with the labor movement. One was some form of systematic economic or spiritual distress affecting the educated directly. The other was the possession by labor, apparent or real, of the keys to the future: its leadership or central position in an ascendant historical formation. At this moment, both conditions are lacking.

The unions have every reason to hope that, under their new national leadership, much can be accomplished; there remains a long and entirely uncharted road to a return to national power, the more so as the reach even of our national state is diminishing. As for the distress felt by the educated, in economic terms it is limited and privatized. Quite apart from the considerable opportunities the cultural market still presents (not least to those prepared to discipline their inner doubts about the direction of our society), the market does not lend itself readily to collective counterorganization. Most of the ascending generation of the educated (who will provide for the public such critical ideas as the more original among them produce) have been inculcated with individualized career ideologies.

No less important, the ties of memory have often been weakened. The grandchildren and great-grandchildren of the New Deal, whose grandparents or great-grandparents were in the ILGWU or the WPA or benefited from the AAA, are often unable to establish any connection between their own lives and the sacrifices of previous generations.

In the circumstances, a stratum of anxious strivers is likely to resort to a classic form of American class conflict: the war of the threatened against the weak. It is in precisely this respect that so many of the neoconservatives are morally and humanly repugnant.

There are some steps open to the union movement that may attract the interest and eventually the support of intellectuals. Contemporary changes in the structure of employment and the nature of work entail problems as diverse as the lack of opportunities for lifelong learning and the precariousness of employment — for all kinds of workers, including educated ones. The increasing role of knowledge in the administrative and productive processes makes it difficult for the employed to refuse to consider the ultimate social uses to which their skills are put.

Questions of the morality and utility of our present scale of resource allocation are raised by the arrogance of capital and its intellectual and political servants. The labor movement can hardly confine itself to questions of hours and wages, employment security, and quality and safety at the workplace. These are decided at the centers of decision in the nation — which have sought to insulate themselves from criticism by presenting themselves as benign and irreplaceable (or by denying that they have any power at all). A larger project by the unions will be needed to capture the imagination of the intellectuals.

One promising aspect of the situation is that many of the offspring of the most exploited workers in the nation, the blacks and the recent immigrants, are using their educational opportunities to assist their communities of origin. The repetition of the experience of earlier waves of immigration may well provide the unions with new cadres — who can join others in a broad coalition for major reforms.

In all of our darkness, there are some rays of light. There are two sources of intellectual — no, spiritual — attitude that may converge to encourage intellectuals to consider the union movement as an ally. One may be termed self-respect, although it is connected to the old question "Which side are you on?" Do the American educated really wish to live in a society in which disparities of life chances continue to widen, in which the pursuit and possession of wealth becomes the dominant if not the sole standard of moral worth? That is a society which would mock nearly everything of value in their own lives — and degrade their knowledge and talents while exploiting and rewarding them.

These aesthetic and moral grounds aside, intellectuals do think. Does anyone with some knowledge of American history, and the history of the modern world, suppose that our nation can go on as it has — with *panem et circenses,* but with decidedly less bread and more circuses? Ever in the forefront of history, we may suffer newer forms of social disintegration — to be followed by the intensification of political fraud and the invention of new servitudes. The subordination of the market by the nation and the extension of citizenship to the workplace remain the unfulfilled tasks of American democracy. They cannot be achieved without the reinvigoration of the labor movement. That is, of course, the job of the unions. Intellectuals, aware of their own social vulnerabilities, might well consider it in their interest to assist in a large process of renewal and reinvention.*

Bibliography

Daniel Aaron, *Writers on the Left: Episodes in American Literary Communism.* New York: Harcourt, 1981.

Daniel Bell, *Marxian Socialism in the United States.* Ithaca and London: Cornell University Press, 1996.

Thomas Bender, *New York Intellect: A History of Intellectual Life in New York City from 1790 to the Beginnings of Our Own Time.* New York: Knopf, 1987.

Norman Birnbaum, *The Radical Renewal,* New York: Pantheon, 1988.

Norman Cantor, *The Sacred Chain: The History of the Jews.* New York: Harper Collins, 1994.

Robert Crunden, *Ministers of Reform: The Progressives' Achievement in American Civilization.* New York: Basic Books, 1982.

Harold Cruse, *The Crisis of the Negro Intellectual.* New York: Morrow, 1967.

Ann Douglas, *Terrible Honesty: Mongrel Manhattan in the 1920s.* New York: Farrar, Straus and Giroux, 1995.

Daniel Ernst, *Lawyers Against Labor, from Individual Rights to Corporate Liberalism.* Urbana: University of Illinois, 1995.

Leon Fink, *In Search of the Working Class.* Urbana: University of Illinois, 1994.

Leon Fink, "Expert Advice: Progressive Intellectuals and the Unraveling of Labor Reform, 1912–15." In Leon Fink, Stephen T. Leonard, Donald M. Reid, eds., *Intellectuals and Public Life: Between Radicalism and Reform.* Ithaca: Cornell University Press, 1996.

Richard Flacks, *Making History.* New York: Columbia University Press, 1988.

Mary Furner, "Social Scientists and the State: Constructing the Knowledge Basis for Public Policy, 1880–1920." In Fink, Leonard, Reid, *op. cit.*

James B. Gilbert, *Writers and Partisans: A History of Literary Radicalism in America.* New York: Wiley, 1968.

James J. Hennesey, S.J., *American Catholics: A History of the Roman Catholic Community in the United States.* New York: Oxford University Press, 1981.

*The author wishes to thank Daniel Ernst for an exemplary critical reading of the text.

Russell Jacoby, *The Last Intellectuals: American Culture in the Age of Academe.* New York: Basic Books, 1983.

Christopher Lasch, *The New Radicalism in America, 1889–1963: The Intellectual as a Social Type.* New York: Knopf, 1965.

Martin E. Marty, *Righteous Empire: The Protestant Experience in America.* New York: Dial, 1970.

Allen Matusow, *The Unraveling of America: A History of Liberalism in the 1960s.* New York: Harper and Row, 1984.

Dorothy Ross, *The Origins of American Social Science.* Cambridge and New York: Cambridge University Press, 1991.

Alan Wald, *The New York Intellectuals: The Rise and Decline of the Anti-Stalinist Left from the 1930s to the 1980s.* Chapel Hill: University of North Carolina Press, 1987.

20

"The Folks Who Brought You the Weekend"

Labor and Independent Politics

Joel Rogers

MY FAVORITE pro-union bumper sticker — admittedly, a small universe from which to cull favorites — identifies labor unions as "the folks who brought you the weekend." The weekend, the eight-hour day, a minimum wage, and too many now-taken-for-granted job protections and social-insurance programs to count. The "folks" (a.k.a. organizations) that did not just pursue a particularistic "contracts are us"/"I'm all right Jack" politics of the organized, but an inclusive "he's not heavy, he's my brother" politics directed to the broadly disorganized working class. The "collection [a.k.a. movement] of many that spoke for all" — from a moral center, a clear sense of everyday if unrealized values, and a confidence in the practical imperative of realizing those values that inspired.

After a long dark night, such a movement may again be dawning. The "new voices" leadership team of John Sweeney, Rich Trumka, and Linda Chavez-Thompson — which ran for office because, in Sweeney's words, "organized labor is the only voice of American workers and their families, and because the silence [under Lane Kirkland] was deafening" — is making good on campaign promises to increase labor's organizing expenditures; upgrade its public relations, program, and political work; build the capacity of regional bodies (state federations, central labor councils); do aggressive out-reach — reflected in, among other things, the composition of executive bodies — to minorities and women; and remake the federa-tion's own organization, starting with the appointment of younger, smarter, more aggressive unionists to top staff positions. Labor is moving again, showing some muscle, and feeling better about itself than it has in years.

For all the good news, however, the bad news is that it may all be coming too late. Labor may be gaining new friends, but some of its old ones — like those in a Democratic administration resolutely am-bivalent about the worth of unions — are increasingly unreliable. Public opinion is vaguely supportive but unconvinced that labor has the answers to what ails it. And labor's real power in the economy is drastically diminished — with private sector union density now down to the pre–New Deal level of only 10 percent, and strikes at their lowest level in fifty years — with no obvious way to increase it. Just to maintain present density levels, labor needs 300,000 new members a year; to bump present levels up one point — and un-ion density is down about twenty points from its 1950s levels — it needs a million a year. Nobody's seen anything like those numbers since the 1930s, and the organization of today's economy is very dif-ferent.

So labor appears ready for change, but it faces a political and organizing climate quite different from the past. It needs a coher-ent institutional strategy — attuned to its present organization and weakness, promising organizing and political gains, premising little immediate help from government, informed by underlying changes in the structure of the economy, capable of getting to scale — for self-revival. And it needs a way, consistent with that strategy, to present itself to the broader public — to reclaim its role as the moral conscience of the nation, to capture and harness the support of the disorganized many for whom it also needs to speak. Labor needs, in short, a new organizing strategy and a new mass politics. Above all, perhaps, it needs to recognize that the two are not independent, that they require each other for success.

Getting Started: A Role in the Economy

Ask the average person what constructive role unions play in the economy, and you'll get laughter, hostility, or a blank stare. This is the first thing that has to change. Unions advance, big-time, only when they do things that not only visibly benefit members or potential members, but benefit the broader society as well — and thereby gain the social cachet and political support they need, in this capitalist world, to defend and grow worker organization. Typically this means solving some big problem in the economy — a problem beyond the power or interest of individual firms to solve on their own, however much the solution might contribute to a dynamic capitalism.

In the New Deal and postwar era, the problem was effective demand. Operating in an essentially closed national economy, where the state relied on fiscal and monetary policy to regulate the macroeconomy, unions demanded and got wage and benefit increases for their members and other workers — partly extracted from firms directly, partly extracted through the state. By delivering solid and rising wage floors, they boosted aggregate demand. That gave firms markets for sales and reasons to renew investment. And that, in turn, increased productivity and lowered the costs of mass-consumption goods, which was good for everyone. The alchemy of Keynesian economics translated worker interests into general interests, with unions as (male, pale, stale, stolid, but still) magicians.

What is the equivalent contribution in today's world, in which Keynesianism is qualified by international capital flows and product competition? Without overstating that qualification (and thus understating the need for demand stimulus) it will likely come as much by changing the competitive strategies of firms, and all that flows from that, as changing the general structure of demand.

There are essentially only two ways firms can respond to today's increased competition. A "low-road" response competes by reducing costs — typically beginning with the cost of fixed and well-paid labor — and compliance with social regulation. Generalized, it is associated with wage stagnation, rising inequality, job insecurity, sweated workers, poisonous labor relations, and degraded natural environments — the current situation in the United States. A "high-road" response, by contrast, competes by increasing quality — with higher wages supported by customer willingness to pay for that quality. Generalized, it is associated with more skilled workers, higher productivity, higher pay, better labor relations, reduced environmental damage, and greater commitment by firms to the health and stability of surrounding human communities (needed to attract and keep skilled workers and managers).

· Firms can make money on either road, but social gains are obviously made only on one, and that road is not widely traveled in the United States. Nor will it be, and we know this, too, if firms are left to their own devices. The reason is that transition to the high road is costly, and staying on it requires a variety of supports — advanced educational and training systems, skill standards and credentialing, integrated labor market services and clear signals on advancement to participants, advanced physical infrastructure promoting dense development, deliberate efforts to upgrade firms and otherwise diffuse "best practice," and, throughout, barriers to low-road defection — that no individual firm can supply on its own. Choosing the high road thus requires a broader social choice to build those supports — a choice that we as a society have failed to make.

Labor's role in the economy, in a nutshell, is to publicize, force, and enable that choice — to close off the low road, help to pave the high road, and enable workers and firms stuck on the first to travel the other. The role requires both a dense and encompassing presence in the economy and political power in the state, which is why the role is uniquely labor's to perform. No other social agent comes close to having the wherewithal for both. But labor's performing this role requires that it break with past routines.

Getting Organized

For starters, labor must change its organizing tactics and its assumed role in economic governance. On these matters, the "traditional unionism" of the postwar period was broadly defined by:

Just service, in majority settings: "Provide members with good wages and benefits, and the unorganized will join up." Effectively, this was the theory of union growth that trade union leadership offered in the postwar period. With the exception of a 1960s' explosion in the public sector, organizing expenditures as a percentage of total revenues stagnated or declined throughout the period. And what organizing that did go on was usually done on a "hot shop" basis, with the goal of achieving majority status in those shops. Majority status was seen as necessary to the economics of servicing, contract enforcement, and the protections offered only "exclusive bargaining representatives" that had demonstrated such status. Where organizing failed to achieve majority support within a limited time, it was generally abandoned. Where organizing succeeded, dues and contracts kicked in, and members were generally demobilized, pending the next contract dispute.

Staying clear of production control: Encouraged by law and their own organizational sense, with rare exceptions (in particular, the building trades) unions steered clear of making demands on issues lying at the "core of entrepreneurial control." They reacted to firm decisions on training, technology, investment, relocation, product strategy, and work organization. They did not typically seek to take responsibility for steering the firm's product strategy or organizing the inputs necessary to preferred strategies. Since they were in a weaker position than the employer, such assumption of responsibility was seen as promising only responsibility, never power, and blurring the distinctions between "us" and "them" critical to maintaining solidarity in the unit. Needless to say, the prospect of changing entire industry strategies was considered even more daunting and unattractive as a task.

Centered on specific sites, and not coordinated: Despite lead agreements, pattern bargaining, and the sectoral jurisdictions of the CIO, collective-bargaining agreements were generally negotiated on a firm-by-firm, often plant-by-plant, basis. Contract administration was highly decentralized, with wide variation in agreements across sites. Within regional labor markets (outside prevailing wage laws for the building trades) little effort was made to generalize wage or benefit norms beyond organized employers. Efforts at multi-union bargaining or organizing were infrequent; murderous jurisdictional disputes were not; and in labor's own structure the internationals fully dominated central labor bodies (state federations and central labor councils), in a "silos of solidarity" model. Finally, again at the regional labor market level, if relations among unions were not close, relations between labor and community organizations were close to nonexistent. There was, of course, "community service," but this was largely confined to charitable works; it did not extend to coordination on political and organizing programs.

For those fortunate enough already to be in unions, or employed in those few sectors dominated by them, this traditional model of unionism worked passably well — in a relatively closed economy, dominated by large and spatially concentrated firms, generally featuring "Taylorist" forms of work organization, occupied by un- or semiskilled labor, composed overwhelmingly of men. But it is obviously disastrous for membership growth, and holds little promise in today's economy — with lower average firm size, more dispersed production, a working class not "readymade" but repeatedly "unmade" through greater educational opportunity, work heterogeneity, and spatial dispersion, composed increasingly of minorities and women, in firms subject to stiffer competition, and policy-makers hostile to union presence or utterly confused about the vital contribution organized workers can make to a productive economy.

Specifically, the service model proves hopelessly expensive and does not produce active and engaged memberships; the two conditions together inhibit organizing, which requires a vast increase of expenditures on paid organizers and recruitment and mobilization of the existing base. Particularly in large units, the preoccupation with majority status imposes too demanding a condition of success, and slows the needed coordination across sites, sectors, regions, and even different branches of large, national, but decentralized employers. It also carries enormous opportunity costs for membership growth. In virtually all workplaces, some significant percentage of workers — typically, about 30 percent — wish now to belong to unions; not letting them do so throws away potential labor strength. Economic restructuring has meanwhile made investment, relocation, technology, and training decisive for member well-being, the defense and advance of which requires that unions be as deeply involved in "baking" the pie as in carving it up.

As a general matter, then, this traditional model needs to be turned on its head — a fact recognized widely within progressive labor, and broadly supported by the new national leadership. Such inversion means:

Everything-that-moves organizing: Locally based organizing staffs and member organizers are a cheaper and more effective way to organize than parachuting international representatives in for hot-shop campaigns. Labor needs to make the development of *in situ* organizing capacity — among rank-and-file members, stewards, local unions — its goal, building on the one signal strength labor still has: the loyalty of its own people. With such built-in capacity more or less permanently in place, the logic of majority-only organizing and short-time cycles on achieving it — mistaken in any case, given the need for expansive reach — additionally fails. It becomes possible to contemplate truly long-term and large-scale campaigns and, within them, clearer focus on the real goal of organizing — which is not to get to contract *per se* but to build the union presence in the workplace. Employees in units still lacking majority status would be given the full rights and responsibilities of other union members, and accreted to the organizing machine of which they are one extension. Reciprocally, the job of "organizer" would become less "parachut-ist" and more "member of the community" — an on-the-scene full-time union activist.

Seeking to control the terms of production: In the supply-side king-dom, the bourgeoisie is king, but only if the serfs let him be. Operat-ing across firms as well as within them, a union movement seriously interested in affecting the design and utilization of human capital systems, technology, and work organization could, in fact, do so. Power in these areas, moreover, could be bargained for power in decisions farther back in the production chain — investment, new technology, and product strategy. And especially in the United States, where employer associations are weak, coordination across firms to supply the needed infrastructure for high-road production and service is something that unions are uniquely positioned to provide. Imagine, then, a labor movement that did provide those inputs (from effective training systems to modernization services and the worker input necessary to upgrading), that offered itself in this way as an ally in production — but only to employers prepared to share power in decision-making and comply with specified wage and production norms. Imagine this sort of deal cut not only with lead firms but with their primary and secondary suppliers as well: that, indeed, union support of lead firms was conditioned on their assistance in generalizing such norms to suppliers.

Spatial and sectoral coordination: To shift strategies and wage and benefit conditions in large industries, those industries need to be organized, and growing variation across firms increasingly recommends that organization really be "wall to wall." Frequently, this simply cannot be done by a single union. Imagine, then, a labor movement that recognizes this fact, and devises joint organizing strategies for sectors; instead of policing existing jurisdictional boundaries, central bodies would monitor their deliberate mutual transgression. Recruited members could be divided up by unions on any number of imaginable justified bases, or thrown into a new pool jointly administered by those contributing to it. And note the tie from organizing to economic restructuring and back. With critical mass provided by pooled resources, organizing campaigns are the natural complement and support to regional skills standards and other aspects of high-roading — especially in metropolitan labor markets — not least because they can foreclose the low-wage restructuring strategy that otherwise frustrates the high-road transition. Reciprocally, labor's active role in shaping labor market administration — in defining job standards and the terms of job advancement, in providing or helping govern the provision of training and other services — provides a natural source of attraction for new members.

Targeted on the metro regions that provide labor's chief area of remaining strength — and thus the natural leverage points for scarce organizing resources — such a new model of organizing would begin to redefine labor's role in the economy as it increased its numbers.

Getting Political

But even redirected organizing energies, expended on a massively greater scale than in the recent past, will in the short term touch only a limited number of people. They will not bring labor back as a generally recognized force for good in the society. Nor will they do much directly to change the background "rules of the game" — the public policy supports to low-roading and anti-unionism — that labor needs to change to bring itself to scale. The United States spends approximately $30 billion annually on "economic development" activity, for example, virtually all indifferent if not hostile to the sorts of development that labor needs. No number of new credit card deals to get resources for organizing can match that. Labor needs to be shaping such policies, redirecting such cash, from inside the state.

For both reasons, then — to build its presence in the society, and to provide direct support for its new organizing — labor needs a political strategy. And labor needs to recognize (as it began to in Labor '96), that strategy needs to be more sophisticated and directive than just waiting for the Democrats to endorse someone and then writing the candidate a check. At present, the relationship between labor and the Democratic Party is an abusive relationship; the way to end abuse in a relationship — whether the relationship itself is ended or not — is to develop the ability to leave it. And at present, the general public knows little of what labor — as distinct from the Democrats — stands for, and thus is ill prepared to stand with it. Labor, in short, needs an *independent, values-based* electoral strategy.

Were such a strategy articulated, it would certainly find a market. Along the way to making American politics ugly, cynical, and vapid, a generation of economic decline and failed government response has also generated enormous implicit support for labor's signature issues — imposing some values on the economy once more, and building a democracy strong and supple and informed enough to enforce them under real-world competitive conditions. The public would like to see some standards imposed on corporate behavior, and it certainly would like to have public (not necessarily governmental) institutions manifestly competent to solve manifest problems. Labor is uniquely qualified to author a politics satisfying these demands. Its core interests are in line with the general public; it commands the most obvious resources (organized people) needed to reconstruct a democratic public administration; and among progressive forces it stands alone in its capacity to carry the message.

Even when it has recognized these things, however, labor has historically held back from taking leadership in such a politics out of fear of doing harm. Knowing the Democrats to be unstable allies at best, it has not wanted to advantage the Republicans. And not being able to afford saying a flat "goodbye" to the Democratic Party, for generations labor — and, with labor, the rest of the progressive community — has concluded that it could not be independent of them either, at least not in the electoral arenas where such independence would be visible to the mass public.

But this conclusion, however long-standing, seems vastly premature. If they wanted to, labor and other progressive groups could find the elements of a progressive independent politics — a simple attractive message, a practical program reflecting its values, trained personnel to run campaigns and ballot initiatives, and some ongoing organization whose support and sanction could keep candidates honest and members of the new electoral formation in touch. And it could do so while strengthening progressive elements now inside the Democratic Party and not advantaging the Republicans.

On message: American political opinion is conventionally mapped on a liberal-conservative axis running from hypertolerant big-government do-gooders at one end to hard-nosed but heartless free-marketeers (joined by some ungodly fundamentalists) at the other. Labor and other progressives are conventionally defined, and accept their definition, as the left wing of this axis, as the all-time redistributionist social liberals, unconcerned with contribution or social order. The definition ensures defeat by ensuring defensiveness about failed policies and cultural distance from the mass public. It should be self-consciously and explicitly rejected in favor of a politics anchored in commitment to democracy, fairness, and contribution. The real fight today isn't between left and right, but bottom and top, between favoring corporate accountability and a stronger democracy (the majority) and those opposed to both (the tiny rich minority and their apologists). Labor should define itself as speaking for that majority, in those terms, not cleaning up after liberals and protesting from the sidelines.

On program: One thing the right does well is work hard in areas of joint concern, not waiting for the resolution of all conflicts before moving forcefully where there are none. Labor and other progressives should do the same, articulating a practical, majoritarian program for democratic and economic renewal out of what virtually all of them already believe. Reform tax and industrial policy to close off low-roading and promote high-wage, low-waste domestic investment and firm organization. This means massive increases in the minimum wage, higher environmental standards for firms, and effective modernization and training services to give workers and firms stuck on the low road the ability to walk the high one. Revitalize our metropolitan economies as model regions of such advanced production — taking advantage of the natural economic benefits of cities now obscured by our endless subsidies to sprawl. Make "equal opportunity" real by wedding it to resources — declaring a "Bill of Rights for America's Children" that provides them all with a "starting even" package of day care, health insurance, safety, recreation, and very advanced high-quality education. Declare America a "lifelong learning" society, first by fundamentally reforming primary education — getting its funding off local property taxes, imposing high standards on teachers and students, and providing links to work for those who don't go on to college — and second by ensuring lifelong learning opportunities for adults through individual training accounts paid off through future earnings. Restore govern-

ment accountability — beginning with serious campaign-finance reform (free media for candidates, limitations on contributions, "people's PACs" bundling those contributions, tax credits for the citizens
making them). Strengthen the organizing rights of workers and consumers and communities — while explicitly assigning them a greater
role in devising and administering "public" programs for economic
upgrading and community renewal. Complete some semblance of a
modern welfare state through single-payer health insurance. Sim-
plify and integrate our tax system to tax both private and especially
social income on a progressive basis, with social income taxed progressively enough to achieve scale targeting of those who really need.
Declare the peace dividend paid for many times against an enemy
that no longer exists. Declare the environmental dividend in energy
and other savings that mass application of current technologies
would permit. Forge a new internationalism centered on "leveling
up" international worker rights and wages.

What is distinctive about this program, apart from the fact that
virtually all progressives adore it, is that a majority of the public also
supports *all* of its planks, and neither major party is systematically
moving to implement *any* of them. Talk about an opening!

On elections: Recruiting from its own and allied ranks, labor
could and should train thousands of fellow citizens in campaign
work — as candidates, campaign workers, precinct leaders, signature gatherers for ballot-initiative petitions, and more — with the
training covering both nuts-and-bolts skills (how to run a meeting,
how to knock on a door, how to target a precinct, how to write a
press release, how to do list management, how to talk in public) and
the general ambitions and programmatic emphasis of the independent electoral movement.

It can then start with the widest and most accessible target: the
tens of thousands of local nonpartisan offices that dominate the
American electoral landscape and generally feature similar sets of
issues. Imagine a training academy for x thousand people recruited
(heavily from labor's own ranks) to run for school boards, city
councils, and county boards, where they learn about regional industrial policy, metropolitan taxation schemes, effective school reform,

sensible land use, best responses to federal cutbacks, and all the rest that they will have to deal with or could deal out after getting into office. Imagine model legislation, speeches, talking points, op-eds, and other supports turned over to these future candidates *en masse*. And imagine running them for local office, with these supports and a sophisticated local targeting and get-out-the-vote operation also supplied by labor and its allies, on condition that they adhere to the program or face a new opponent next time. The New Party has been running candidates principally in these sorts of races over the past few years. Operating with almost no resources, we've elected two thirds of the some two hundred candidates we've put up. If it's clear that we can win with our values intact, why not take the effort to scale?

In partisan races, labor should of course continue to issue report cards on available electoral choices, giving voters instruction on whom they should vote for if they share its values. But also, depending on the strength of its local organization, it should enter Democratic primaries with its own or allied candidates, or — assuming New Party success in its current effort to restore cross-nomination rights nationally — cross-nominate its favored major party candidate on its own ballot line, or run its own people on those lines where it thinks it can win. Again and throughout, the culture of the effort could be to "do no harm" and not let the perfect become the enemy of the good. Intent on expanding its capacity to win, where it and its allies don't have that yet, labor should indeed generally support the lesser of the available "evils." Throughout, it should advertise its new electoral efforts as what they are — value-based building, not spoilage.

Labor should also use state and municipal ballot initiatives and referenda to frame debate and to change policies that corrupt legislatures won't. Ballot initiatives on campaign-finance reform in term-limited states where thousands of seats open up in the next few years, turning their plan to obliterate incumbent Democrats into an opportunity for progressives. More "living wage" campaigns banning public grants or government service contracts to employers paying poverty wages, or increasing the minimum wage directly.

"Children first, prison last" initiatives on state spending. "Take you out of the ball game" initiatives directed at stadium owners getting public subsidies, declaring that if they threaten to move, we'll simply seize their assets. "Maximum wage" initiatives declaring that no firm should receive public subsidies or expense executive salaries if its CEO makes a certain amount more than its entry-level workers.

Assert the people's voice. Change the rules of the game. Show labor's values and its base. Have some fun along the way. All at relatively low cost.

On organization: Eventually this should be a mass-membership organization with a national executive consisting of representatives of organizations providing some stated measure of ongoing support, itself gradually joined by elected representatives from states where we achieve a specified significant level of membership. But it could begin simply as a coalition, with list-sharing and other coordination on joint projects. It should not, however, be another "one letterhead, one vote" coalition. Power should be proportionate to contribution — in members, money, or some other recognizable currency. Any alternative would not be democratic and would fail for want of commitment by those with something real to offer.

And who might the different allies be? Along with labor itself, anyone and everyone who agrees to work together on these terms. New Party, Citizen Action, ACORN, Greenpeace, Clean Water Action, U.S. Public Interest Research Group, NAACP, NOW. A range of people obviously big enough to stand for something, and for once standing together in the electoral space where the mass public can find them.

A formation like this — an electoral alliance of progressive forces in the country, a progressive version of the Christian Coalition and GOPAC — would not solve all the problems of labor or of other progressives. But it would begin to give some organizational coherence and punch to what are now largely wasted assets — millions of such progressive votes, and the millions of votes of those who agree with this simple progressive program even if they'd never call themselves "progressives." It would permit labor to take some power and show that its values work — in sustainable development, school reform, campaign finance — particularly in those metropolitan areas where its new-model organizing would be concentrated and is in need of precisely this sort of support. It would vastly increase the supply of trained operatives and potential future candidates. It would, by making electoral activity real, force improvements in program thinking and message. Not to be slighted, by giving ongoing life and purpose to some shared activity among labor and its many potential allies, it would vastly improve their relations with one another and cement their programmatic alliance. And, most obvious (and irrespective of final decisions about long-range strategies on minor-party building), it would send a powerful wake-up call to Democrats.

Above all, however, such an effort would simply broadcast, in arenas where the message could be heard and acted on, that "labor was back" with a constructive program of broad appeal and manifest general benefit. What that would mean for labor — in terms of public visibility and esteem and associated reduced organizing costs — is an unqualified good. What it would mean for currently disorganized progressive forces is that they would finally have some visible focus and concrete means of coordination. What it would mean for the country is that business's domination of American public life would finally be questioned again — by the same folks whose concern with basic human happiness should be manifest from all sorts of gifts they've brought in the past.

21

Audacious Democrats

Cornel West

THIS IS a propitious moment in the history of this country, as unionists and intellectuals come together to energize and galvanize a tradition. It's a tradition of struggle, struggle for decency and dignity, struggle for freedom and democracy. There is wind at our backs even in this dark and difficult time. Let us never forget that. It's a tradition that has the audacity to wrestle with the most fundamental question of what it means to be human, namely, the problem of evil. How will we respond to unjustified suffering and unwarranted pain and undeserved harm and unnecessary misery? There is still too much suffering. There is still too much harm. There is still too much misery. There is still too much pain in America and around the world.

It's difficult for fellow citizens and fellow human beings to take us seriously, because we are the audacious radical democrats who say we confront the dark realities of life at the end of a ghastly century. We haven't forgotten the two hundred million who have been murdered in the name of some pernicious ideology. We'll never forgive the Nazism at the heart of so-called civilized Europe and the Stalinism at the core of so-called emancipatory Soviet Union. We'll never forget that European colonialism and imperialism have left such scars and wounds in Asia and Africa. We won't forget the patriarchy that has left such bruises on sisters in all social systems. We won't forget the homophobia that's closeted so many gay brothers and lesbian sisters.

But here we stand at the end of this century and say, "We are going to keep the radical democratic tradition alive, come what may!" We're going to keep it alive. Which means that we're going to love and respect our fellow citizens and fellow human beings enough to tell them the truth about their situation. We will tell them that unregulated, unedited, and unfettered capitalism is killing us! It's killing us! We'll tell them that the vicious legacy of white supremacy is still alive. It's suffocating us. And this practice of male supremacy is still at work. It's stifling us. The invidious ideology of homophobia is crippling us. And this is not cheap PC. This is a fallible focus on human suffering!

Let's tell our conservative fellow citizens that we're talking about what the great artists have always talked about. We're talking about what the great Eugene O'Neill grappled with as part of that rich Irish tradition of struggle that Brother John Sweeney is part of. The grand John Sweeney, at this point. And it's true that he is where he is for a special reason at this point in American history.

In 1946, when the greatest American playwright returned from California after twelve years of silence with his new play, *The Iceman Cometh*, Eugene O'Neill told the press he was short with words (like John Coltrane), but he spoke through his art. Didn't like talking to the press too much. They said, What is the play about? He said, It's about one question: What does it profit a nation to conquer the world and lose its soul?

And the iceman has been at work in America in the last twenty-five years. These have been icy times in this country. We recognize that we are at the crossroads, the fork in the road in the history of this very precious yet precarious experiment in democracy. We could well be witnessing the embryonic stages of the disintegration and disillusion and decomposition of American civilization. That is a real possibility. Civilizations wax and wane. They come and go. There's no guarantee that America will make it into the twenty-first century with its radical democratic tradition alive unless we do something about it. No guarantee.

This particular moment is the most frightening and terrifying moment in the history of this country. There's no external enemy to unite a people who hides and conceals its own suffering and misery. No communists. Forced to look at ourselves. Very few want to speak candidly about the relative economic decline in this nation, the slow-motion depression, the silent depression that has been ravaging Chocolate Cities since 1973, the levels of unemployment and underemployment not reflected in the statistics of the Department of Labor, which do not account for part-time workers looking for full-time jobs or those who have given up looking for jobs. They don't want to talk about the dilapidated housing and the decrepit school systems that break the motivational structures of so many young brothers and sisters of all colors. Don't want to talk about the inadequate health care and unavailable child care.

And yet we hear, over and over again, "The economy's stronger now than it's been in thirty years." Who are you talking about? The top 20 percent? Yes. The top 1 percent? Euphoric. One out of five brothers and sisters of all colors in the labor force work more than forty hours a week, do not receive one penny from the federal government, and still live in poverty. Still growing every day. And yet 1 percent of the population owns 36 percent of the household wealth. Sixty-two percent of the wealth accrued to that 1 percent between 1983 and 1989. Two hundred and five percent increase in corporate profits since 1980. Four hundred and ninety-nine percent increase in the salaries of CEOs, and yet 25 percent of all of America's children live in poverty and 42 percent of brown brothers and sisters live in poverty and 51 percent of black brothers and sisters live in poverty, in a nation predicated on the promise that the future would always be better. Something is wrong in America. Talk about democracy, but it's really oligarchy, plutocratic, to some degree pigmentocratic, when we talk about the economy.

We know that the social structure that once looked like a diamond is beginning to look more and more like a pyramid. That it creates depths of economic insecurity and anxiety and makes persons feel that things are out of control. It's human — all too human — when things are out of control to want to scapegoat the most vulnerable because of the cowardly streak in all of us. We want to look down to the powerless rather than look up to the powerful. We can focus on the immigrants, especially brown immigrants. How long have you been in? I'm third generation. I'm glad Great-grandma got in. But we're closing things up now. We can target the sisters of all colors. Push them back into the kitchen and into the labor force. Make things difficult for the brothers who can't be manly. Or maybe it's those gay brothers and lesbian sisters, you know, that 3.5, 4 percent who stepped out of the closet and the whole civilization began to decline. Or it's those black folk. They're the ones. Two hundred and forty-four years of chattel slavery. Eighty-one years of Jim and Jane Crow. Every two and a half days some black child or black woman or black man was hanging from some tree, that strange fruit that Southern trees bear that Billie Holiday sang about, and we finally break the back of American apartheid and just begin to get, not a foothold, but a toehold on the main road. And yet, target them — making special pleas, excessive demands, black folk taking over.

I was talking to some reactionary white brothers the other day. They said "Black folk taking over. They're responsible for me losing my job." Then I replied, "Well, how many black folk own production units in your town?" "Well, none that I know of." "Oh, oh, oh. Okay. Oh, I understand. I understand. I think you need a more complex analysis, brother! I'm sorry you don't have a job, even given your reactionary politics. You're still a human being. I know you suffer, too." He said, "No, it's that affirmative action that did it." I said, "Oh. How many black folk in your workplace?" "There's four out of eighty." "Oh, they're taking over, aren't they? Oh, that affirmative action. That's something else. I bet they're all in senior management, huh? Oh, yeah. Uh-huh."

But, of course, he is searching too. Trying to make sense of his pain. We can't leave those brothers and sisters to Rush Limbaugh. There is some way we can create a bridge for those folk. How do we broaden their vision and analysis? That's the challenge. And we do so by being candid about our own history.

A revitalized labor movement is the prerequisite for rejuvenated social motion and momentum in this country. But at the same time, let us not fetishize the labor movement and ascribe these magical powers to it as if we were just waiting for them to descend from heaven. They're made up of fellow human beings, too. And they have to struggle within their own ranks with the same forces that are in the larger society. It's just that they happen to be a group of Americans who tilt in a radical democratic direction to the degree to which they know that their relative powerlessness at the workplace means they're unable to live lives of decency and dignity without being organized and mobilized and bringing power and pressure to bear against management.

Which is to say that the revitalized labor movement is a necessary condition, but not a sufficient condition for the fundamental transformation of American society. Very important. And it's here that we must wrestle with the deep cultural crisis that is very real and cuts across ideological and political lines. We're witnessing in our society the relative erosion of the systems of caring and nurturing, with devastating impact on children. More and more shattered families and neighborhoods. Neighborhoods becoming 'hoods now. Weakening civil institutions. Making it difficult for all of us, but especially young people, to gain access to the very preconditions of what it is, in part, to be human, namely, those bonds of affection and affirmation, of people who care for you and love you and nurture and give you sense of possibility and self-confidence. Those networks of support and those ties of empathy and bonds of sympathy.

The labor movement in this sense becomes more than simply an economic affair concerned with class struggle at the workplace, as important as that is. It's also a cultural space for people who care about you. People who could bring out the best in you. And how rare it is in America, given the fact that we are more racially segregated now than we were in 1965, even given the overcoming of legal segregation, that there is a public space where we can enter without humiliation, where we can engage in give-and-take and argument mediated with some respect, rather than the ugly name-calling and finger-pointing that constitute so much public conversation these days.

What public spaces do we actually have in which we don't have to deny but can transcend our racial and gender and sexual orientational identities? Where we're not just clients of a constituency but actually citizens in the making? And by citizens I mean public actors. Focus on public interest to generate new public action and respond to public problems. Which is to say, be able to bring together persons of different cultures and heritages. Not in order to celebrate some kind of ethnic smorgasbord-like picnic but to focus on something bigger than us. Something bigger than us that accents the best in us, namely, the democratic identity, the radical democratic identity. How crucial.

The great John Dewey, in his classic of 1927, *The Public and Its Problems,* says that if you show me a democracy that proliferates publics and constituencies and identities, but does not have a democratic public wherein they can enter in order to focus as radical democrats on problems that affect all citizens, show me a democracy that cannot engage in high quality public conversation about those public problems and I'll show you a democracy sliding down the slope to chaos and anarchy. That's John Dewey in 1927, and it still resonates so deep in 1997.

Let us never forget the unprecedented unleashing of capitalist forces and the creation of a market culture that becomes so obsessed with buying and selling and promoting and advertising, that yield market moralities and market mentalities become hegemonic. Hedonism, narcissism, I want pleasure now. I want power now. I want property now. Your property, I've got a little technology (e.g., a gun), too. I'm saying in part that the ultimate logic of unfettered capitalist forces creating a market culture is the gangsterization of a culture in which people feel as if they will attempt to get over by any means. And gangsterization of culture may be reflected and refracted in part in so-called gangsta rap. But we know that there's gangsta mentality shot through every institution in this society, from White House to statehouse to city hall to church, mosque, synagogue, educational institution, and so on.

The only countervailing forces against gangsterization on a local, regional, national, or global level are democratic practices and procedures. Countervailing forces that attempt to render elites account-able. Democracies are very rare in human history. They tend not to last too long. America's the oldest surviving democracy. And for many people it seems as if it may be running out of gas.

When we look back at those few experiments in democracy, we see two fatal viruses sitting at the center, poverty and paranoia. Increasing poverty generating deeper levels of despair. There will never be enough prisons and police to deal with a grand avalanche of despair and paranoia. That increasing paranoia generating deeper levels of distrust. And no democracy can survive with pervasive distrust. It creates a culture of cynicism. We think it's clever to avoid humiliation, and therefore we identify with aggression and sidestep sympathy and empathy. Cynicism, fatalism, pessimism, addiction, addictive personalities, strategies for survival in a market culture, but taking us away from this tradition, this radical democratic tradition of struggle.

First and foremost we must attempt to reconstitute this grand tradition by beginning with something profoundly un-American, a sense of history. A deep sense of history. We must highlight nonmarket values in a market culture. Nonmarket values like love and care and concern and service to others, nonmarket values like solidarity and community and fidelity and loyalty. Even on the interpersonal dimension, which must not be overlooked, because we must deal with one another and we will have disagreements. But nonmarket values like gentleness and kindness and sweetness and tenderness, which make so much of life worth living.

We say that we will attempt to be courageous. Not simply a matter of standing up for our convictions, but also having the courage to attack our convictions sometimes. We could be wrong. We're demo-crats. We could be wrong. We'll listen to one another. We'll push one another. We'll unsettle one another for a greater good.

And more than anything else at this moment, we'll attempt to project a sense of hope. And by hope I do not mean optimism. I do not think at the moment that there's enough evidence that will allow us to infer that we can win. Not at all. We must cut against the grain. Hope looks at the underdetermined evidence, the flimsy evidence, and says we will make a leap of democratic faith beyond it. We will believe enough in each other to acknowledge that, even if our numbers at the moment are small, by witness, by discipline, by struggle, we will exemplify this democratic tradition in such a way that it may become contagious, it may provide an analysis of why we're in such pain. It may provide a way out, some vision as it were. Somewhere I read that where there is no vision, the people perish. People are perishing. And vision is not a vision thing, as the fellow citizen who lives in Texas, George Bush, said; it's a power. Convince persons that they could do things when they have concluded that they could not. That's the fundamental challenge.

Let us go forth, with our sense of history expanding our nonmarket values, in a courageous manner, self-critical, self-corrective, and with a sense of hope, acknowledging that there may be limits we know not of. That we can laugh at ourselves and our own contradictions and still keep keeping on. Let us keep our heads not so much on the ground but to the sky, as Earth, Wind, and Fire would put it. Let's keep our hands on the plow, the way Mahalia Jackson used to sing with such power and poignancy. Let us keep our eyes not so much on each other's inadequacies, but on the prize, something bigger than us and grander than us that can appeal to the better angels of our nature, and maybe then we can meet the challenge. But whether we can or not, let us all go down fighting.

Contributors

Paul Berman is the author of *A Tale of Two Utopias* and a contributor to *Dissent, The New Republic, The New Yorker,* and *The New York Times Book Review.*

Norman Birnbaum is University Professor, Georgetown Law Center. He was a founding editor of *New Left Review* and was on the editorial board of *Partisan Review* from 1971 to 1983, and is presently on the editorial board of *The Nation.* His book on European socialism and American social reform, *After Progress,* will be published in 1998.

Ron Blackwell is director of corporate affairs for the AFL-CIO.

Michael Eric Dyson, Visiting Distinguished Professor of African-American Studies at Columbia University, is the author of four books, including the best-selling *Race Rules: Navigating the Color Line.*

Bill Fletcher, Jr., is director of education for the AFL-CIO.

Eric Foner is DeWitt Clinton Professor of History at Columbia University.

William E. Forbath is professor of law at UCLA and the author of *Law and the Shaping of the American Labor Movement.*

Steven Fraser is executive editor at Houghton Mifflin and the author of *Labor Will Rule: Sidney Hillman and the Rise of American Labor.*

Joshua B. Freeman is associate professor of history at Queens College, City University of New York, and the author of *In Transit: The Trans-*

port Workers Union in New York City. His forthcoming book, *Working-Class New York,* will be published in 1998.

Betty Friedan is the author of *The Feminine Mystique, The Second Stage,* and *The Fountain of Age.* She is also the founder of NOW, National Women's Political Caucus, and NARAL.

Todd Gitlin is professor of culture, journalism, and sociology at New York University. His latest book is *The Twilight of Common Dreams: Why America Is Wracked by Culture Wars.* He is also the author of *The Whole World Is Watching, Inside Prime Time,* and *The Sixties: Years of Hope, Days of Rage.*

José La Luz is associate education director of the American Federation of State, County, and Municipal Employees (AFSCME), and formerly the national education director of the Amalgamated Clothing and Textile Union (ACTU).

Manning Marable is professor of history and director of the Institute for Research in African-American Studies at Columbia University. His forthcoming book, *What Black America Thinks: Race Ideology and Political Power,* will be published in 1998.

David Montgomery is professor of history at Yale University. His latest book is *Citizen Worker: The Experience of Workers in the United States with Democracy and the Free Market During the Nineteenth Century.*

Mae M. Ngai is director of research and policy at the Consortium for Worker Education in New York City and a Ph.D. candidate in history at Columbia University. She is a founder and member of the national executive board of the Asian Pacific American Labor Alliance, AFL-CIO.

Karen Nussbaum is director of the Working Women's Department at the AFL-CIO and has also served as director of the Women's Bureau, U.S. Department of Labor.

Frances Fox Piven is on the faculty of the graduate school of the City University of New York and co-author, with Richard Cloward, of *Regulating the Poor.*

Joel Rogers is professor of law, political science, and sociology at the University of Wisconsin-Madison, and chair of the New Party.

Richard Rorty teaches philosophy at the University of Virginia.

Lillian B. Rubin is the author of a number of books, including *Worlds of Pain, Families on the Fault Line,* and *The Transcendent Child.* She is senior research fellow at the Institute for the Study of Social Change at the University of California, Berkeley, and a sociologist and psychotherapist who lives and practices in San Francisco.

John J. Sweeney is president of the AFL-CIO and the author of *America Needs a Raise: Fighting for Economic Security and Social Justice.*

Robert W. Welsh is executive assistant to AFL-CIO president John Sweeney.

Cornel West is professor of philosophy of religion at Harvard University and the author of *Race Matters.*